# THE LONG SONG OF TCHAIKOVSKY STREET

# THE
# LONG SONG
*of*
# TCHAIKOVSKY
# STREET

a Russian adventure

## PIETER WATERDRINKER
### TRANSLATED BY PAUL EVANS

SCRIBE
*Melbourne • London*

Scribe Publications
2 John St, Clerkenwell, London, WC1N 2ES, United Kingdom
18–20 Edward St, Brunswick, Victoria 3056, Australia
3754 Pleasant Ave, Suite 100, Minneapolis, Minnesota 55409, USA

Published by Scribe 2022

**N** **ederlands**
**letterenfonds**
**dutch foundation**
**for literature**

This publication has been made possible with
financial support from the Dutch Foundation
for Literature.

Typeset in Adobe Garamond Pro by the publishers

Printed and bound in the UK by CPI Group (UK) Ltd, Croydon CR0 4YY

978 1 912854 07 3 (UK edition)
978 1 950354 88 7 (US edition)
978 1 925849 13 4 (Australian edition)
978 1 922586 30 8 (ebook)

Catalogue records for this book are available from the
National Library of Australia and the British Library.

scribepublications.co.uk
scribepublications.com
scribepublications.com.au

*For Julia*

*Today, there are only happy hours*

Hildegard Knef

# CHAPTER ONE

One morning in late October 1988, this dapper-looking guy from Leiden asked me if I might be able to deliver 7,000-odd bibles to the Soviet Union. I still haven't got a clue how he found me. Back then, there weren't many people in the Netherlands who spoke Russian and had visited the USSR. I'd only been once myself, more than seven years before. But if there's one thing that life has taught me, it's that the way the world works is totally arbitrary.

I was twenty-six and I'd just moved back in with my parents after living for more than a year on the Canary Islands and a little mountain village on the Spanish mainland. Now I was back in my dire childhood room, three and a half metres by two.

'Can I come in for a moment?'

The man had damp, black hair, carefully combed over to one side. His parting looked as if it had been branded with hot tongs. He was wearing a tan mac with matching buttons.

'My parents aren't home,' I replied. 'They're in Haarlem, at the hospital.'

He hadn't come to see them; he'd come to see me.

'Siderius,' said the pre-war apparition.

A few seconds later, he was sitting on the couch, spreading out in his mac so that he resembled a bird of prey on its nest; he lit up

1

a cigarette and blew the smoke out through his hooked nose.

'I don't have very much time,' Siderius began. 'And the matter I've come about is quite simple. Could you take delivery of a shipment of Russian bibles in the Leningrad harbour in — let's say — three weeks?'

The question was absurd, preposterous.

I nodded absently; the cigarette smoke floated between us like a blue lace curtain.

'The Lord Our Father and Creator, who sent His Only Son into the world to save us, is in dire straits. The East is adrift. I assume you've been following. But just as in warfare, we'll rejoice only once victory is achieved. What I'm about to tell you is secret, or, to put it in a way our friends at the KGB and the Stasi might understand, *classified information*! Can I have a glass of water? I have to take my pills ... Gout, it's the toothache of the joints. When I get an attack, I just want to die ...'

When I came back from the kitchen, the man drained the glass with a grimace and then told me about something I'd never heard of before: the large-scale, illegal transportation of bibles to the Eastern Bloc. Sometimes on the border between Finland and the Soviet Union people would release balloons with bibles strung to them, in the hope that these would come down somewhere in the realm of the Anti-Christ, the Red Empire founded by Lenin. But most religious contraband was distributed by road, using specially converted luxury cars, mini-buses, and the odd motorbike with sidecar, which the religious activists, generally of a Protestant persuasion, would drive to East Germany, Hungary and Romania.

It was pretty risky — there was the threat of arrest and prison. The East German border guards, with their Alsatians, were feared the most. They were always ready and waiting to check under cars with mirrors, and tap the chassis with small hammers, searching out secret compartments, where seditious anti-socialist writings, porn or bibles might be stashed. The perfect cover was a family — a happy, child-blessed family on its way to the fields, the woods or the beach for a holiday in the Model State. Siderius had often gone east as well, but he'd had to quit the missionary work after his wife had fallen ill. The final approach to the border was always preceded by a prayer in God's free and open country. And lo, the guards never once found a bible secreted behind a kitchen wall, or under the fold-away beds in his VW camper van.

'So, you'll do it?'

Siderius's right hand was gnarled with growths like big, red peonies. He twisted his wedding ring so forcefully that he seemed to want to tug it off.

'What do you mean exactly?'

'Take delivery of the 7,000 bibles in Leningrad. You do speak Russian? You have been to the Soviet Union?'

Siderius stared at me almost imploringly, a heavenly radiance in his deep-blue eyes.


The next day, Siderius was waiting for me outside Rotterdam Central station. We drove through the pounding rain to Pernis in a small car to meet the organisation. He began saying how the political plates in the east were shifting, like grain on a ship. 'But you have to understand the danger a ship at sea is in once the cargo in the hold comes loose? It could end up in a watery grave!'

Siderius told me how, over the years, a bible-smuggling rivalry had grown up between the churches. He was Dutch Reformed himself, but among the reformed faiths various denominations had gone into business for themselves, even the Mormons and the Baptists.

Competition had kicked in.

'The church council sees the situation as open warfare. It's now or never. The struggle and ammunition must be stepped up at the front. Smuggling bibles in by mini-bus just isn't getting the job done fast enough. Our Marxism-enslaved brothers and sisters must be provided *en masse* with spiritual nourishment, with hope and light. What I'll show you in a bit is only a trial delivery, 7,000 Russian bibles, cleverly concealed under a couple of tons of Zeeland spuds. If this mission is a success, there are 80,000 more waiting in a warehouse in Gouda, to go via Leningrad to Moscow, the Urals, and villages deep in Siberia. The other reformed churches are planning something with a ship too, but they're keeping as quiet as the grave. They're so sly!'

We went to a silo where potatoes were stacked like coal. There, he introduced me to three middle-aged men in long overcoats. They shook my hand in silence, with distrustful, furtive looks. Then they began to coo in the corner like pigeons, until the one in the middle said, 'Fine, Siderius, if you'll vouch for this brother, we'll take you at your word.'

And then he led us in prayer. For the success of my mission.

I hadn't prayed since I was a child; I shut my eyes for a few seconds. With hands clasped, I studied these believers: good, strong, solid Dutch profiles, as though chiselled from stone.

I was to be paid for my flight, visa and hotels. I went for the adventure; beyond that, God himself would reward me.

A week and a half later, I found myself in the corridor of an old people's home in Leningrad, breathing in the human stench, the reek of sickness, deprivation and decay. I'd lugged along six packages of Cyrillic bibles, each containing twelve copies wrapped in brown paper, past the guard in the hall, up to the second floor, to this universe with its fatsias and its unbearable fragrance.

The director of the home, a middle-aged Russian woman with a forbidding purple hairdo, was standing by a serving trolley with rubber wheels.

'Lina, could you clean this thing for once! It's covered in splodges of porridge and soup. What kind of mess is this? Quick, a damp cloth! What will our guest think?' The director struck the metal push-bar of the trolley with a wooden ruler. 'I'm going to count to three! Don't make me angry … One! Two! And that is …'

A skinny girl of around twenty-five, who was fastening the bottom button of her sea-green apron, flew out of the door as shifty as a weasel. She said, 'I heard you, you know! I was just looking for a clean nappy in the laundry. We don't have any incontinence pads left … There are three women on Ward 7 …'

'What are you cackling about now? Come on, *davai*, a damp cloth!' the director commanded. Her name was Ms Lentova. 'This foreign gentleman has brought us bibles.'

'Bibles?'

'Yes, you do hear me, don't you?' The director's ruler now lolled affectionately on her ample bosom. 'Bibles, classy books …'

The young sister mumbled that it would have been better if I'd brought nappies, and also syringes, gauze, dressings and plasters. This morning, she'd again been cutting sheets into strips to bind the legs of the old-timers, as if she were helping wounded soldiers at the Front.

She disappeared and came back with a cloth that she'd held under a scalding-hot tap. The steam rose from it as she cleaned the trolley.

'There! That's done!'

And she disappeared again.

Ms Lentova, in her black pencil skirt, scratched her bare calves with her ruler. She nodded at me encouragingly. I piled up the bibles on the trolley like merchandise. Ready to hit the road.

Because of the fatsias, which were growing furiously in jungle fashion towards the ceiling, everything was bathed in a greenish glow. Cockroaches marched from underneath the plinths, not furtively, but well-ordered, as though arrayed for battle, as if they were the true masters of this building, who at best tolerated the people here. Pensioners in quilted dressing gowns shuffled by with dead-fish eyes, trembling, as though sedated. They passed me as though I didn't exist, as if they sensed with some animal instinct that I wasn't bearing anything essential.

I could only slip a bible to the odd one or two. Most were wary, and didn't want to have anything to do with me. An old Russian woman, hairless as an ape, shuffled from the toilet to my trolley. She sniffed the pile, and asked how much a book cost.

'Free,' I said. 'These bibles are a gift from the Dutch faithful to the Russian people.'

There were almost no staff to be seen; occasionally, the odd woman would shoot by in the same sea-green apron and paper cap as the girl who'd wiped down the trolley for me. One would be carrying bedding, the other a bedpan, and yet another a plastic container, in which all sorts of small dark-red bottles rattled. The expressions on the faces of these women were invariably set to intense. They seemed more like prison guards than nursing sisters.

'Who are you?' one of them barked at me as she came around the corner carrying a zinc tub; I had almost bumped into her.

I told her.

6

'Does Lentova know about this?'

I nodded.

'Why don't you go and stand outside a church? What use do the people here have for a bible? They're all nearly dead, aren't they?' Breathing heavily through her nose, the sister took a book off the pile. 'But they *are* nice sturdy books. They'll light up the hearth nicely. First-rate briquettes! Free, you say? She grabbed another six, stuck them in the zinc tub between her feet, then lifted it again and headed off on her wooden-soled slippers, which clattered like castanets.

Since my departure three days before, nothing had gone as Siderius had sketched it out in Pernis. The flight to Leningrad was changed at the last moment — no longer direct, but with a stopover in a chicken-coop hotel at the airport in East Berlin. The only towel in the bathroom was stiff with dried semen from the previous guest.

Then, the contact person who was supposed to pick me up in Leningrad was nowhere to be seen. At the airport, I took a taxi. I drove through the murky November night to my hotel, as though through a wartime city. The chicken coop that I now ended up in looked almost identical to the one in East Berlin. There was a stench there, as if a hundred sweaty miners had just rinsed off. And there were no towels at all.

The contact person, named Pozorski, didn't show up the next day either. In my hotel room, I called the man's number, which Siderius had given me, about seven times. The other end of the line was stone-dead. I finally decided to go to the harbour myself, on the off-chance, taking one of the Volgas that were standing stationary, like patient horses, in front of the hotel with their engines running.

The city of Leningrad, once known as Saint Petersburg, had passed me by in a whirl seven years earlier, with its décor dilapidated down to the last plinth. I'd found everything so ghastly that on my return I immediately swapped my Russian studies for Law. I could never have imagined visiting the Soviet Union again. But the segue across time was flawless: it was as if I'd never been away.

The driver calmly ferried me out of the street. It was 10 am, but it seemed almost evening. Skirting the potholes in the road, we drove along the park fence, with nothing there but fir trees; printed in copper capitals along the entire length was:

SCIENCE, SPORT AND THE ARMY –

LONG LIVE THE FOUNDATION
OF SOVIET POWER!

The shadowy forms of workers were gathering together on a street corner, supping beer from jam jars, tapped from a yellow container truck by a woman who was wearing a white jacket. She looked like a milkmaid on her stool.

'Where exactly do you need to be in the harbour?'

I had no idea; the ship with the bibles concealed among the potatoes had arrived three days earlier. Just before my departure, Siderius had told me that everything had gone like clockwork so far. Maybe something had gone wrong, and Pozorski, the brother in faith of the Dutch believers, was waiting for me somewhere on the waterside.

We drove past Stalinist office buildings, Czarist palaces and Soviet residential blocks; the same uniform lamps shone from the windows as at my hotel. People slunk by on foot anxiously, keeping close to the fronts of the houses where they merged, like chameleons, into the décor with their dark-brown and grey camouflage colours.

'Did you know that Casanova was here once?' the taxi driver suddenly offered.

'Really?'

'Yes, Casanova, the seducer! But everything was still under construction then. This city was once Europe's new housing project. Can you imagine? And now we live in a coffin. Yesterday, my wife had to stand in a queue for three hours for six eggs. That's two eggs an hour! Casanova thought it was grim here ...'

A mist of dust and decay had settled over the entire city. The roads and streets were as good as deserted. The occasional jam-packed tram slowly glided along with a grating groan. There were hardly any cars. The masters of the highway were monstrous trucks with rattling, empty flatbeds, the drivers moonlighting as cabbies *en masse* because the factories around the city were on their last legs and there were scarcely any goods to transport.

'Here for business?' The driver had stopped his Volga on an unpaved road, covered with rained-on sand and gravel, in front of the harbour entrance, which was walled up with concrete blocks.

'No, for bibles ...'

I managed to get into the harbour premises by bluffing that I had an appointment with the director, waving around my foreign passport, and handing out Marlboros to guards left and right.

It seemed more like I'd walked into a scrapyard than a harbour. The quays reeked of fuel oil and were strewn with rusty iron reels, containers of pressed aluminium, mountains of shredded copper, screws, nails, and pipes. A silvery-white sheen fumed from the concrete lampposts. It gave the surroundings a gulag quality. Occasionally, a crane moved languidly in the distance, and from a dry dock you could hear the hollow clack of hammers. The longshoremen were sitting on low walls or on wooden cable reels, playing cards; the smell of alcohol wafted amid the fuel oil and scrap metal.

Suddenly, a siren went off. No one even looked up.

'So you want to speak to the director?'

A man in a brown woollen suit was standing in front of me. He had a bushy white moustache. His bald, mouse-like skull had paper-thin, yellow skin stretched over it, like a corpse's. Beside him was his clone, thirty years younger.

Both had moist dagger eyes.

'Here he is, your director,' the elder man said. 'At least of this section. We recently split the whole place up into sections. The fatherland is on the march; everything is in flux. We are living through great times! Nikolai Borodin, a pleasure. And this is my son, Andrei … What are you here for?'

I told them. The harbour director looked at me almost passionately, with his gummy grin. Bull's eye. I'd managed to get hold of the right person! He liked foreigners. This harbour was the gateway to the west. And that had been its intention when it was built.

'How do you know Pozorski?' he asked.

I wanted to tell him, but the son who had been eying me in silence suddenly came to life, asking in an unpleasant falsetto, 'Do you have the bill of lading?'

I patted the inside pocket of my coat.

'Let me see …'

The director swiftly snatched the title deeds for the 7,000 bibles out of my hand. 'Excellent, we'll give Pozorski a call, that dozy idiot! He's an old comrade of mine … A top guy … We were stationed together once, as petty officers in Leipzig … And then one day …

Anyway, I could tell you some priceless stories …'

We walked past mountains of granulated copper, beneath the cries of filthy gulls, to a small brick building where an old Mercedes was parked between the Lada wrecks.

The whole time, the director was giving the workers that he passed a bollocking. They were drunks, loafers, layabouts; if it was up to him, they'd all be kicked out of here.

It was stifling hot in the cramped harbour building. A fax machine was proudly on display on the table, in the centre of an otherwise empty office, and a fax had just come in.

'We do everything here by fax!' The director violently ripped the glossy paper out of the machine. 'What an invention! Now I can't get by without it!' He studied it for a couple of seconds, squinting short-sightedly at the letters. 'Nikolai, this is from Hamburg … The Jerries have agreed the price for the aluminium … Have Nadia draw up a contract right away …'

A half hour later, my contact drove up at the wheel of a clapped-out Mercedes. Beside him sat a Russian Orthodox cleric, about 50 years of age, with a goatee like an old Billy goat hanging scraggily over his habit.

'Pozorski,' said Pozorski, introducing himself.

With his handsome face, he looked like an actor; he was wearing a bright purple leather jacket with a chickish-yellow fur collar.


The ship from Rotterdam had unloaded its cargo of Zeeland spuds in Denmark. There, it had loaded deep-frozen fish and set course for the Leningrad harbour. The ship was sailing under Polish colours; those on board were Polish too. I followed the harbour director and Pozorski to the quay, where the colossus was moored up between the cranes. The hold was as big as a factory shop floor; the 600 boxes of smuggled bibles in the corner were barely noticeable. Russians clad in rags were busy in the twilit catacombs of the ship, like human pack animals, lugging metal pipes on their shoulders.

'And now we'll sort out the importation.' Borodin glanced around quickly in triumph, fixed his sights on one of the luggers and barked, 'Hey, you there! Go and call Smirnov!'

A minute later, we were joined in the hold by a Russian with an owl's face, sweating in a uniform that hung from his body like a sack. Borodin nodded at the stacked boxes of bibles.

'You have the bill of lading?' the customs officer asked.

'Here,' said Borodin, handing the uniformed Russian the paper that he'd taken off me earlier.

'And the certificate of receipt?'

'Of course.'

The customs officer fished a small round stamp from his trouser pocket, which was hanging from a thin chain; in the metal cap was an ink pad. In a flash, he'd stamped a pale-red hammer and sickle on the bill of lading and the receipt, and in Cyrillic, the letters: CCCP.

'So ...' The harbour director stuffed the papers into the inside pocket of his tobacco-brown jacket. 'You see how efficiently things are done around here? And that's just the goods that the Soviet authorities have officially banned.'

The customs officer immediately slunk off again.

Pozorski spoke, 'Tonight we're going to make a toast. To the first good catch ... You know restaurant Nord?'

Even before I'd left the harbour premises, Pozorski and the priest, who turned out to be named Father Alexei, had put 150 boxes of bibles on the train to Moscow, where the books would be sold on the new free market.

'Sold?' I asked.

'Don't worry about it,' Pozorski said in a soothing voice. 'Of course, you'll get a share of the profits. A new day has dawned. We are good for the people. Goodness is our guiding principle! Those 7,000 books are child's play, of course. But I understand that there are another 80,000 bibles on the way from Rotterdam. Look, they can fetch us some pretty rich pickings. Rounded off, and despite the rate of the ruble, and the misery in this country, we should be able to turn a dollar profit on each book. Isn't that right, Father Alexei?'

The cleric nodded. On his left cheek was a wreath of brown pimples and moles. I thought of my promise to Siderius, and to the members of the church council praying in the warehouse in Pernis.

'Keep your mouth shut about it though ...' Pozorski looked at me inquisitively with a frown. 'Tell me, you did come to this damned country to make some cash, didn't you?'


That afternoon, I wandered for hours through the centre of Leningrad. The façade of the famous Hotel Astoria was clad in scaffolding. A new spirit was sweeping the country; the hotels were being done up at a rapid rate. But the streets around them did resemble a coffin, as the taxi driver had put it. A stone coffin. It began to sleet; I nipped into the Gostiny Dvor shopping centre on the Nevsky Prospect. Here, too, in this grandest shopping temple in the city, there was scarcely a thing to be bought. The visitors flitted past me on the parquet floors like hungry animals.

Middle-aged women jostled before a rack of aubergine-coloured raincoats that had apparently just arrived, hurling curses, and clambering over each other's backs to get at them.

'We are a country of magicians!' Pozorski told me that evening with a grin. 'You can't buy a tomato in the shops, but somehow the fridges are always full. But the greatest trick is yet to come!' We were sitting on the balcony of a restaurant called Nord, an establishment with an erotic cabaret, lively music and a menu as big as a newspaper.

'But shoes?' I asked.

'It's true, you can't find them anywhere.'

'And umbrellas?'

'Nor those! There's absolutely nothing left! *Nitchevo, nichts!* But with your help, we'll soon do something about that. With imports from the West! I can already feel the vibrations of the new age steaming towards me. But be patient, we're still a bit early ...'

While the dishes of salads, smoked salmon, and Volga sturgeon and bottles of Soviet champagne were brought in, Pozorski told me what he and his partners had been doing for the last year: exporting old metal, scrap that was practically lying around in this country for free, which fetched a fortune in the West.

But they expected even more from imports.

Drunk guys hoisted themselves from tables, their hands stuffed with dollar bills, to snag for the night the skeletal beauties who were hanging around by the bar. The restaurant was, after all, a surreptitious brothel.

The next morning, I called Siderius to report in; I had to wait on my bed for an hour to get a connection to Leiden. I kept quiet about the fact that 600 boxes of bibles had disappeared from the hold of the ship to be sold on the grey market via Father Alexei's religious network.

'So it's all going excellently?'

'Excellently,' I lied to the overseer of the Protestant community of Leiden.

A plan had suddenly come to me to hand out the fifty boxes of bibles that I'd managed to hang on to at the harbour in old people's homes. To at least preserve something of the original aim of the mission — to get the books to ordinary people. The administrator in my hotel helpfully jotted down a few addresses for me; I jumped into a taxi with six boxes of bibles and ended up at Ms Lentova's home.

I went back the next day to finish my work.

I arrived on the ward for the clinically insane. It was marked with a little lit red-glass sign. There was a reek of boiled cabbage, urine, faeces, and the ferrous stink of blood. The whole time, I breathed in through my mouth. Sometimes, I couldn't hold it anymore and sucked in the stench of people who were leaking from every orifice, whose mouths released nothing but foul gases before they were put in the coffin or in the fire.

Apparently, darkness was curative for these pensioners, who had been possessed by a mental hell; they lay, in shambles, or sat together on beds and tall chairs in the turquoise twilight.

I wheeled my cart into Ward 3; I mechanically pressed bibles into the hands of people whose faces I could barely discern. A god-awful groaning arose from a bedstead by the window. I drew closer. It was an old man, skinny, nearly naked, with a snow-white Neptune's beard. His pupils rolled around in his eye sockets like big marbles in an empty shot glass, but he appeared not to see me. His arms and legs were bound to the slats with rubber belts.

I turned my trolley around, determined to continue my trek and to get out of this lurid human warehouse, when in the corona of a bedside lamp the apparition of a woman appeared. She was ancient, with a narrow face and long girlish hair, so intensely white that it seemed almost blonde. She fixed me with her almond eyes, which gleamed like precious stones in the semi-darkness.

'What's your name?' she asked calmly.

I told her.

'*Pozhaluysta*, please, take me with you ...' she said.

'Where to?'

'Outside.'

The sibylline apparition continued to fix her irises on me imploringly. My ears flushed, I felt nauseous — just like when I fell in love for the first time.

'How strangely you're looking at me!' Her Russian had an old-fashioned clarity.

I nodded like a bashful schoolboy.

'Pokrovskaya ...' The old woman slowly stretched her skinny hand out towards me. 'Nadezhda Petrovna, but just call me Nadia ...'

It took me over half an hour to persuade the director. She asked me why I'd chosen this half-baked old woman in particular. But I didn't really know myself. I only felt I'd be committing a crime if I refused her humble wish. Ms Lentova fixed her eyes on me, full of mistrust, as though my request was premeditated, as though I'd only set up my whole bible operation with this one aim: to get her permission to take this extremely elderly lady out for a stroll through the city. Did I understand what I was asking? She was 81 years old and didn't have any family. The only ones she could rely on were the Soviet authorities — in fact, Ms Lentova herself, the director of this home.

Madam Pokrovskaya had been sectioned nine years earlier, after she'd spent months on a park bench, wearing an astrakhan fur hat in spite of the summer heat, swigging from a bottle like a slattern, among other mostly male freeloaders, bums and professional alcoholics. One day, she was picked up by paramedics, put in a cell to sober up, disinfected and then brought here, where she howled and resisted until she was drugged senseless.

'She's completely insane,' Ms Lentova continued with her cautionary tale. 'She lives almost entirely in the past. Sometimes she thinks the last czar is still alive! That old soubrette can't even walk three steps in a row. How am I supposed to rustle up a wheelchair for you to go outside? They aren't free, it all costs money …'

She asked for US $150. This was a lot of money for both of us, but I felt I had to do it. I took out my wallet and laid the ten-dollar notes on her desk.

'OK, it's a deal …' The notes disappeared in a flash into her décolleté. 'Come back tomorrow at around twelve.'

The next morning, I wheeled the mysterious woman outside in a chair. The wheels ground the frozen pavements. Ms Lentova had given me a pouch with a syringe; if her patient grew aggressive, then I was to give her an injection.

That whole night, I'd barely shut my eyes because of the hotel whores, who kept phoning me with their honey-dipped voices, interrupting my slumbers. Meanwhile, I was tormented by my crisis of conscience. I knew almost nothing of Siderius, but he'd put his faith in me. Faith that I'd betrayed because, the previous afternoon, I'd called Pozorski to say he could have my remaining bibles to flog.

I wanted to get out of the country as quickly as possible.

'Ooooh!' Madam Pokrovskaya cast her mother of pearl eye-sockets towards the grey skies in delight. 'What lovely fresh air! My sweet city ... Where shall we go?'

The chair's wheels shot off in every direction; I had to use a lot of force to direct it.

'Well, where are we heading to, my little swallow?'

We were surrounded by a wasteland of housing blocks, with plumes of smoke in the distance. The centre was fifteen kilometres away.

'You tell me,' I said.

'To the corner of Rubinstein Street-Nevsky Prospect ...' Madam Pokrovskaya replied, revelling in a sable jacket, with matching hat that she'd been given on loan by the home. 'How old are you, by the way, dear boy?'

Twenty-six, I told her.

'My first lover was 40. I was a girl of 17 at the time. He was an American ...Yes, handsome Americans suddenly appeared among all those revolutionaries in their black coats. To give us food! Suddenly, my family was *boo-shwa* ... Papa, Mama, Natasha ... We lived on Rubinstein Street ... and then one evening they were taken ... They simply forgot about me! But I wasn't a real bourgeois, just an adopted orphan ... They thought I was the child of one of the maids! At the time, all of the guys called me "my little honeypot"... Eh, what are you doing now?'

I flagged down the first lorry that passed. The driver was prepared to take us into the centre for thirty rubles. The wheelchair disappeared among the spades, shovels and wheelbarrows in the back. Madam Pokrovskaya had to be lifted into the cabin, which was tricky, but she laughed her head off the whole time. The driver, a thick-set Tatar with a face as round as a penny, was quite amused.

When the Soviet truck pulled off again, Madam Pokrovskaya rubbed her almost transparent hands in glee. 'When I was 17, I was in Moscow for the first time, on the train, at a party with Soviet commissars and Americans. The drinking that went on! The champagne corks flew like bullets! A hideous city, Moscow ... Hey, look, we're riding like sovereigns!'

The Tatar changed gear with great bravura. Every time he swept around a bend, I grabbed hold of the elderly Russian lady by one of her sable sleeves, asking myself how I could have been seduced into this absurd act. The enchantment of the day before, in the turquoise twilight, when I'd had the impression that I knew the old lady, and we were mysteriously connected across the bridge of time, had long since dissipated.

Madam Pokrovskaya asked the Tatar for a cigarette; she recklessly blew the smoke towards the windscreen, which was rattling wildly. She started to give the driver directions and then said she wanted an ice-cream. And where in Saint Petersburg could you get a good liqueur these days?

'To the Astoria!' she ordered the Tatar, as she chewed on the *Papirosa* cigarette that dangled from her lips.

I told them that the hotel was closed for restoration.

We passed a classical governmental building with peeling yellow plaster and white colonnades. A blood-red banner was flapping from the zinc shingles bearing the slogan: HONOUR

TO LABOUR! When we drove onto the bridge across the Neva towards the English Embankment, Madam Pokrovskaya took off her fur hat. Her bun fell loose. That angel's hair again gave her face a girlish quality.

Madam Pokrovskaya began to mutter to herself out loud. Her Russian still had a remarkable clarity, but there was no following what she was blathering about. She was saying something about ice choppers on the Neva, about her papa ... Where was her dear papa? They cut ice on the river in winter; whole chunks, a metre square, which were carried off to the cellars by horse-drawn sleighs ... To make cool drinks and ice-cream in the hot summers, dairy ice-cream! The Saint Petersburgers were crazy about their ice-cream. One day, her papa had drowned — I could make that out from what she was saying. He'd plunged into the hole in the Neva that he'd cut himself ... With his stupid drunken head! Her mother came in, 'Papa's gone, he's dead!' And not long after, her mother died too, of cholera; hot water was handed out for free on the street corners to combat the contamination, but it didn't help. And a year later, she was living with the Pokrovskis on Rubinstein Street, real Christians. She was lovingly adopted, but a couple of years later they were all dead too; only she was left alive.

'Hey, coachman! You're going the wrong way, it's to the left here!' she yelled at the driver in a feudal tone.

'What? *Shto?*' The Tatar gave me an asinine look. 'Are we going to the Astoria or to Rubinstein Street?'

'To the Karavannaya!' Madam Pokrovskaya commanded again. 'I want to go to Masha! We're going to play some lovely piano and dance ... And then afterwards, Mama and Papa will come to pick me up. Gee up, coachman, let's get on! To the Karavannaya!'

'What? Oh, maybe you mean Tolmachyov Street? I know where

that is. That used to be called the Karavannaya.'

When a moment later the Tatar didn't see a hole in the road in time and we were shaken up as if in a tumble-drier, the elderly Russian lady accused him of being a simpleton. The driver hit the brakes in the middle of the Nevsky Prospect and calmly asked us to get out. No, he didn't want money off us anymore. He was an honourable Soviet worker! He wasn't going to allow himself to be insulted!

I had to take the wheelchair and the ancient passenger out of the truck myself.

A moment later, Madam Pokrovskaya nestled into the wheelchair without complaint. She tugged her fur hat halfway down her parchment cheeks, mumbling that there was snow on the way, and announced that we definitely had to drop by Friedländer in the Passage, Nevsky Prospect 48. She desperately needed a new warm shawl and underwear. The fact that the drapery-shop Friedländer, which I'd once seen in sepia-tinted photos, had closed seventy years previously at the command of the Bolsheviks seemed to entirely elude her.

As soon as she said anything, she immediately appeared to forget it again. Her little green eyes darted back and forth like nervous silverfish. As I pushed her past the city blocks, where the patina of Italian pastel gleamed through the Soviet grime, she saw things that weren't there. She said we'd have to watch out for the tram in a bit: those buggers always came tearing round the corner! She looked at the people numbly passing by with the marks of disillusion and want in their eyes, and gave them an astonished, almost insolent, challenging stare.

I pushed the elderly Russian lady in the direction of the Moscow station, repeatedly drawn towards the road by the rocky right wheel.

The usual queues were standing outside the state shops. There was one person on the street flogging potatoes, carrots and onions from a crate. The authorities turned a blind eye to the primitive street trade. There was nowhere to sit down.

Just then, my eyes settled on the opposite side of the Nevsky Prospect; although the front of the Hotel Europe was also clad in scaffolding, the dark-yellow window of the restaurant section beside the street was filled with the silhouettes of people.

'Where are we going?'

'To Europe ...' I wheeled the chair off the pavement and onto the road.

'Do they have ice-cream?'

'Of course!' Still leaning against the wheelchair so that it wouldn't topple over because of that one unruly wheel, I drove the aged Russian over the greasy asphalt.

'Oh, delicious!' Madam Pokrovskaya whooped. 'But do call Mama and Papa ... I have enough two-kopek pieces! So that they know where I am ... That I haven't gone to the Karavannaya, to Masha, but we're having ice-cream ... Bastard!' Just before we reached the other side, a shit-coloured Lada almost dinged us. 'Bastard! Viper! Foul communist!'

The doorman at Hotel Europe shut the door as soon as he saw us approach. I rapped my knuckles on the glass, on which the name of the hotel was written in gold ornamental letters.

'We're closed!' came the response from behind the door.

'I think you're open.'

'No, closed!'

'Well, who's in there then?'

'Foreigners ... We run on foreign currency ...'

Everybody wanted hard currency then: dollars, Deutschmarks,

even guilders. I took a wad of Deutschmarks out of my trouser pocket, fanned them out and held them flat to the glass.

The door opened as though it were automatic.

'Bibles, hard currency …' Madam Pokrovskaya was nothing but admiration. 'My lad, you're an artist!'

The doorman in his bottle-green service coat helped me to lift the wheelchair over the granite doorstep, grumbling. It was smoky and stifling in the pillared dining room. There were a lot of guests seated between the faded-red velvet walls; indeed, they were mostly foreigners.

As soon as we'd taken our place at a table in a corner, Madam Pokrovskaya's craving for ice-cream dissipated. Wasn't that chicken she smelt? She wanted to have a roast chicken, with sautéed potatoes. And what wine did they have here?

'What wine would you like?' A waitress had descended on us. She scrunched up her snout with disgust, as though an old woman in a wheelchair didn't belong here at all.

'Red,' Madam Pokrovskaya said decisively.

'Sweet or sour?'

'Sour? Child, have you no breeding? You mean "dry" surely? Dry, of course …'

I had a beer. A little while later, Madam Pokrovskaya was happily consuming her wine and chicken opposite me. She was holding a drumstick to her mouth with both hands, like a harmonica.

'How do you know my husband?' she asked.

I looked at her without understanding.

'How is that cursed war going? Is there still a war? Thank God I was able to escape. Leningrad … Yes, I was able to get out in time with my husband, Dima … To the Urals, and then on to Siberia … The city of Tomsk … The summers there are blistering!

But we always ate well … My Dima's a wonderful fellow … He had a portrait of Stalin tattooed on his back … A waster, a fraud, always running after women … Do you think I don't know that? But he isn't a murderer! And he always thought I was the most beautiful! So, tell me, how do you know each other? From Berlin? You do come from Berlin? I knew it right away when I saw you, a handsome young German! Dima brought me back cases full of things from Berlin. Beautiful towels, shimmering material for dresses, shoes, exactly the right size! And German porcelain … I think that Lentova nicked it all off me. Don't you think so too? That bitch! I was playing with Natasha … and then you suddenly walked into my room with a trolley full of bibles. But I've no desire for a bible … I've always hated God. And God me! And certainly when I went to work in that house, there in Tomsk … My husband swore to me that it was necessary, for the money … And what's more I was helping the men … Small beer — a bit of fun before the wretches left again for the front! But what filth! *Hitler kaput!* Do you know whether that skunk has actually been defeated now? Every spring I saw the coaches pass by in the street. A whole cortege! The czar's furniture being conveyed from the Winter Palace to Tsarskoye Selo. The horses left hard yellow turds behind them … The boys started pelting each other with them … That was always in April … Then Papa, Mama, Natasha and I went to the dacha for the first time. We had a car, a French one! I was in a cell for two years, then four years in a colony, innocent … And me praying that that fellow of mine wouldn't do anything to my daughter … I know how these men are! But what on earth are you doing with those bibles? Why don't you find yourself a nice girl? There are enough walking around. But do watch out for diseases! Oh, oh … Dima took Mila away from me, I think Brezhnev was already here then … Hey, Madam, what good liqueur do they have here tonight?'

Ms Lentova had been right. Time was all jumbled up for this poor old woman, and she was becoming more and more excitable. In spite of her fragile appearance, she had a loud contralto voice. The guests kept turning their heads in disapproval. I ostentatiously checked my watch, and after half an hour beckoned to the waitress for the bill, saying that it was high time I got the old woman back to the home.

'Son of a bitch!' Madam Pokrovskaya seemed to ignore my words completely. 'Did he send you here to spy on me or something? I'm on to you, laddie! With your bibles! Yes, my husband sent you after me. To interrogate me. But why did he take Mila away from me? My daughter, my sweet child, my sunshine …'

I was about to ask the manager to call a taxi when a Russian entered the dining room with a swarthy actor's face and a purple leather jacket with a chickish-yellow fur collar. Pozorski was accompanied by a skinny girl who looked like she'd just been yanked out of a schoolroom.

I tried to make myself as small as possible. The next morning, my flight was leaving for Amsterdam. I'd rather not have anything else to do with my bible contact, with his corrupt way of doing business, and his import plans.

'Well, well … You do have taste, sport. These days, this is by far the best establishment in the city!' With a nod of his head, Pozorski directed his nipper to a table, where the child sat down demurely. 'And who do we have here?' Charmingly, with feigned interest, he looked at Madam Pokrovskaya with his brown, puppy eyes.

The Russian lady, who was born pre-revolution, glowed like amber. She held her hand out haughtily towards him, gave her name, and asked whether the general had sent him to save her.

'Of course, dear lady …' Pozorski had immediately surmised her condition with his intuitive cunning; he played along exquisitely. 'The general sends his regards.'

I said I was sorry, but it was sadly high time that I took her back to the home.

The scream that arose from Madam Pokrovskaya's throat bordered on the surreal — a human siren. While all eyes in the dining room were now fixed on us, it appeared as though the elderly Russian lady was trying to wrestle herself out of her wheelchair. She begged Pozorski to take her with him, and again started calling me a fraud, a friend of her husband's … The son of a bitch that had taken Mila away from her! He had been sent by the general?

'Take me with you!' Madam Pokrovskaya grabbed Pozorski's arm. 'The general is the only one who can bring Mila back to me!'

Then, something strange happened. Her eyes went completely white in their sockets; foam appeared on her lips. The poor lady was having one of the fits that Ms Lentova had warned me about.

'What an idiotic female!' With a gesture of disgust, Pozorski rid himself of his hysterical countrywoman. 'So, are we seeing each other tonight in Nord? We really have to talk!'

A sort of death rattle arose from the lips of the pensioner. In panic, I directed Pozorski to the leather case in the side pocket of the wheelchair. He stabbed the pre-filled syringe into her thigh like a poniard dagger, straight through the material of her dress, yelling that this person wouldn't wake up again for a century.

Twenty minutes later, the old lady woke up in the taxi. A snow storm had started up; the driver struggled along the road in the swirling whiteness. She was lying with her head in my lap, on the rocking back seat. First she opened one eye, then the next. I was about to brace myself, but a smile appeared on her lips, like a just-woken child.

'Are we going to Papa?' she asked.

I nodded.

Back in my hotel there were two messages: a telegram from Siderius that said that the church had given the green light for the shipment of another 80,000 bibles, and a reminder that Pozorski had left with the receptionist by phone, saying that he expected me that evening in Nord.

I tore up the notes. My decision was final. I was flying back the next day, never to return to the USSR.

I didn't know that my Russian years were only just beginning.

# CHAPTER TWO

My wife and I were carried on the stream of human beings, out onto the teeming street beneath the night sky, which was olive-green and black, as always at this time of year. Autumn in Saint Petersburg – the theatre season had just begun.

The theatregoers were being whisked away by taxis and limousines with their headlights dimmed. Inside them young women, thinner than paper, quickly folded themselves into back seats, with the paunches of men trailing after them, heading for supper somewhere in the city.

We'd been to see *Giselle*. We walked home from the Mariinsky Theatre, in the embrace of the city palaces, and onwards through the ever-emptier streets higher up, where I was overcome by angst.

I thought of Flaubert, who was a close friend of Théophile Gautier, one of the writers of the libretto of *Giselle*, which had premiered at the Paris Opera in June 1841 and had been performed again on this dark and cloudy September evening 175 years later. The prima ballerina had been buried beneath flowers, and there had been a standing ovation of at least fifteen minutes. We'd paid a hundred euros altogether for the cheap seats.

But the view was phenomenal: we were sitting right beneath the sky-blue, domed ceiling with the fresco-like cherubim; below, to the left, was the czar's box with its gilt and blue velvet. The chandelier was the absolute showpiece; it had lit the faces of anyone and everyone who had played some role in Russian history, and also the nameless, countless horde.

We slowly strolled down Dekabristov Street. Julia asked why I was still so silent and sombre. She started talking about the star of the evening, a ballerina trained in Saint Petersburg, who practically only ever performed abroad. My wife was fanatically proud of her, as if she were her own daughter.

In the meantime, I was still lingering with Gautier and Flaubert. The creator of *Madame Bovary* had had quite a time of it! In his twenties, he was suddenly struck down with epilepsy. Then shortly after, his father had died, and Flaubert's sister Caroline, who'd just given birth to a daughter, weakened with puerperal fever and died soon after. The writer, his brother, his mother and the bawling infant were left behind. The sister was laid in her coffin in her bridal gown and thus interred. 'My mother is like a weeping statue,' Flaubert wrote to a friend. 'What a household, what a hell! And me? My eyes are as dry as a marble statue …'

And that was the way you had to live, not bellyache, but be brave. Carry on.

Then, on a square near St Isaac's Cathedral, there was the sound of a loud thunderclap. I'd been in war zones a couple of times on account of my work as a journalist; I'd learned to determine the origin of a strike unerringly.

But this time I did err.

The rain began to clatter, to bucket down. It fell vertically from the sky like cold, liquid steel. We bolted to the revolving door of the Astoria; a guy was just coming out through the glittering glass.

He dashed straight to a white taxi in his sodden shoes; it was parked in the middle of the street with its lights flashing.

'Where do you need to go?' he gasped through the window.

'Tchaikovsky Street 40,' I said.

'OK, get in.'

We drove past the Moskovsky Station, and a little while later we were standing in front of our apartment block. There was a sweet scent in the street from the bread factory across the road, which was already running at full kilter. Behind us were the city barracks. Bread and soldiers – everything within a hand's reach.

The lift in our lobby was out of order again. We calmly climbed the smooth, worn granite steps of our showy staircase.

Once inside, my wife jumped straight into her dressing gown, and talked reassuringly to our three cats, who wound themselves around her feet, their tails up, six sapphires fixed on her in absolute adoration. She went through to the kitchen to make tea, as she dried her long dark hair with a rough white towel. She asked if I'd like some tea too, though she knew I never drank it, except when I was sick.

'Do you really not want tea?'

'Really I don't ...'

The white wines at the theatre had been pretty unimpressive, as usual; my alcohol level was low. I hurried to the fridge, poured a glass of wine and walked over to the fireplace. A little while later, the ash logs that I'd bought earlier that day were flickering and flaming in their marble home. They began to give off a scent; my face caught their warm glow.

My wife was now nestled in her bucket seat, the cats sprawled to the left and right of her, and on the back of her chair, like live hot-water bottles.

I crept behind my desk, which was over by the window, with its view of the dark courtyard. The water was thundering down, gargling out of the organ of drainpipes and echoing off the walls; the pipes were so wide that a dwarf could easily disappear down into them. We heard a few fresh thunderclaps from the direction of the Neva. I flicked on my green-glass reading light. My desk was an antique battleship with ornamental legs, covered in open books, papers, old theatre tickets, train tickets, photos, pieces of amber that I'd picked up on happy days on the Baltic coast. It was a total mess, but I had written a few books on it.

By now, Julia had turned on the overture to *Giselle*, which we'd just been listening to, and it boomed through our high room.

I furtively glanced at my wife, wreathed in a loop of cats; she was dark, handsome, classical, illuminated by the warm yellow glow of a tombac lamp. My parents were two thousand kilometres away, buried in the Dutch dunes. Julia's father and mother were dead too; we didn't have any kids. All in all, an uncomplicated existence. Nonetheless, I was again overcome by angst — a bleakness that had been my companion all my life, and which I'd occasionally tried to fight, but which kept coming back like a chronic skin disease.

'Genius, eh, this version?' Julia glanced up at me from the French cookbook that she was slowly leafing through.

I got up, fetched the wine bottle from the fridge, sat back down behind my desk, topped myself up, opened my laptop, and checked my email for the first time that day. I read:

> *Hi Piotr,*
> *We had a great idea here at the publisher's last week.*
> *Next year, it'll be a hundred years since the outbreak*
> *of the Russian Revolution. We were having a bit of a*

*brainstorming session and we thought wouldn't it be nice if you wrote a book about it? Not too weighty though. Try to keep it personal. When the anniversary comes around, we'll be drowning in commemorative books, of course. We want to chart our way through that mountain of publications — as far as press attention goes — and we can only do that if you keep it personal. Personal, personal, personal. We'll need to know soon, by the way, because even though the spring catalogue's not quite finished yet, we're already busy with the autumn's.*

*I haven't heard from you in ages, but I hope you're doing well.*

A half-charred block of wood dropped onto the glowing red hearth-plate like the casing of a launched grenade. I got up to attend to it with a poker. Our marble surround was a veritable masterpiece; on the mantel there was a pair of swallows, busy feeding their three young in a nest. We were almost certain it was the work of an unknown Italian artist. Occasionally, I'd run my hand over it to feel the craftsmanship and the smooth finish.

I chucked the wooden grenade back onto the fire, dodged out of the way of the tangerine-coloured sparks, then tossed on a fresh block of the ash and jiggled it up with an iron poker that had once stoked the fire of a house in Enkhuizen. It was an heirloom from an aunt. At a certain point, almost everyone becomes the collector of the precious debris of other people's lives. Some of the plates in our kitchen had been my parents', the knives and forks too. Our German sideboard came from Kaliningrad, where Julia's grandparents had lived for the longest part of their lives. And now our two-room apartment was full: with books, books, books, lots of paintings, an Art Nouveau mirror, precious photos, Julia's collection of teapots, her grandmother's dark-blue glass ashtray, an antique French tombac clock on the mantelpiece, plaster busts of composers (two of Wagner) and other bric-a-brac that made you wonder where it would all end up one day. Sometimes, in my very bleakest moments, I could see the junk-shop dealers in their overalls coming in, wearing their dirty shoes. This childless couple had died. And with their shoes they'd soil our parquet, which we'd always lovingly maintained, with dollar signs in their eyes. What would happen to the life we'd accumulated? To the things here on my desk?

My blood was pounding in my temples. I clicked away from my publisher's email, swallowing a lump in my throat as dry as dust, and for a moment I stared at a little bookcase containing all the books I'd written over the last twenty years, ten in total. But it had all been for nothing; I'd been consoling myself with an illusion.

'How's the wine?' Julia asked.

'Delicious …' I opened the laptop again and decided to answer the email right away, before I headed to bed.

> *Dear E,*
>
> *I find it a bit awkward answering this, as I'd already told you I've quit writing. After almost twenty-five years, I'm giving up. And that has nothing to do with the intensely corrupt Dutch literary world, where a little gang of frightened, mutually sodomising gatekeepers gets to make or break books and thus lives too. It's more the fact that …*

Just then, there were a couple more thunderclaps; this time not from outside, from the direction of the Neva, but from somewhere downstairs inside the building. The force was so fierce that the cats immediately went flying, each to a different corner of the room, leaving my wife flabbergasted in her dressing gown. I quickly told her to stay where she was — I'd check what was going on. I slipped on my shoes, went down the staircase and halted halfway. One of our neighbours, from the *kommunalka* — communal flat — below ours, was standing on the landing in a blue-and-white striped sailor's top, hacking up an antique sideboard with an axe.

'No, not Mama's dresser!' came his wife's voice through a gap in the door behind him.

'You foul street-walker, I'll show you!' He raised the axe high above his fiery-red, moustachioed head, grimacing in his rage at the piece of polished cherrywood furniture. 'No, not Mama's dresser ...' the man imitated his wife's voice out of key. 'But why not? You slut!' The axe-head fell again, the splinters and brass fittings flying every which way. 'Here it *goes*, Mama's dresser!'

His wife's alcoholic clown's face poked out through the gap between the two paint-peeling salon doors of the apartment. She watched in silence as her husband continued his destruction; the top of the flaming-red furniture was entirely in splinters.

'There you go, you slut! That'll teach you! And from now on, if you don't do as I say, it'll all end up the same way, you hear me? Everything! We're selling this dump ... This mildewed cage is driving me mad ... I'd rather have a hut in the woods than stay here any longer ... Sell up ... Or else it's going, everything!'

I heard the lift switch on above me; apparently it was working again. The metal doors opened. Zinaida Petrova stepped out wearing a fox-stole around her throat and spreading a pungent cloud of perfume. She was the mother of the famous opera singer who lived on the top floor of our apartment block.

'Gennady Nikolaevich!' the sprightly Russian lady yelled at my downstairs neighbour in rebuke, which immediately made him stop his senseless act of destruction. 'What *are* you doing?'

Her inky Caucasian eyes spewed fire.

'Chopping wood for the fire.'

'Chopping wood?'

'Yes, firewood! This dresser was my mother-in-law's, that witch! She was a witch and my wife is a witch. Oh, if only I'd realised it sooner ... How daughters take after their mothers ... Now she has the same fat arse and pig's snout as her mother. But this is excellent kindling!'

'Why here?'

'Where else?' Panting heavily, and every moment looking as if he might depart this life, Gennady Nikolaevich lowered his axe lamely beside his leg like a Neanderthal with his club.

'This is a communal area ... Do I need to call the caretaker? Or the police? Why ... ' Zinaida Petrova suddenly turned to me. 'Why didn't you put a stop to this?'

I said I'd only just arrived, that I ...

'He wants to chuck everything out ...' The clown's head in the doorway came to life. 'Someone's finally shown up who wants to buy our twenty-four square metres ... And what do we get in return for it? Not even a dog kennel on the outskirts ...'

For a moment, my downstairs neighbour's drunken gaze drifted over the carnage that he'd wrought, as if the scale of it was only now dawning on him. And as he half turned his sea-dog's head towards his wife in the doorway, he spoke. 'Sooner a coop with its own privy than always having to sit in the shitty stench of twelve others ... I want out of here!'

'Oh, our lovely dresser!' The downstairs neighbour stared

flummoxed at her husband, her chubby chin flopping over the door-chain. 'Why this, my love? My dead mother's dresser ... Firewood? My dear Gennady, we don't even have a fire? What have you gone and done? It's all ruined. And this pair here!' Raising her voice, she suddenly turned on Zinaida Petrova and me. 'Yes, you there, in your fancy apartments, you've got your great fireplaces! But everything was ripped out of ours ages ago ... The twelve of us here behind one door, we could just die beside our stove ...'

'That's why, Masha ...' My downstairs neighbour fixed his moist eyes on his wife remorsefully. 'That's why I wanted to sell the place too ... Better some shack on the outskirts than ...'

'Fine, Gennady, fine! I'll have another think about it,' Masha the clown answered. 'But first put down that axe ... And go and get me something to drink at the kiosk. I'm dying of thirst! See if they have that plum liqueur ... And in the name of the devil, what are you two still gawping at?' She angrily addressed me and the opera singer's mother again, who nervously picked at the fox-stole around her neck. 'Off with the pair of you! These stairs are a communal area. Do you hear me? Com-mun-nal! If my husband wants to come out here and chop up a dresser with an axe, then he's well within his rights to do so!'

Zinaida Petrova slipped into the lift after casting a helpless, quizzical look at me. I slowly climbed the stairs past the broken window, behind which the rain was still clattering from the eaves and gargling down through the drainpipes.

Julia was in the shower. When she came out in her bathrobe and terry slippers amid a halo of steam, I told her what had happened. 'Poor buggers,' she mumbled, as she disappeared into the bedroom and asked if I'd soon be coming too.

First, I finished my email to my publisher, quickly downing

two glasses of wine as I did so. Red. Red wine is the best to help you fall asleep.

Just a short while before, I'd received a message that my contract at the newspaper — which still had a year and a half to run — was probably not going to be extended. Print was a sinking ship. Freelancer-freeloser. What was I supposed to do? I hardly had any pension. For twenty years, I'd faithfully dedicated myself to writing novels just about every day, despite the daily issues, the political crises, the press conferences, the travels, wading through war zones as a reporter. But I'd earned less from literature than €300 a month, on average. Old age was gaping up at me like a ravine. I would be leaving my wife behind 'unprovided for', as they say. It was over; I'd have to start doing something else quickly.

After I'd told my publisher of my decision a week before, I finally told Julia that I was quitting writing too. I was one of the absolute dregs of literature.

'Now you listen to me closely …' my wife said.

Then she gave me both barrels.

The next morning, my brother-in-law Alexei came to visit. Julia had taken our middle cat, Ljòlja, to the vet's, all the way over behind the Vitebsky Station. She messaged me from the waiting room, saying it was chock-a-block, that they had to do an emergency operation (a whimpering sheepdog had just been brought in), and there was some apple pie in the fridge for her brother. I made coffee and gave my brother-in-law a generous slice of the apple pie, with lots of raisins.

He devoured it as though he were starving. Since my father-in-law's funeral the summer before, I'd only seen him a couple of times. For a Russian, my brother-in-law looked remarkably youthful. He still had all his own hair, full-bodied and in good condition in spite of his being past fifty. It was evenly dark, without the least hint of grey. But I could see deep torment in his light, greyish-green eyes.

He'd worked for the same company for years, carrying out the quality-control of the fruit and veg that came into the harbour in Saint Petersburg by ship. The reports were written up in Russian and English. I'd once seen one of them, and had been deeply impressed by the tables, the temperature coefficients, PH values, fungi, bacteria, and other matters. When, several times, the shelf-life of some products that had been brought ashore proved to be disappointing, he was sent abroad to do the sampling at the place of origin. In this way, he spent three weeks in the north of Morocco for the orange harvest, and in Chile for the kiwis, and he once spent three months in a hotel in Vlissingen, from which he trekked into the Zeeland fields every day to check the onions and carrots that would soon be harvested. In spite of his highly specialised work, my brother-in-law didn't earn much. He lived with his wife, Tanya, in a run-down, two-room apartment on Vasilyevsky Island, sixth floor, with no lift. Then one day, when the ruble collapsed again, he was fired. What was he to do? He had a bit of capital, a few thousand euros, and together with his wife and son, Dima, he started a little business from home, in glycerine, which was used for all sorts of things in Russia: from making shampoo and soap to pimping Russian wine. He bought his ware from a Flemish factory, somewhere around Ghent. He couldn't buy in large stocks because capital was tight. A loan was out of the question — the interest that the banks charged could run as high as 20 per cent — but they managed to get by. After a year, my brother-in-law bought a second-hand car. He even went on holiday to Spain once with his wife. But then the crisis struck again: the ruble dropped by 50 per cent against the euro. His wares had to be paid for in foreign currency, while the contracts with his buyers had been drawn up in rubles. They squeezed him more and more; as a small supplier, he was no match for the big boys.

And in this way, it ultimately all went belly up.

'I find this difficult to admit, but … to be honest, I'm flat broke …' My brother-in-law carefully scooped together all of the crumbs from the apple pie with his fingertips, then swiftly lifted the saucer to his mouth and licked them off like a dog.

He'd paid off all his debts; the second-hand car was sold. And now he owned nothing. And yet, Alexei hadn't thrown in the towel. He had a plan — a great plan to earn a living and fulfil an old dream. He wanted to buy a second-hand sailing boat with an old school friend: a great boat, a golden opportunity, it was now or never. My brother-in-law had all the papers you can get for sailing at sea. In the final years of the Soviet Union, he'd taken part in regattas, and despite all of his financial problems, he'd always kept up with the sport. Things might have been going badly economically in Russia, but there was an abundance of people with money in the city. Many were planning to buy sailing yachts, but they didn't have the necessary papers. He wanted to start a sailing school with his old school friend; first, here on the Gulf of Finland, maybe later in Italy, Spain, warmer waters … It was really a golden opportunity, my brother-in-law continued breezily. The boat was eleven years old, but still in excellent condition. A beauty! Thirty thousand euros. His friend would put in ten grand, they could borrow another ten from the bank, but first he'd have to come up with ten himself … Well, then he thought …

I walked into the kitchen and came back with the coffee pot and the rest of the apple pie. My brother-in-law again greedily attacked the pastry that his sister had baked, and said, 'I'll pay you the money back as soon as possible, of course. According to our calculations, we should be able to pay back half by the end of the summer, if it's a good season. It's a real beauty … The *Nautilus* — a great name!'

Fifteen minutes after her brother left, Julia came in with the cat basket. Her face was red, not because of the sudden cold, but because she'd been crying.

'Ljòlja.' Slowly, my wife lowered the checked cat basket down by the strap. Behind the netting was the whiskered snout of our middle one. 'There's something terribly wrong with Ljòlja … Oh, what should I do?'

Of course, I promised my brother-in-law I'd help, but there was one complicating factor: I didn't have the money. While Julia began calling her girlfriends around the world — the Russian-Jewish diaspora — to ask about the best way to treat Ljòlja's stomach ailments, I was totally knocked off track for days following Alexei's request; the existential despair had entirely returned. I was well over fifty, I'd worked all my life, and I wasn't even able to help a family member in need. What sort of a failure was I? And this despite being at the threshold of the gates of wealth a couple of times in my life. I'd had a sniff. Like lots of my friends, I could have been a millionaire. If I'd just gone about things better. If I'd been more egotistical. Harder, craftier. But over the years, I'd accumulated nothing but debts.

I was cantankerous, grim, I could hardly bear my wife's silent grief about our sick cat, and so around eleven in the morning I headed out onto the streets with a hangover, puzzling how I could come up with the money. Should I take up my publisher's offer after all? Yet another book. Where would I find the strength? I changed tack out of necessity. I wrote to my publisher agreeing to write the book, with the working title *Revolution*, to be delivered no later than 1 September 2017, for an advance of ten thousand euros, non-refundable.

Only fifteen minutes later, I received the following:

> *Hey guy!*
> *It's great you're taking it on! But what do you mean ten grand? You know how tricky things are in the book trade? Ten grand: that would mean us having to shift at least five thousand just to break even. Considering your previous sales, that isn't all that realistic. Shall we round it down to five grand?*

They finally agreed to the ten grand, but on the proviso that, if I didn't hand the book in on time, I'd have to pay back the entire advance. The contract was scanned, I signed it, sent it back, and the advance was deposited in my account by expedited transfer. Every day, I went to the *bankomat* in Mayakovskogo Street, until one afternoon I could hand over an envelope to my brother-in-law containing one hundred €100 notes, green as linden leaves, which came out of the wall as though freshly printed, in the marble doorway where the heater was always on.

I'd rarely seen anyone happier than Alexei. Not only that: we'd heard from the vet that Ljòlja's stomach troubles perhaps weren't as bad as they'd first appeared. Julia literally jumped in the air with delight.

My brother-in-law immediately wanted to celebrate the upcoming purchase of the boat. He took us to a restaurant with singing gypsies and paid the bill, smiling generously; after all, he'd been given an envelope that afternoon containing a sum that he'd have had to work at least six months for.

The next morning, still feeling groggy from the vodka, which I usually didn't drink, I realised what I'd done. I was planning to take the train to Moscow the next day, where we rented a second apartment where I wrote, and where months of work now awaited me. I was overcome with dread. Where was I supposed to find the time for this book? I'd never had the luxury of only having to write, but I'd noticed that I was growing older; it was getting tougher and tougher to keep so many different balls in the air.

This advance had got me into a terrible mess.

When I went out onto the street that afternoon, there was a golden autumn mist hanging over the city. In front of our door, a woman was selling smoked Murmansk stockfish from a crate. The smell reminded me of Volendam eel. I usually turned right here, past the old fire station, city palaces and what used to be the Austrian-Hungarian embassy, to where the street meets the Fontanka and the Summer Garden, then along the linden avenue opposite the Mikhailovsky Castle as far as the Moyka, where I would drink coffee at Singer on the Nevsky Prospect, with a little something on the side — my daily outing when I was in Saint Petersburg.

'Wouldn't you like some fish?' asked the woman sitting on the stool beside the crate of fish from the Barents Sea. 'You won't find any better.'

The fish looked like clubs that you could beat someone's head in with, also golden yellow now. The whole of creation suddenly appeared to be golden yellow. I declined, and didn't turn right for some reason or another, but left, in the direction of the Tauride Gardens. How many months did I have, actually? More than ten. For a writer, that was quite long, but I wasn't a real writer. Real writers could live off their work, they were asked to give readings, almost earned more from talking about their books than from the books themselves. Waiting for me shortly would be swirling Moscow, with all its press conferences, meetings, *vernissages*, the issues of the day; before you knew it, a rebellion or a war would have broken out somewhere, although I'd decided never to cover a war again. Ultimately, war and sex are for the young.

We lived at number 40 Tchaikovsky Street. For some years, a florist had been housed on the ground floor of number 58, in the same kind of stately, neo-classical building as ours, but more drastically run down – the peeling stuccowork fell into nets attached to the façade, like boulders in Southern Europe. In the florist's window there were depressing bouquets, as though they'd once been laid on a grave, and someone had given the order to have them pinched and spruced up with misting water and plant feed, to get them ready for re-sale. The building's wrought-iron gate led to the courtyard that housed the notary's office where Julia and I had once sat in the waiting room between the hacking pensioners, in the oppressive searing heat of an August day, to hear that issuing a death certificate for someone whose body was never found — in this case, my wife's first husband — was well-nigh impossible.

There was also a black granite memorial plate on the front of the building, engraved with this gold-coloured text:

*Vladimir Ilyich LENIN lived in this house from 31
August to early October 1893. It was during this period
that he began his work in Saint Petersburg on the foundation of the Russian Social Democratic Labour Party.*

The October Revolution of 1917 began with Lenin. The son-of-a-
bitch from Simbirsk, who'd given the order to wipe out innocent
people like cockroaches, to beat in the brains of the bourgeois
scum, to humiliate them and not spare the bullets; he'd once lived
a couple of doors down our street. I'd walked past so often. I knew
quite a lot about Lenin. A couple of years earlier, I'd written a
novel about the embalming secret of his mummified body, which
was still lying in state in a glass sarcophagus in the mausoleum on
Red Square in Moscow. Would I have to get mixed up in all that
misery again?

I'd used a lot of quotes in the novel, about how dirty the revolution
was, with lots of allusions to Russian literature and history, which
sadly only a few in the Netherlands had understood. Couldn't they re-
publish that novel, with an eye to the coming hundredth anniversary
of the revolution, which began under Lenin's leadership, and was
the greatest crime in human history — apart from the Holocaust?
Maybe I could shift another five thousand of them: ten grand in
royalties. Then I'd be free of the burden I'd taken on.

I'd always known, or rather I'd never *not* known, what had happened
here in Saint Petersburg, in this city that had become my home
over the years, more so than Moscow. From those first decades
after its foundation in 1703 to this very day. As a teenager, I'd read
about uprisings, revolts, frenzies. By now, I'd experienced them in

my own life too. Not the uprisings that took place in Paris, with students waving around crowbars and throwing bricks, or the so-called 'left-wing revolts' in Amsterdam, where more rubbers were discharged than rubber bullets, but the kind where there was real shooting, where people were killed, and rulers were toppled.

A man walked out of the florists with a face like a pug with a heavy cold, wearing a lead-grey overcoat. He wasn't holding a bouquet that reminded one of a floral creation once stolen from a cemetery, but an actual funeral wreath, which was bigger than a bicycle wheel. He quickly carried on, keeping close to the houses, in the direction of the Tauride Gardens. The low-hanging, golden sun penetrated my back without providing any warmth; because of the glare from the windows, it occasionally seemed as though the sun was shining straight into my face, so every now and then I squinted my eyes.

Tchaikovsky Street wasn't named after the famous composer, whose music I was quite a fan of and who had lived elsewhere in the city for years, but after some communist or other. Before the revolution, our street was called Sergiyevskaya Street, and was home to some illustrious and delightful occupants. Among them, the poet and writer Zinaida Gippius, a friend of Alexander Blok and Andrei Bely and dozens of other writers, thinkers, philosophers, politicians and artists; she eventually died in Paris in 1945, destitute and entirely disillusioned with life, like so many Russian émigrés. I thought of her briefly every day. Almost no one had experienced the revolution of 1917 from so close at hand and had described it as minutely as she had done in her diaries. Sometimes, she mercilessly depicted and unmasked her contemporaries, such as the radical cleric Georgy Gapon, alias Father Gapon, who in 1905 — in a beard and long white habit, and holding a crucifix aloft — had led a column of thousands of impoverished workers over the Nevsky Prospect through the freshly-fallen Saint Petersburg snow to the Winter Palace, to demand better living conditions of the csar.

He'd drawn up a petition for the oppressed, which read:

*SIRE*
*"We, inhabitants of Saint Petersburg, who come from various quarters, our wives, children, and helpless elderly parents, have come here to YOU, SIRE, to seek justice and protection. We are poor and oppressed, we toil endlessly, and we are degraded (...)*
*We are being suffocated by despotism and our lack of rights, we are gasping for breath. Oh, SIRE, we have no strength left. We have reached the limit of our endurance. We have come to that terrible moment when it seems better to die than to continue in our unbearable sufferings ..."*

Shortly before, Japan had wiped the floor with Russia in war in a humiliating fashion, and many could remember all too well the famine of fourteen years previously; people had died like flies all over the country. Those who rebelled had been finished off with bayonets, bullets and the noose. In the meantime, the export of grain by the government continued, and the aristocracy blissfully carried on with their privileged lives of balls, hunting parties, banquets and concerts.

On that Sunday in January 1905, the pealing of the clocks rang out over the entire city; the golden domes gleamed. The czar and family man, Nicholas II, was residing with his wife, the newly-born Tsesarevich and four daughters in his palace at Tsarskoye Selo — walking through the white woods, playing dominoes, smoking, writing his diary. While men, women and children from the workers' quarters were walking over the thick ice of the Neva in their Sunday best, in the direction of the centre, to take part in the demonstration that had been brewing in the caverns of their city for weeks.

Father Gapon cried out to the assembled masses, 'Would the police and the soldiers dare to stop us, comrades?'

'They won't dare!' hundreds of voices chanted together.

Gapon: 'Comrades, would we be better off dying for our demands than carrying on living as we have?'

'We will die! We will die!'

'Do you swear to die?'

'We swear it!' a chorus of voices rang out.

'Let everyone who swears ...' Gapon requested, 'Let everyone who swears raise their hand ...'

The czar, in the comforting bosom of his loving family thirty kilometres away in his country estate, issued the order to kill them.

The imperial guard rapidly mowed done forty of the poor devils, a few of them holding icons aloft; hundreds of people, including many children, were wounded. Elsewhere in the city, there were more horrible butcherings. The Cossack cavalry mercilessly hacked at their own people, just as in previous centuries and in the century to come. 'There is no God, there is no czar,' Father Gapon murmured after looking around helplessly at the bloodbath. Ultimately, though, he would come out of it alive. A theatre barber cut off his hair and beard, and hid him.

To be honest, I'd always considered the radical cleric, who'd set up societies and tea-houses in the city with dance evenings, readings, and other edifying entertainment for 'decent workers', to be quite sympathetic. But according to Zinaida Gippius, he was one of the many secret agents paid by the czarist secret police, the Okhrana. She called the whole history of that day foul and terrifying. In the end, Gapon was murdered in a Finnish dacha by a member of the socialist-revolutionary party.

Would I have to delve into all that business again for this damned book?


The revolution of 1905 was the prelude to the one of 1917: quite soon after that 'Bloody Sunday', the revolt spread to the countryside, where the peasants, who often didn't live any better than their emaciated cattle, got a sniff of the weakness of imperial authority and grasped their chance. The estates of the aristocracy went up in flames; with rags on their feet, and armed with pitchforks, knives and flails, the rabble stormed their masters' salons — though serfdom had been abolished in 1861, they'd always remained their masters — which smelt of perfume and Egyptian cigarettes, and were adorned with Empire furnishings. Grand pianos, paintings, books, and pottery were destroyed or stolen.

The revolt spread to Warsaw, Riga, Odessa — cities that were still part of the Russian Empire. In the last of these, sailors on the battle cruiser Potemkin began to mutiny; the revolt also broke out in the ranks of the army. Many of the estate owners who'd managed to survive now experienced their personal *boulevard of broken dreams*: in their youth, in the final decades of the nineteenth century, many of them had been progressives. They had joined the '*Going to the people*' movement, heading for the villages to teach the needy how to read and write. They'd secretly flirted with revolt, covertly donated money to terrorists. Out of a sense of guilt. It was this eternal sense of guilt — about their own privileged lives, and the misery in which the masses found themselves, as well as the need to make atonement — that not only determined much nineteenth-century literature, but also their concrete acts. There had been terrorist attacks, like the one on Czar Alexander II in 1881. And now, while the horde was rushing on with pitchforks and torches to set the whole place alight, they suddenly realised what a monstrous visage the populace had. The intelligentsia came to their senses, withdrew, and often became arch-conservatives themselves.

The czar did make a minor concession: in 1906 he formed a Duma. A phony parliament, housed in the Tauride Palace, once a present from the empress Catherine the Great to her lover, Prince Grigory Potemkin. But precious little changed. The opulent life of the czarist elite continued: aristocratic balls, entertainment in societies, brothel visits to red-velvet men's paradises with their dimmed lights and gold-rimmed mirrors, lavish dinners, the building of houses and country houses, and holidays on the French and Italian Riviera.

Meanwhile, the Jews in Russia were having a very hard time. Czar Nicholas II passionately supported the 'Yid'-bashers in the Black Hundreds. Pogroms broke out over the whole country. Rapes, plunder, murder. Jewish girls as young as seven were impaled by Cossacks on quivering lances. Elderly men and women were tossed onto bonfires. The Jews were apparently set on undermining all of the Christian states in the world, including the Russian Empire — you only had to study the document *The Protocols of the Elders of Zion*, a favourite reading material at the court. In the higher circles of Moscow and Saint Petersburg, but also in the provincial cities, it became *bon ton* to be an anti-Semite. Meanwhile, both the popular press and the brand-new Duma began to bang the nationalistic drum. The Ottoman and Austro-Hungarian empires were on the verge of collapse. Russia had been focused on the glistening wreckage for some time, particularly control of Constantinople and the passage from the Black Sea to the Mediterranean via the Dardanelles. The call grew ever louder for an association of the Slavic peoples to support their Slavic blood-brothers in the Balkans, in their struggle for independence. After the nephew of the Austrian emperor, Archduke Franz Ferdinand, was assassinated by a Serbian nationalist in 1914, people passed through Tchaikovsky Street to gather at the Austrian Embassy, a hundred metres from my house, with clenched fists, calling for support for Serbia.

Then World War I broke out.

On 1 August that year, the czar called for a general mobilisation.

There was great euphoria in Russia, as in Austria-Hungary and the German Empire. A day later, the people cheered the czar when he made an appearance on the balcony of the Winter Palace. Just like elsewhere in Europe, it seemed as though everyone was *thirsting* for war. 'What is a fatherland, exactly? The people or the state?' Gippius pondered in her diary. 'Both. But if I hate the Russian *state* now? If that state is in opposition to my people in its own country?' She believed that everyone around her had gone insane, including the intellectuals and writers who supported the war and had voluntarily joined up.

The czarist army was actually a farm-cart army, with lots of plumes, golden epaulettes, colours and flags; an operetta cavalry from the nineteenth century. In 1914, it had just 679 motorised military vehicles and two ambulances. The Russian peasant soldiers, who'd been plucked from the villages for the slaughter, like rabbits from a hutch, fought in the trenches over the next few years without sufficient ammunition, underfed, desperate, often bare-foot. They again died by the bushel. Fury spread over the battlefield. While they were ordered into hails of bullets, the muzzles of guns and minefields, their officers, who were members of the aristocratic and privileged classes, remained safely far behind the front, drinking Bordeaux and puffing on cigarettes. The downfall had begun. The wall of the German army and the wall of the internal revolt were pressing closer together every day, as Gippius would note. The czar, who didn't understand one iota of military affairs, quickly appointed himself commander-in-chief at the head of the armed forces, an idea that had been whispered into his ear by his wife, who in turn had been whispered to by Grigori Rasputin, who she'd become addicted to because she was convinced that God had sent her this Siberian fool and erotomaniac to cure her son's haemophilia.

In February 1917, the city, which by now had been re-named Petrograd, once again broke out in revolt, with workers, soldiers, shrewd politicians and an army of opportunists making common cause. The czar, whose position had become untenable because of the scandals surrounding Rasputin and the dramatic losses at the front, abdicated a few days later in the sumptuous luxury of his train carriage. The epicentre was my neighbourhood around the Tauride Park, where Zinaida Gippius lived. From her view of the gateway to the park from her *bel étage*, she'd recorded her experiences and insights into the people and politics of the day — which were like waterfalls of clarity. She felt that Russia had clearly grievously sinned because the cup that it had to drink from was so bitter. Rasputin had been poisoned a month earlier during a drinking bout at the Yusupov Palace, and was finally shot and murdered. According to Gippius, Rasputin was a complete illiterate, an alcoholic, bumpkin, and perverted clown, and a skirt-chaser, who was driven by unbridled lust, vanity and fear, but he had an ingenious sense of time and place, and had climbed on the back of an entire populace and ridden it around in a princely fashion. In her estimation, he was a dead-ordinary, and insignificant, sly peasant, who was a dime a dozen, debauched, a lecher who had been pampered by his admirers — with the czarina as the focal point — who gave him silk and velvet shirts, bonbons, flowers and their vulvas; he was a mischievous courtier who'd helped drive his country towards the precipice with his chicanery, intrigues, nominations of ministers and advice to the czar, the full extent of which was only now becoming apparent.

At the end of February 1917, a bread riot broke out in the city; the call for peace and a speedy end to the monarchy grew ever louder among the vanguard of intellectuals, city proletariat and peasant soldiers who'd returned fresh from the front. 'A collapse is coming! It's coming! A revolution, or an insane riot,' Gippius wrote at the start of the month. And indeed, a couple of weeks later, the first incidents of disorder broke out. 'The general consensus is that it began in the Vyborgsky district, as a result of a bread shortage. Here and there, trams were stopped and smashed up. People were also reputed to have murdered a police commissioner (…) "Old Cossacks" reappeared, galloping along the pavements with whips, crashing into women and students. I've seen it for myself in Sergiyevskaya Street.'

There were once again lynchings, the first murders. After the general rehearsal of 1905, the definitive settling of accounts was now taking place. Meanwhile, the theatres and restaurants were buzzing. To the very last moment, the wealthy, the aristocrats in the city, were abandoning themselves to waves of pleasure, and orgies; entire fortunes were lost in casinos.

While Gippius was sitting writing in her *bel étage*, the composer Sergei Prokofiev was stepping onto the little bridge at the Summer Garden, less than five hundred metres away, on the other side of my street. He too kept a diary and noted what he witnessed in the last days of February 1917, before the abdication of the czar. The revolt grew grimmer by the hour. The centre of the city was transformed into an army camp. Snipers had taken up positions on the roofs; crossroads were blocked off. Machine guns were set up on the Nevsky Prospect and near the Winter Palace; everywhere Cossacks patrolled on horseback. The czarist troops had moved the front against the Germans to the heart of the city. To fight against their own population. Sunday the 26th would go down in history as the second Bloody Sunday, after a trainee regiment began shooting at a crowd of workers that had advanced on the centre. At least fifty people — men, women, and children — were killed in a bloodbath on Znamenskaya Square, now known as Uprising Square, where Julia and I take a stroll whenever I'm in Saint Petersburg, to shop at the Finnish supermarket, Stockmann. At the moment that the slaughter was taking place, Prokofiev was sitting at home working on a violin concerto; only in the afternoon did he go out for a walk. 'Everything was very peaceful and I even thought that the rumours of shooting were a slander (…) In the evening, I went to Zakharova to play bridge and cards. There was an indescribable vitality on the streets: a people was astir as though on Easter Vigil.' But a day later, the composer, a scion of his class with a certain natural *sang-froid*, was confronted by violence after all. 'A guard at the library said that a real battle was raging on the Liteyny, near the Arsenal, where there was heavy gunfire because of soldiers who'd gone over to the workers.' He'd been at a general rehearsal of the opera *Eugene Onegin*, put on by students from the conservatory. When a little while later he was walking past the Summer Garden to the Fontanka, he stopped on the bridge because he heard the energetic rattling of rifles. 'A worker was standing beside me. I asked him if I could cross the Fontanka. He answered enthusiastically, "You can, go on. Our side has broken the line." "Which Our Side?" "The workers with rifles and the soldiers who've crossed over to our camp" (...) A bunch of madmen, I thought! I didn't know that the revolution was focused so directly on its target.'

Because the sun had set so early, my street was bathed almost entirely in an orange-red glow, an autumnal radiance in which the approach of winter was already apparent. I remained standing for a moment in front of the chocolate-brown building where Zinaida Gippius had lived. There was now a little café on the corner, with a spa salon next to it — you had to go down a stairway in front — where expensive cars stopped day and night and men got out, rang the bell of a silver door and disappeared behind it. Oh, even Gippius would never have imagined what was awaiting her, this city and this country, despite all her historical awareness, her understanding of human nature and her predictive gifts. At first, it all remained reasonably calm. 'Columns of armed workers, soldiers, and every other possible category of person passed our windows,' she wrote on the morning after Prokofiev's walk. 'All the cars are being stopped, the soldiers are dragging out the passengers, firing into the air, getting in and driving away. There are a lot of cars with red flags turning off towards the Duma.' And in the afternoon, she wrote: 'A delegation of 25,000 mutinying soldiers has now advanced on the Duma, dismissed the guard and taken its place (...) A bizarre procession is passing our windows: soldiers without guns, workers with sabres, lanky boys, and even children of seven or eight, with bayonets and poniards. The only doubts left are about the artillerymen and a section of the Semyonovsky Regiment. But the entire street, down to the last beaming woman, is convinced that they too will fall in "behind the people".' Later that day, the Peter and Paul Fortress would be taken; the revolutionary troops established their base there. But the centre of the uprising would remain the Duma building, the Tauride Palace. In the following days, an orgy of violence broke loose over the entire city, where everyone was an outlaw; houses, shops and public buildings were plundered by drunken rebels, and people on the street with a *booshwar* appearance (the wealthy, the intellectual, the sophisticated) were set upon; soldiers and officers who'd remained loyal to the czar died a terrible martyr's death; aristocratic girls were raped by pariahs, while working-class girls sometimes made love in public with opportunistic thieves, sticking up their middle finger at the old order (just as some burglars took a leisurely crap on the tables of their victims before leaving the building).

The anarchy spread to Moscow and the rest of the country, but it was chiefly Petrograd that was the stage for scenes that always remained with me, and which through the years had become part of me. Such as the bloodbath in the Hotel Astoria where officers and their families had dug in, and where the machine guns were finally turned on them from the street as the building was stormed and the mob pressed inside, ripping to shreds the luxurious palms, mirrors and furnishings, plundering the wine cellar and going from room to room plugging the representatives of the *ancien régime* or skewering them with bayonets. All of these images, just like those of the horrors of the nine-hundred-day siege in World War II by the Germans (in which a million people died) never left my thoughts. Whenever I tossed a log onto the fire, with its chiselled swallows feeding their young, I often asked myself who might have lived here during those awful days.

'The Bolsheviks were waiting yearningly for the arrival of Lenin,' Gippius wrote in March, shortly after the czar had abdicated. 'Will there be a return of Caesarism, autocracy, monarchism?' And then one day in April, he came, he arrived, the new Caesar, the autocrat, the monarch of retribution and misanthropy: 'And now we have him, Lenin … Yes, the scoundrel has come after all! The reception was pompous, with floodlights and everything. But … he came *via Germany*. The Germans rounded up a whole gang of these "dangerous" rogues, and gave these characters an entire train, and sealed it (to make sure that German territory wouldn't be infected by them), and then dropped them in our lap: there you are, enjoy.'

A white Mercedes stopped in front of the spa salon with a young man behind the wheel and an older one on the back seat. The older man got out, went down the steps, the silver door opened as though by appointment — as if someone inside were peering at the street through a camera — and then immediately closed again. Before dusk fell, I at least wanted to take a walk, to stretch my legs. Tomorrow, I would have to travel deep into the country via Moscow to the Urals, leaving Julia and the cats behind. This was how our life had been over the last twelve years. My wife absolutely loathed the capital, the racket and the filth, and the flat that I'd rented there amid the exhaust fumes, to earn my keep.

The lake in the park was as smooth as a mirror. Three grave-looking schoolgirls with books under their arms were walking in silence around it. A homeless man was lying curled up in the grass in a drunken stupor. Through the trees, the green dome of the Tauride Palace gleamed. Until 1990, it had housed the party school of the

Communist Party; now it was the seat of the inter-parliamentary body of the ex-Soviet republics, which had been independent states since 1991, a reality to which the current masters in the Kremlin were still not entirely reconciled. For a number of years now, a counter-movement had been mobilising, as counter-movements had been mobilising throughout the entire old continent. History doesn't repeat itself, Mark Twain once said; no, history rhymes.

I hurriedly walked back out of the park, the leaves rustling under my shoes. There were still barracks in the high, broad Zakharyevskaya Street, just as in Gippius's time. A group of recruits were strolling by listlessly; etched into their pale faces were their poor nourishment and needy youth in the provinces. Meanwhile, a blaring, commanding voice rang out from a courtyard that I couldn't see, followed by the drumming of feet and a mighty cry, arising from hundreds of throats — all in unison and echoing. This street wasn't as nice as our Tchaikovsky Street, which was right behind it. In spite of the fact that they were camouflaged by the best set builders at the Kirov Theatre at that time, some of the barracks had still been hit by German bombs in World War II. Some new buildings had sprung up here and there. It was a miracle that our building had been entirely spared, from the stained-glass windows in our living room to the courtyard below.

'Saint Petersburg played a crucial role as the centre of all these events,' Zinaida Gippius wrote of those revolutionary days of 1917. 'But inside Saint Petersburg itself, there was another, separate centre: from the very beginning, the revolution had taken place in the area around the Duma, that is to say: in the vicinity of the Tauride Palace. The straight streets running towards it were just like arteries in those February and March days of 1917, through which life-giving blood streamed to the heart, to the great palace of the days of Catherine the Great. I looked on at how the old palace, which had risen from death to new life for a short time, now slowly died again, I saw how the city died ...'

And it was precisely in these arteries that I was now walking and living, almost a hundred years later: an excellent starting point for a *personal* book about the Russian Revolution of 1917. You buffed up your own life with a little patina, borrowed an abundance of what others had written, with liberal citations, made up a bit if need be, and mixed it all together like the ingredients of a thick, hearty soup, *et voilà*: it was as if the book had written itself.

I swiftly walked on, my ticking footsteps echoing off the granite façades of the barracks. I bought a bottle of Chilean white wine at a grocer's. On a hope and a prayer. There were three conscripts standing in the queue in front of me in their green battle dress, all barely eighteen. They were bareheaded. On their skulls there was a dark sheen like sandpaper. One was holding a fried fish in a plastic bag, another a pack of Latvian biscuits, and yet another two rolls of pink toilet paper. They were standing at the cash register *en groupe*, and their coins lavishly tinkled. They'd put their wares on the counter, plucked some small change from each other's hands, counting it out loud. The checkout girl, who was around their age, waited patiently, her slant Tatar eyes surreptitiously inspecting the boys' physiques. They were thirty-nine rubles short. I put down a five-hundred ruble note and offered to pay for them. The poor buggers, ready to fight for the fatherland if need be, now slunk off almost jubilantly.

When I got home, Julia was sitting in her chair. It was already dusk, but all the lamps in the living room were off.

'Don't you notice anything?' she asked.

I looked around.

'Ljòlja,' my wife sobbed. 'She is so ill. I've just come back from the vet's. She's there now on a drip. I can pick her up at eight. I left my shawl behind so that she has my scent. Where have you been?'

I told her.

The bottle of Chilean wine turned out to be dire. I poured it down the sink, then went out again and bought a bottle of Chablis at the off-licence opposite the German consulate on Furshtatskaya Street.

It was exorbitant, but divine.

# CHAPTER THREE

When I returned to the Netherlands from my failed bible mission in Leningrad, in the autumn of 1988, there was a sad piece of news waiting for me: my father's intestinal cancer had returned. My mother told me in passing, hesitantly, almost with a degree of shame. My father smiled and tried to keep up a strong front when he was around me. Once again, there was a tension around everything, a doom, a fear. I didn't know what to do; every afternoon, I walked for a couple of hours over the beach and through the dunes.

'What will you do next, my boy?' my father asked.

I didn't know.

One morning, a week later, Siderius suddenly appeared again at the door. This time, my parents were at home; there was no escape. Once again, the church leader from Leiden nested on the couch like a bird of prey, in the same raincoat, after having introduced himself to my father and my mother and amicably shaken their hands like they were old acquaintances. 'No, thank you. No coffee … A glass of water … The doctor thinks I should drink lots of water … Gout … The malady of the drinker … But I haven't drunk a drop in my life …'

Siderius began to tell my parents all about my recent success in the Soviet Union, proudly, as if he'd been there himself. His church contacts on the ground were absolutely lyrical about my work. He had come to take me with him to a warehouse in Gouda, where 80,000 bibles were waiting, packed and ready to be speedily shipped to Leningrad.

'You have a wonderful son, a soldier of God, I can tell you that,' Siderius said, while my parents sat there beaming.

Suddenly, he fell quiet, then looked around for a moment enquiringly, as though he'd heard something, and asked in a light-hearted tone who in this room was ill.

My mother glanced at my father, turning pale.

'Brothers and sisters …' Siderius began. 'Keep quiet, God knows and sees everything … God is love. He has a plan for each of us. Keep quiet, dear people, let us pray …'

He clasped his hands together and closed his eyes. As he directed himself to God in a ceremonious, semi-singsong voice — lips trembling, knuckles white from clenching — my parents looked at each other blankly, as though involuntary victims of hypnosis. When I was younger, my father had sent me to a Christian grammar school in Haarlem, purely on account of the good quality of the education. But for his whole life, he'd absolutely loathed everything to do with the church, after he'd had to look on during a Christmas service as a six-year-old, while rich classmates were allowed to grab cranes, racing cars, and fire stations from under the sparkling Christmas tree, squealing with joy, and he (the son of a mason) and all the rest were given an orange with a green crêpe paper ribbon, which he'd tied around it earlier that day in school handicraft.

The prayer went on for several minutes. Siderius appealed to the Almighty for forbearance for suffering, and if necessary, resignation. I was worried for a bit that my father might get up, stamp on the floor, grab the man by the collar of his raincoat and chuck him out of the door. I now projected onto my father the helpless aggression that I felt about fate.

'Amen ...' Siderius concluded his monologue to God.


Two weeks later, I was once again on the plane to Leningrad, despite the promise I'd made to myself never to return to the USSR. Life had taken me for a ride. I'd been unemployed for months, had tried to do anything to escape an office life; I couldn't bear the silent, gruelling sorrow of my parents; and what's more, I'd be paid for this mission: a thousand guilders.

This time, the flight didn't have a stopover in East Berlin. I landed in a white arctic hell. Standing on the steps that had been wheeled up to the plane, the frost cut through me like a knife. Steam rose from the mouths of the border guards, as though they were on fire inside.

Pozorski was waiting for me in the sweltering arrivals hall, dressed in a Turkish woollen peacoat, accompanied by the emaciated blonde teenage girl.

'When are the bibles arriving?' he immediately asked.

I thought they were already here, I answered. Siderius had told me before leaving that the shipment of bibles had left Rotterdam by sea nine days earlier, concealed among a load of coal.

'Natasha ...' Pozorski shoved the blonde forward, like a slave trader at market. 'She'd really like to meet a foreigner. For her languages.'

'Hello ...' she said, looking at me with eyes like oysters.


The bibles finally arrived, not in Leningrad, but in Arkhangelsk, where by his own account, Pozorski's partner Borodin had now gained an influential position, and lorries were waiting to distribute the 80,000 holy books all over the country.

The girl with the oyster eyes, who entertained me in my room for two nights and an entire afternoon while the snowstorm assailed the windows outside, had now made herself scarce.

An hour later, Pozorski was standing in the lobby, waving an envelope, a smile from ear to ear on his face.

'I told you, didn't I?' he began. 'We don't cheat anybody — goodness is our guiding principle!'

He gave me the envelope and announced that he was taking six months off. He'd just been granted an exit visa after months of waiting, and he was going to set up a network in Prague, Berlin and Budapest for his future import business. As soon as he was back in Leningrad, he'd get in touch with me. He promised me golden times.

The money would be enough to get by in the country for a long while. My visa was valid for a month. I decided to go to Moscow, where I'd previously been for two days as a first-year student, in the spring of 1981, and which had struck me as much livelier than Leningrad.

The night train arrived in the capital at quarter past seven in the morning. Figures in fur bobbed by on the platform in the misting frost. Icicles were hanging from the station roof, big and sparkly, like chandeliers in a ballroom. But here in my compartment it was still warm; the samovar was steaming and whistling softly. Beside it sat the trolley lady who'd woken me up at six-thirty and brought me tea in a glass with a metal holder — an elderly Russian lady, wiry, agile, with a hyper-sophisticated appearance despite her apron. She reminded me of Madam Pokrovskaya. Remorse now overcame me. Why hadn't I popped by to see the old woman before I left Leningrad? On her ward for the clinically insane? To bring her bonbons, a bottle of perfume, the nylon stockings she'd spoken about. Things you could only get hold of in the foreign-currency shop at the end of the Nevsky Prospect. After our short joyride through the city more than a month earlier, I'd more or less dumped her. As soon as I'd helped her out of the taxi and wheeled her into the lobby of the home, Madam Pokrovskaya completely lost her senses; amid the green twilight of the fatsias, she again began screaming, crying for her child, lashing out aggressively, after which a scurrying nurse sedated her for the second time, and she was carried away like a rag doll. I never went back to the home; never spoke to her again.

But that's not the only thing I'm sorry about in my life.

I was just exiting the scarlet train-carriage with my case, when somewhere in the teeming masses a little further off, I heard Dutch voices. The brown coal smoke of a slow train caught me in the face; a porter with a trolley stacked with snow-covered suitcases almost bowled me over. I walked on, then I stood still. A young man who I'd guess was a little older than me, at around 30, with a fur hat over a puffy, blushing face, was saying goodbye to a group of Dutch tourists.

'Thanks, thanks again!' A beefy blonde woman threw herself into the young man's arms and gave him three smacking kisses, after which a gentleman with grey boyish hair in a duffel coat helped her into the train.

'So someone will be waiting for us there?' another person asked.

'Don't worry! Someone will be waiting to pick you up in Leningrad! Have a good trip!'

'Thanks, Ragnar!' said a woman with an imitation-fur construction on her head. 'They were wonderful days! I'll never forget those drunken musicians in that restaurant!'

And so it went on for a little while.

I was still smoking in those days; I lit up a cigarette and watched the scene from behind a pillar, enjoying the freezing cold and the nicotine after the oppressive night in the sleeping compartment. Then the doors closed with a pneumatic hiss; rising water vapour froze into glistening crystals, and the train started up. When the carriage containing the Dutch people had disappeared, the young man took the fur hat off his head, adjusted the red-silk lining, and put it back on, then he made out as though he were heading for the exit, when suddenly he turned and came towards me with great strides.

'Why are you spying on me?' he asked in Russian.

'Good morning,' I responded in Dutch.

'God damn …' he shot back.

His name was Swindleman — Ragnar Swindleman. After he'd bummed a cigarette off me, we walked out to the street through the imposing station hall, with Lenin in the middle on a granite plinth.

'Where are you staying?' Swindleman lifted his gloved hand; a couple of seconds later, a Volga obediently came to a stop beside us.

I went along on a whim.

'Okay, get in …'

On my first journey through a wintry Moscow, I felt intensely happy; there were Communist slogans everywhere and almost no cars, as though the grand décor of the city was for us alone. It was just like two years before when I'd left the Netherlands for Tenerife, where I managed to get by for a year and a half as a recreation leader at a holiday hotel. Then, as now, a heavy weight dropped from my shoulders. It was as though my father were no longer ill; as though the Netherlands no longer existed, with its office life that had always struck me as the most awful horror.

'So, this is Moscow ...' Swindleman said.

He began to question me, asking where I'd learned my Russian, then raised his eyebrows in admiration and jealousy when I told him about my years in Spain, and had to laugh out loud about my history with bibles. Then he began to tell me things about himself. He turned out to be an even bigger windbag than me. Before we'd arrived at Hotel Intourist on the Gorky Street, he'd told me he had a job for me; he'd been looking for someone like me for months. I'd come as though sent by God.

The job was as a rep for a Dutch travel agency in Moscow. Because of the newly increased interest in the Soviet Union, Swindleman could no longer manage all the work on his own. The groups kept coming, to see for themselves the miracle of Gorbachev's reforms — *perestroika* and *glasnost* — as well as the golden onion domes and the museums. In addition to guiding tours, I was supposed to develop new destinations with him, and also procure enough hotel space, which was growing scarcer by the day. The monopoly of the state tourism monolith, Intourist, had rapidly disintegrated in that year of 1988. Previously, you went to the main office directly opposite the Kremlin, handed in a wish list to an official for a plane, bus, train, boat, or other mode of transport, and a guide in the language of choice — and it was all arranged. But everything had begun to slip; there was a gradual revolution taking place in the country. Piecemeal alternatives were springing up alongside Intourist. Competition was growing. The communist ban on making a profit, on setting up your own business, was now eroding. And who profited from that? Those who were closest: the professional communists. Across the entire country, organisations like the Academy of Sciences, the railways, the state circus, even the army-owned hotels, sanatoriums, and other residences, which were meant for USSR personnel, started to open up to that new Soviet phenomenon: consumers. For a gratuity, high officials and military figures rented out hotel space in the name of the state to little businesses that they'd set up with their friends, who in turn sub-let them for ten times as much. But it was clandestine: it was still semi-illegal. And you couldn't just break into it; you had to have the right contacts.

'Do you understand?' The evening after my arrival in Moscow, Swindleman took me along to a bathhouse to introduce me to some of the delights. Naked and with a face like a buoy, sitting beside me in the *banya*, he was furiously flapping a wet towel over his head — the hot air grew even hotter and scorched my skin. 'You haven't even asked me what you'll earn. I'll tell you straight: nine hundred guilders a month, a pittance. They're misers in the Netherlands! But there's something else that I'll tell you later. By the way …' Panting, he began to rub the sweat off his chubby body; everything was flowing onto the pale birch wood of the sauna benches. Then he started talking about the plans he had for importation, about the fortunes that could be made in the long term.

It was as if I was listening to Pozorski in Leningrad.


And so a period in my life began of almost uninterrupted travel. First, I went back to the Netherlands to extend my visa, to fill in my parents, and to apply to the tour operator in the east of the country – they seemed thrilled that another idiot had turned up who wanted to spend his days in the USSR.

Two weeks later, I was sharing a room long-term with Swindleman in Hotel Intourist. It soon became clear that I'd never actually see him. When he was out and about with a group of tourists in the immense country, I was meant to stay in Moscow, and the reverse. We alternated; our work contacts were by phone and fax. It was a chronic disaster because the phone connections in the Soviet Empire were absolutely lousy, with constant static on the line, and they would suddenly get cut off, or take half an hour to connect. I picked up groups of tourists at the airport, guided them to their hotels, maintained contact with the travel organisations and the local guides. More and more often, I went travelling with them. Professional Dutch tour-guides were meant to take away the fear that the majority of our clients still felt about the Soviet Union. Swindleman had already been here for two years. He'd developed a certain sense of *ennui*; he preferred organising things in Moscow. In the beginning, I made the six-hour trip a few times by train from Moscow to Leningrad. After a couple of months, I travelled with the same ease as Swindleman, back and forth between Moscow and the Baltic States, Siberia, Georgia, Ukraine or Uzbekistan. Everywhere in this country of eleven time zones, whether in the metro, in the houses, in the passages of the hotels, in aeroplanes, trains, schools or hospitals, there was the same sickly smell – a mixture of garlic, stale sweat, the reek of rotten fruit and, in short, a foul human odour emanating from the citizens, because soap and other hygiene products were massively rationed, or simply unobtainable. Women were forced to use cotton wads for sanitary towels, and when these had run out, they often used newspaper. My descent into the hell of the old people's home in Leningrad, wheeling the trolley of smuggled bibles through the passages full of cast-off people, turned out to be a *pars pro toto* for the entire country.

Our work was a collaboration, partly with Intourist, partly with rising new 'cooperative companies' led by shady types who I had to spend nights with in restaurants — as there was no contract to be had without building up trust in advance. They were smoky places like grottoes, with seas of light behind the shadowy façades, lively orchestra music, and a surfeit of food and drink. Guarded by geezers in black leather jackets with ape-like heads, this was where young women and girls guffawed down to their uvulas, acting like signposts for the night, while the world outside was covered in grey twilight, a realm that at any minute would further disintegrate — you knew it, you could feel it, like dogs feel the approach of an earthquake long before it actually strikes. By now, the ruble was almost worthless; there was hyperinflation. Western goods were like gold ingots. For six cans of imported Carlsberg (which I could buy for ten dollars in the foreign-currency shop next to the hotel where I lived), I could sometimes fill up the tank for the driver of my tourist bus with three hundred litres of diesel. No one stuck to the rules.

It was during this time of scarcities that the large-scale grasping began — the mass theft, the marauding — just as in the years immediately following the revolution of 1917, when workers and soldiers began to plunder the bourgeoisie. With the blessing of the brand-new revolution behind them, they had burst into houses with carbines, dragged men, women, the elderly, and children out onto the street, taken possession of their antique furniture, their tableware, silver, paintings, tasteful photos (with palm trees in the background), crystal paperweights, and other luxury items, or smashed them for revenge or out of pure loathing. Finally, after so many centuries of exploitation and degradation, it was their turn. To dominate, to humiliate. The aristocrats and the bourgeoisie were put to work with snow shovels in the freezing cold, dressed up like monkeys in workers' garb, or the workers had them lick clean freshly-shat-on toilet seats with lips they'd bitten to bits from fear, egged on by young factory girls as they allowed a grinning comrade to grab their smouldering crotches. Some were stabbed to death right away, executed, or else taken to a cell or a prison camp, in Petrograd, in Moscow, and then the rest of the country. But very soon after Lenin's putsch in the autumn of 1917, a schism opened up between the people — those useful idiots who'd carried out the dirty work — and those who'd got their hands on real power, the career Bolsheviks in their long black leather coats, stamping their boots, with loaded pistols on their baldrics, the commissars.

Only a few outsiders witnessed this, but they were there. One of them was George Nypels, a reporter who saw how the young revolutionaries travelled through the country like barons and baronesses with their 'nauseating' excesses. 'They comprise a new gentrified caste in Soviet Russia, a caste that can do anything and is allowed everything, who travel in first class carriages and live first class too, who eat and drink and smoke: things that a proletarian in his factory can only dream of, just as with a bourgeois. Russia has degenerated into a dictatorship of the new caste.' The stolen household wares soon appeared in open-air bazaars. The flea-market as a metaphor for the revolution! And those who hadn't fled or been murdered, who concealed their origins, or simply couldn't believe that it would be their turn one day, now sold the last of their things on the street. To survive. In 1919, Nypels visited the

Sukhareva market in Moscow, where the street trade still hadn't entirely disappeared, in spite of communism. He wandered past traders of embroidered Russian tapestries, blue mink, astrakhan and Siberian opossum fur, balalaikas and gramophone players, before finding himself in the bourgeois section where — in his words — and according to Marx's dictum, the dying capitalist class was selling off the last of its personal possessions. 'Turban hats, gold rings, bottles of perfume and hair lotion, manicure and curling instruments, gold cigarette cases, silver samovars and gaiters. The knick-knacks of the middle classes were being spirited into the pockets of the peasants and the workers, and so the ex-bourgeois earned their bread and meat.'

Now, the same street trade was being conducted at full pelt in Moscow, Leningrad, and also Kiev, Minsk, and Yalta, which smelt of oleander and the sea, and all those other places I stopped at in the latter years of the USSR. But this time, it wasn't the possessions of the aristocracy and bourgeoisie that were being frittered away, but the paraphernalia of the Soviet Union, a scene similar to a chock-a-block church where the priests made their daily offerings to a God that nobody actually believed in any more. The God of communism. The things being sold included the complete collected works of Lenin and Marx; castings of their heads in bronze, plaster or brass; Soviet porcelain; statuettes of steelworkers, peasants, sporting heroes and ballerinas; the oxygen masks of MIG fighter pilots; Communist Party decorations; Orders of Lenin and other medals; night-goggles, German helmets, baldrics and other extraneous spoils of the war of the Russians against the Nazis; but mostly watches that the commandos in the Red Army had worn — and all of this was done preferably speedily and exclusively with foreign currency.

I was witnessing historical times, and I knew that I was witnessing historical times — on the train, off the train, on the plane, off the plane, sometimes spending days in the diesel stench and drone of long-condemned boats. The work totally consumed me, slowly drained me physically. At first, the tourists were mostly left-wing intellectuals, later they were middle-of-the-road intellectuals, and soon a mix of doctors, bookkeepers, teachers, bakers, stevedores, anyone who wanted to witness the miracle of the transformations in the east. My tourists looked on from behind the windows of a BOVAG bus that had travelled over from the Netherlands, with a chemical toilet and a coffee maker for fresh coffee, as it floated through the broad Moscow streets, full of nothing but Ladas and Volgas, which were covered in the winter with grey mushy snow like papier mâché, under a grey sky, with red pendants everywhere. They watched their fellow man wrestling under the last spasms of communism, queuing in front of shops, wearing clothes — overcoats, shoes, and headwear — that had gone out of fashion thirty years before in Amsterdam, London, and Paris. They watched from the windows with interest, as though observing fish in a dirty deep-sea aquarium. How did these people keep going? Why didn't they rebel? But they'd already rebelled, that is to say: the system had rebelled for them, from above, even if the cesspool had only been opened a little, and a counter-reaction to the first reforms was a continual threat.

At first, Mikhail Gorbachev was as hesitant about the reforms that he'd set in motion as Nicholas II had been. Just like the last czar, whose power rested on an all-oppressing system of terror together with the privileges and fairy-tale opulence of the aristocracy,

Gorbachev at first also obstinately refused to really take an axe to the system. This was the system that had, for seventy years, preserved a privileged lifestyle for the upper echelons of the party — the communist aristocracy — who could readily charter aeroplanes for their personal use, force subordinates into sex, and who lived in state residences with staff, just as the grand dukes had once done in their palaces.

'*Esteemed comrades! Dear foreign guests!*' Gorbachev had said in a lengthy speech at the State Kremlin Palace in 1987. '*Seven decades separate us from the unforgettable days of October 1917, those legendary days that were the starting point of a new age of human progress and the true history of humanity. For mankind, October was truly the hour of its genius and its shining dawn.*' Among his audience were tyrants and dictators like Honecker, Castro, Ortega and Ceaușescu. To their utter astonishment and horror, the Soviet leader suddenly began listing the crimes of Stalin. '*Many thousands of party members, as well as people that weren't, were exposed to repression en masse. That, comrades, is the bitter truth. The guilt of Stalin and his close collaborators in this mass repression and lawlessness towards the party and the people was immense and unforgivable ...*'

But Gorbachev left Lenin intact, the bastard that started it all, the mass murderer who called for the shooting of *more* professors in his telegrams. A psychopath riddled with misanthropy and spite, whose mummified body is, as I'm writing this, still lying embalmed for posterity in a glass sarcophagus in the mausoleum on Red Square. Gorbachev even lauded Lenin for still being the sacred font of inspiration: '*Neither the greatest errors, nor the aberrations from socialist principles that took place, can divert our people and our country from the path that we took in 1917 (...) We are travelling to a new world, the world of communism. We shall never diverge from that course ...'*

Meanwhile, you could pick up a bronze bust of Lenin on the street for six packs of chewing gum. The country, still officially on its way to perfect communism, was a brothel — in the literal sense, too. Legions of girls and young women went down on their backs for a few packs of nylons. I was approached by seedy characters. Sometimes I too felt like a seedy character, as I plied my trade in theatre tickets. Everyone wanted to go to the Bolshoi Theatre in Moscow, or the Kirov in Leningrad, to see a performance of *Swan Lake, The Nutcracker* or *Giselle.* The golden czarist splendour had never disappeared under the communists; all that had been destroyed by the Nazis in World War II was quickly restored to its full glory. In Moscow and in Leningrad, a permanent battle raged for theatre tickets. These were dirt cheap in rubles, but you couldn't get them anywhere. Corrupt theatre cashiers engaged in a vicious trade with black-market dealers. The majority went to the state organisation, Intourist, which sold the tickets to foreigners for international currency. A ticket that wouldn't even have cost the equivalent of twenty dollars at the ticket office would pass from hand to hand for eighty dollars.

It was Swindleman who introduced me to the art of fleecing tourists. As justification, he pointed to our absurdly low salary from the Netherlands. Just like him, I soon made contacts in the theatre box offices. I took them out to restaurants, pampered them in all sorts of ways, and after that they mostly came back with lists of things that they sorely needed: nail polish, eyeshadow, lipstick, French perfume, the necessities for female hygiene, *dessous,* underwear for their husband or boyfriend, socks, a piece of edible cheese, medicines, the eternal nylon stockings, digital watches, sometimes a pair of stylish shoes, and other things. I was invariably embarrassed by the banality of it all. In exchange for these items, they sold me tickets in rubles, which I stamped in my hotel room with PAID IN FOREIGN CURRENCY, after which I could vary the price in dollars. I usually let the travel groups know immediately on the day of arrival that — given the chaotic situation in the country — a visit to the theatre was unfortunately almost entirely out of the question, a tombola, but of course I'd try. But that couldn't be true? Now that they were here, they definitely wanted to go to the theatre. I understood, I understood. I repeated that I'd do my level best. A day later when they asked me how things were going with the tickets, I'd shrug my shoulders in torment, mumbling how things were looking very bleak. And so I ramped up the tension until the liberating tidings came ('My dear people, I can hardly believe it myself, but I have forty tickets for *Swan Lake* at the Bolshoi Theatre this evening!') and in the bus or in the breakfast room a cheer would rise, applause, and I was figuratively tossed in the air. In one evening, after deducting expenses, I'd sometimes make a thousand US dollars.

Meanwhile, everywhere in the country, people were in discussion, in the middle of the ice-cold streets, in the metro, on factory shop floors, under the dismal fluorescent light of government buildings, in cinemas and theatres. Every day, there were new revelations, new facts, new rumours. People would nervously grab newspapers out of each other's hands, as soon as the other person had finished reading. I didn't miss a single issue of *Ogoniok*, or *Little Flame*. After I'd switched to the Law faculty in Amsterdam, I'd kept up my Russian for my entire student days by conversing for one hour twice a week with Mr Panteleyev, a Russian who'd fled to the Netherlands after the Hungarian Uprising in 1956. It now came on in leaps and bounds. I was terribly conscious of how deep I'd sunk, but in spite of all the travel, the organising, the haggling, the focus on earning money, I still continued to be a sort of intellectual.

The press had exposed the cloaca of history, and every day it revealed fresh dirt about the repression under Stalin — the mass murders, the penal camps — which made the air in the country grow thicker, heavier, while everyone was actually gasping for more oxygen. But people also talked plenty about the present, they debated the future with heated voices, clenched fists and chins in the air. When I happened to be back in Moscow for a couple of weeks, while Swindleman was roaming around elsewhere in the immense USSR, I often went to the Dom Kino auditorium, which was misty with cigarette smoke. It was the trade-union home of the Soviet film-makers, not far from the square with the statue of Mayakovsky, which was one of the nests of the revolution in the country. An eddy of budding politicians, students, intellectuals, artists, housewives with handbags on their laps, workers who actually looked like workers, with chafed hands in greasy jackets and exhausted staring eyes, prisoners who'd been released from prison camps, provocateurs and quiet agents of the KGB. For the first time, I saw Andrei Sakharov, the Nobel Prize winner and father of the hydrogen bomb, an old grey-white bird with big glasses and a sloppy grey suit, who'd been released two years previously from his exile in Gorky, now Nizhny Novgorod on the Volga. He occasionally nodded off, like a somnambulant czar of the conscience; he mostly kept to the side of the auditorium above where the speeches were delivered. They addressed the necessity for further reforms, both in agriculture and industry, and more influence within the still all-powerful Communist Party. Usually, I didn't understand half of it. People debated about concrete legislative proposals, procedures, and people who I'd never heard of. In the years before and after the revolution of 1917, things had gone on in the same chaotic way, in little auditoriums, at secret meetings, and eventually on factory shop floors, cinemas and theatres.

The revolution held a remarkable attraction for young girls. Russians of my age and younger, who often wore the same dresses, pinafores, and sweaters as my mother had in photos from her youth. They looked out expectantly from under the canopies of their eyelashes with admiring expressions at the procession of men and women trotting on and off the podium. The horrors of the Stalin years were now coming to light, in poems, in stories, in the testimony of victims, through reading out documents and lists of victims that had only just surfaced from the partially opened archives. People listened in silence, open mouthed, sometimes sucking on a cigarette, their folding chairs dusty and squeaky under their bums, with varying expressions of repugnance on their faces, as they heard stories of how people — men, women, soldiers, officials, teachers, workers, and others — were taken from their homes by Soviet-Gestapo types. Leaving behind their screaming families or dumb with fear and dismay and — after noting the name, date of birth, and sometimes also being weighed for the administration — often an hour later, they were shot in the back of the neck and piled into a lorry like tree trunks, together with their fellow victims, who'd received the same treatment shortly before or shortly afterwards. Then they were driven amid droning and a diesel vapour through the nocturnal streets, with houses on both sides where people were already asleep, or still drinking tea in the kitchen, or reading books, or drowsing by the radio, or making love, to finally reach a place outside the city, and to disappear into a ditch, already dug, with the season's earth tossed over it. Often, they were cremated first, in underground ovens, long before Auschwitz, and afterwards the ash was poured into pits, stamped down and covered with a layer of asphalt. A woman of about seventy — a survivor of the gulags — sketched out the Bosch-like scenes of a Siberian women's camp, where girls were forced to crawl naked over the snow or through mud for the pleasure of the guards. Yet another — a man with a professor's face — told how one day, as a young man, he was put on a ship in the Far East, with hundreds of other men, a ship full of white slaves on its way to the coal mines in the far north, and how a quarter of them — almost without food, and in rags — died of the cold and diphtheria, and how the majority were soon transformed into a knot of writhing flesh, sweating, stinking, bleeding, and at each other's throats to survive, growling, scratching and biting like beasts, but how others were actually able to preserve their calm, their peace, their humanity. He also spoke about something that I would often hear and read about later in different versions: how guards, wrapped up in thick furs, would bind prisoners to a post naked when it was forty below, all for their own amusement, or as a retribution for transgressing some prohibition. Then they'd spray them with water so that they were soon transformed into gigantic icicles, white transparent lumps of amber, not with a fly, a bug or a beetle inside that had hardened in the resin millions of years ago, but a person, who a little while before had been breathing, screaming.

And all this was related there in the house of the cinematographers.

One morning, I found myself right at the back of the auditorium, where at least eight hundred people were sitting jam-packed together, listening to a woman who'd walked onto the stage with a bony gait. She had the figure of an Olympic shot-putter, wearing a formless moss-green dress, with short hair that was more yellow than blond, over a strikingly pale full-moon face, and she completely held the audience under her spell with her masculine gestures and powerful voice from the moment she began to orate. She spoke about the need for further, far-reaching reforms, in politics, the economy and in social structures, but emphasised that the Soviet Union was an empire of different peoples; violence had already broken out in Nagorno-Karabakh between Azerbaijan and Armenia, and there had been deaths. The dangers of racial hatred, of the march of the plague of nationalism, and even a major war were ever-present threats.

Suddenly, a commotion broke out in the auditorium.

'Shut your trap, you Jew-faker!' some guy cried out.

A group of men that were sitting on folding chairs to the right of the stage rose amid a clamour of shrieks. They unfurled a banner and stormed the stage; the one at the back tripped on the stage's steps and stumbled. The presidents of Israel and the US were pictured on the banner with gigantic noses, gambling, like crooked pickles, amid a shower of dollar signs.

A Russian in a black leather jacket, with a black T-shirt underneath, and black shoes gleaming like black signet rings, started yelling that the whole meeting was a pack of Jews. That the freemasons and the 'Yids' wanted to drive the country over the precipice, that they were intent on the destruction of the USSR; that the Zionist clique wanted to hand the Russians over to the Americans, to the Capitalists, to make the country their colony for raw materials … After which they'd …

'Citizens! Citizens!' The woman on stage barely seemed affected by the pandemonium that had broken out. 'Citizens! Let's talk to each other in a civilised manner …'

But the guy in black shouted back, 'Civilised? You want to drag us lock, stock, and, barrel to the grave. Civilised? You just carry on with your civilisation! One day, I'll see you in front of a firing squad!'

The auditorium remained motionless; eventually, the agitators were taken away by three black suits. This was democracy; the woman on stage continued her oration. As long as order in the auditorium wasn't disturbed, everyone could say what they thought or felt.

'You carry on, Galina!' A flaming red-headed woman in one of the front rows had stood up. 'We're hanging on your every word!'

'Thank you, citizens ... Where was I? Well, if we're talking about the nationalist dangers that are threatening us now ...'

In those days, I was always enveloped in a scent of *eau de toilette* and soap, I still am as it happens: one of my little acts of revenge on life. Although not inexperienced, I was unbelievably shy. But amid the fire of these meetings, borne on the hot air of the approaching revolt, so to speak, girls drifted towards me like dragonflies, and they took me to student digs on the Lenin Hills, or to little rooms in suburbs that I can barely call to mind.

When there is unrest in a country, sex thrives.

Following my initial meeting with Swindleman, I was on the road continually for a year and a half, between my stays in Moscow.

I did the Great Soviet Union Tour seven times, an enterprise that lasted three weeks, beginning in Leningrad and proceeding by plane to Kiev, Simferopol in Crimea, Tbilisi, Tashkent, Samarkand, Bukhara and Irkutsk, from where you took the train westwards again via Novosibirsk to Moscow. The number of participants never amounted to more than about twelve, and there was always a woman from Intourist as a guide. In truth, I didn't need to do much at all, except organise things a bit and chat to the tourists, who were usually interesting, interested, and friendly people. Some of them had specific wishes, such as a couple from Overijssel with a Polish surname who, come what may, were determined to visit the synagogue in Bukhara, a city that with its minarets, azure-blue mosaics and depressing Brezhnev buildings rose like an eclectic *fata morgana* in the blinding sun of the hellish-white desert, an enterprise that was viewed by the authorities with suspicious eyes in 1989. I talked to three Jewish boys there, aged about ten, all with dark, deer-like eyes in intensely pale faces, who dreamt of emigrating to Israel because there they could shoot at Arabs without penalty. They grinned while making violent gestures in the air; the schoolboys play-acted pulling the triggers of their machine guns at a passing car. That evening, I was lying in my stifling hotel room, with the cries of a muezzin outside, plagued by a swarm of bluebottles and recovering from awful diarrhoea, when someone knocked on the door. As soon as I opened it, three Uzbeks in grubby green linen suits literally almost knocked me over. The anti-Semitic virus that was raging in the capital had also spread in this direction. It was fed by newspapers, politicians, and national movements that seemed to spring up out of nowhere, but in fact were built upon rotten old czarist foundations.

'What were you doing with those Jews this afternoon?' The eldest of the two stared at me threateningly with a mouth full of golden teeth. He was in his forties, with the face of a villain from a Soviet film, Russian-speaking with a thick Central-Asian accent.

'Nothing, nothing at all, I was there purely as a tourist.'

'Papers!' The Uzbek quickly flicked through my passport and asked, 'What's this? You're an Israeli spy!'

'You're mistaken.'

'Do you think I'm a moron? I've just come back from an official trip to Moscow. Israel doesn't have a consulate there. But who gives Jews their exit visas? The Dutch. You're all spies!'

These two guys grabbed my arms in this miserable room that was full of buzzing flies. My on-looking mind was suspended somewhere near the ceiling, and I was staring downwards, as though at a poor vaudeville performance. The eldest yanked my trousers and pants down, and pointed at my genitals with his quivering finger.

'Didn't I know it? A filthy Yid!'

I'd been circumcised as a baby, purely for reasons of hygiene.

'Fuck your mother! As long as we never see you again, there at that synagogue! Otherwise, we'll have you transported immediately!'

And they vanished again, the three Daltons, leaving me aghast, my pants around my ankles.


Usually, travel stories are deathly dull, so I won't trouble you any further here. Still, I'll never forget that day in April 1989 when I landed at Tbilisi airport at 4 pm and I'd had to wait nine hours at Simferopol with my group; the flight kept getting postponed by Aeroflot, without them letting us know why. In the cramped waiting area, the stench, the racket, the reek of sweat, were scarcely bearable. Passengers for the next flight to Moscow scuffed up and down, lay on benches, or on the floor with baskets of live poultry, buckets of pickles, baskets of apples, pears, strings of onions and garlic, potatoes and other foodstuffs that they were taking on board the plane as hand luggage to flog in the capital. You could buy a ticket for the price of three roast chickens. My tourists gradually started to show their displeasure towards me, though they knew there was nothing I could do. Some were already beginning to mumble about compensation. It turned out nice people could turn into insufferable arseholes. For a while, there was talk of us being sent back to Kiev or Moscow. Eventually, we were herded like human cattle into an Antonov propeller plane, with relief on the faces of the ground crew. When we were flying over the mighty, snowy mountain peaks of the Caucasus, though the continual racket of the ancient, rattling crate was deafening, the sun briefly made it sparkle with silver and liquid gold.

It was my fourth visit to Georgia. By now, I knew quite a few people, I'd even had a brief flirtation with a waitress, amid the intoxicating scent of peaches in the botanical garden on the mountain that looked out over old Tiflis with its orthodox church domes, minarets, and a synagogue with a glittering roof. I looked forward to the terrace outside Hotel Iveria, at the end of the central Rustaveli Avenue, just past the opera house, where the successful local men, who were fashionable and mostly dressed in black, spent the whole evening dining among string musicians, popping the corks of Soviet champagne as loudly as possible and singing, while the waiters continually brought in new dishes, like stage servants with their props, as well as stone pitchers of white and red wine, which they filled by plunging them into the oak wood vats that were picturesquely lined up against the wall and decorated with grapevines. In Moscow, even the worst sort of sausage, a small chicken, or an orange had become rarities. Even if you had money, you could barely get hold of food without the right connections. Here, there seemed to be a surfeit — dishes of citrus fruits adorned the tables, together with *Khachapuri*, cheese-filled bread fresh from the oven, spinach with garlic and pomegranate seeds, boiled chicken in a nut sauce, *shashlik*, fresh aubergines; my mouth was already watering.

But as soon as we landed, with the engines roaring, brakes screeching, and shaking as though we were sitting on a rickety merry-go-round, something seemed wrong. We had to remain seated — even the cabin staff weren't allowed outside. After half an hour, the whining and complaining started again. What kind of lousy operation was this? For breakfast, we were given mineral water in a poisonous-green plastic beaker that tasted of iron. The air in the Antonov soon grew thicker; when someone quietly broke wind, the smell lingered for ages. Those that smoked began to smoke, including the stewardesses and the pilots who had come forward. I wiped a circle with my fingers in the condensation on the window beside me; peering along the wing, with its propellers, I could make out a busy commotion down on the concrete field. Three helicopters came flying up. While the rotors continued spinning, soldiers with flapping green gear and proto-Slavic features jumped out, and immediately disappeared from sight. Army jeeps drove up and away; a monstrous cargo plane landed. Soldiers also disembarked from it through a rear ramp that was lowered to the ground like a ferry. It was followed by armoured cars.

Only after an hour and a half were we allowed out. But contrary to what was promised in the itinerary, we weren't driven on the Icarus bus directly to Hotel Iveria in the middle of the old city centre, past the stone camel humps of the seventeenth-century bath houses with their sulphurous spring waters, but to a sanatorium from the 1970s, three-quarters of an hour further, located high in the mountains, with a view of a medieval church in the distance. On the wall by the entrance were portraits of Lenin, Marx, and Engels, with the following slogan: *Onwards to a shining future under the banner of Marxism-Leninism!* Rooms had been made ready for us. However, in the Spartan passage there was only one communal washroom with seven shower heads, and the toilet-paper in the WCs consisted of torn shreds of *Pravda*. The white steel beds in the narrow little rooms resembled those in a hospital. Photos hung on the rough, green, lime-washed walls of smiling medical personnel — men and women with paper caps on their heads, the majority with thick glasses — and below was a list of 'procedures' that you could have done in this institution entirely for free: blood pressure readings, removing callouses from hands and feet, correcting the vertebrae, ingestion of oxygen cocktails, massages and medicinal hot baths, the unlimited purification of the system with Georgian green tea, walking in the park ('nowhere is the air as pure as in the Caucasus — the air here is so delicious that you could spread it on your bread!'), and there was also a sort of miracle mud, which came out of the ground locally and could be applied both rectally and vaginally with special East German tampons to prevent the development of internal growths (*profilaktyka*), or else treat pre-existing abnormalities. I got the impression that the building had been cleared in haste for our arrival, which turned out to be the case: it was a sanatorium for workers and their families from the mining city of Norilsk above the Arctic Circle.

We were given a light meal of mash and pale sausages in a canteen-like dining room, with a mosaic of little stones on the wall, on which a steelworker and a factory girl were kissing. It had nothing in common with the refined and delicious Georgian kitchen. It was practically inedible, and once again there was the sound of mumbled complaints in my direction. A professor of sociology, in his fifties and a prominent citizen of our capital, took me aside when I went to the toilet. He spoke as a representative of almost the entire group. 'After waiting for half a day in the Crimea, we've just about had enough now. This isn't a hotel, it's a sort of hospital! According to the programme, we're supposed to be taking a tour of the centre of Tbilisi tonight. And afterwards, dining in the roof garden of our hotel. What kind of organisation is this?'

I told the professor that I was sorry, that I'd try to get some clarity and hoped that everything would be sorted out as quickly as possible. Three women from the group, sisters and farmer's daughters from East Brabant, who'd won the lottery and decided to spend their money on distant exotic travels together, were actually quite lyrical. After the meal, they'd thrown themselves into the medical programme with gusto. They had male masseurs trotted out, with moustaches like variety artists, took a sauna, walked around the terrace outside in absurdly baggy bathrobes with flapper-like bravura, even though it was already chilly and dusk, while the rest of the group sat together grumbling in the recreation room, or reading or playing chess, or slipped off to the ascetic rooms for an early night. The local guide who'd taken us from the airport to the sanatorium in the bus, a girl of a poignant, almost biblical beauty, kept as quiet as the grave. Was the hotel in the centre fully booked? And what was the programme for tomorrow, actually? Her lips trembled, as if she wanted to say something, but quickly thought better of it. Tomorrow at nine o'clock, she said with faltering hesitation, she'd be in the lobby to give me more information.

Because the sociology professor had let me know that he was considering making a claim on behalf of the group, due to the lack of entertainment, I feverishly tried to get in touch with Swindleman in Moscow. I wasn't able to call directly. I put in a call via an operator; it was only after three quarters of an hour that a connection was made.

'How are things going there?' Swindleman began cheerfully.

I told him what the matter was.

'Stay calm … I've been expecting a call from you. It seems a bit chaotic in the centre of Tbilisi at the moment, a terrible mess … I don't know exactly what's going on. But the centre is supposedly occupied. Where are you now?'

I told him.

'Compensation? Just let the guy keep harping on. And don't tell them anything. Intourist has the right to alter the travel itinerary at any time … That's even in the travel conditions, so don't worry … But I don't like what's going on there. Have you already called Timur, by the way?'

Damn it, I'd completely forgotten. Timur was a Georgian history student, a friend of Swindleman's, who organised optional excursions for us, and we split the profits fifty-fifty. I'd brought along six new videotapes for him, Betamax, gold around here.

'Call Timur as soon as possible! Everything here's running like clockwork, but soon we'll have to have a chat about the future. Or do you want to be a wage slave for the rest of your life? And, by the way, I'm in love, my friend … Dark, petite, eighteen; *fresh from the sixth form*, as we used to say in Groningen. But a panther in bed! Anyway, good luck there, it'll all fizzle out … Everything always fizzles out …'

Ten minutes later, I had Timur on the line. I told him that I'd arrived and had brought the videotapes with me. But however mercantile he usually was — he always sold the videotapes on for dream profits — this time he hardly seemed interested. Didn't I know what was going on in the country? The whole Rustaveli Avenue had filled up and the most awful rumours were going around. 'Where are you? Why are you there? Yeh, yeh, of course I know the sanatorium … It's three-quarters of an hour's drive, but I'm on my way …'

An hour later, Timur was standing in the lobby with the profiles of Lenin, Marx and Engels and the slogan about the shining future, along with his friend, Bagrat, a bear in a leather jacket with close-cropped hair.

'I've brought them for you anyway,' I said, as I handed over a bag to Timur with the six videotapes.

He took it in silence, and gave it to his mate, like a prince who'd been given a gift and then passed it along to his lackey, unmoved. Timur was nervous; he walked straight back to the exit, mumbling that he had to return to the city quickly. He'd come to pick me up to show me, as a westerner, what was going on. Even in Moscow, people didn't quite know what was happening here.

A doorman in a grey jacket, with round glasses, sprang up from his easy-chair behind the reception desk, where he'd apparently been perched like an old owl taking a nap on a branch, when he noticed that I was heading out with two guys. He ran after me, panting, and called me back very courteously, and laid a hand on my shoulder to keep me there. What was this? As a guest, I didn't have the right to leave the sanatorium without permission. The safety of the clientele was paramount! Instructions from the authorities. The man spoke lousy Russian, burring, the grammar so mangled that even I noticed it and it was almost comical. Timur turned around, fired off a few words in Georgian, and the doorman slunk away immediately, as though bitten by a watchdog.

'If we're stopped, act as if you're deaf and dumb, a deaf-and-dumb Latvian.' Timur and I sat in the back of the ramshackle, petrol-reeking Lada. 'On the way, there were soldiers everywhere. Damned if it doesn't look like war …'

We hurtled down the mountain at a furious speed, over the same road, along a ravine that I'd crawled up that afternoon in the

Icarus bus with my tourists, with everyone holding their breath.

Bagrat was a student friend of Timur's, who came from Batumi. The nocturnal landscape loomed in the sheen of the mint-green moon, but the dizzying depths didn't seem to bother him. He hit the gas, braked, hit the gas again. Timur was talking constantly. Until then, our conversations had been mostly about money, about his wish to visit the West one day, whenever we'd earned something from an excursion with my tourists to a tea plantation, or to an open-air folklore performance, where moustachioed men in Kaftan-like black jackets showed off their martial dancing arts with daggers and clattering sabres. Now, all fired up, he was speaking solely about politics, about the future of his fatherland. The whole situation had definitely shifted, there was no stopping it now. He'd taken a lead with a few friends from the faculty. Over the last few days, the Rustaveli had filled up with demonstrators who demanded full independence from Moscow, copying those in the Baltic States. The decades of subservience, terror, and the suppression of the Georgian language and culture had lasted long enough. Didn't I know that they had been cultivating grapes and making wine here when people in Europe were still wandering around in animal hides?

We left the Lada in a side street that rose at an angle, lined with fine houses with verandas. The neighbourhood was wreathed in darkness because of the scarcity of lampposts, with only the occasional yellow-lit shop, no wider than two doors, where despite the late hour, they were selling flat, round loaves. We walked the last five hundred metres. Six months before, I'd seen demonstrations in Vilnius, Riga, and also Moscow, of mostly small gatherings of people with flags and banners who were making all sorts of demands — *Down with the dictatorship*

*of the communists! The truth about the camps! Long live freedom!* —
and which were usually brought to a quick and efficient end by
the police or plain-clothes security people. When we approached
the centre of Tbilisi, though, I had the impression that we were
entering a human beehive, a swirl of sound, of movement, of
music and yelling. An ocean of people had washed over the
Rustaveli. Lying on the steps of the governmental building, with
its austere architecture, were men, women, young people and also
children half-wrapped in blankets, getting ready for the night.
Timur had urged me not to speak Russian; I moved through the
crowd as though I were deaf and dumb. Occasionally, there was
the waft of food smells; they were warming soup on fires. The
round loaves of bread that I'd seen earlier were being passed from
hand to hand filled with pieces of tomato and roast meat. Nobody
drank, other than tea and water. Eight years earlier, I'd witnessed
the euphoric human mass on Museum Square in Amsterdam,
after they'd marched in a procession through the city protesting
the deployment of cruise missiles. This was different from that
casual display of protest then. Here, there was the unmistakable
odour of approaching doom hanging over the cacophony. The
demonstration had clearly been going on for a while and fatigue
was seeping from the hollow eyes of some of them. A revolt was
brewing. Bagrat was immediately swallowed up in the throng.
I followed Timur's small figure as he moved towards a group of
fellow students waving flags. They greeted him like a hero. A little
further on three girls were playing violins with verve. A cleric
in a black habit was advancing very slowly and the crowd was
parting respectfully before him. With his cascade of thick, bronze
strands of hair, his beard resembled the ancient Greek god Zeus.
He held up a silver cross with inlaid gems for the people, so that

they could all kiss it. After a little while, I also lost sight of Timur. On the way, I'd seen armoured cars. Only after a little while did I realise that a whole army of security forces was stoically spying on the demonstrators from a ridge. I struggled a few hundred metres further in, failed to spot Timur anywhere, and struggled back. Suddenly, I was no longer a deaf-and-dumb observing eye. I became conscious of my physical presence and was overwhelmed by a cold panic.

When Timur woke me at six the next morning with a call, I had to think for a second before I could remember how I'd got back to my sanatorium the night before. The Bakelite telephone on my night-stand had yanked me viciously from a dream.

I'd run into a bald Abkhazian in a stinking alley that had been transformed into a public latrine, after being swept from the Rustaveli by the mass. He'd driven me back to the sanatorium for $50 and insisted that I polish off half a bottle of cognac with him in the lobby, which I didn't dare to refuse. The doorman in his grey jacket was still lounging half asleep in his chair behind the desk, but got up occasionally to re-fill his coffee cup with booze, while he and my driver described the commotion in the city as a crime by a bunch of idiots.

'Where are you?' Timur asked in a panicky voice.

'Back in my sanatorium,' I murmured.

'I looked for you everywhere … Oh, it's awful, terrible … Those bastards! Those filthy, rotten bastards. From now on, it's war!'

I gathered from his words, despite his interrupting himself and jabbering at someone else in Georgian — and with the sound of agitation and even screaming in the background — that a couple of hours after I'd left, at a quarter to four in the morning to be precise, the Red Army had gone into action to clear the Rustaveli. When the droning armoured cars steamed over the asphalt to crush anyone who didn't spring aside, as though under steamrollers, the patriarch of the Georgian mother church had appealed to the crowd through a megaphone to leave the boulevard in a final attempt to avoid a bloodbath. But the demonstrators had dug in. The army began striking at the defenceless men, women, and even children with clubs, bludgeons and razor-sharp trench shovels; others succumbed to the tear gas, and yet others were trampled in the stampede that broke out in the panic.

There were tens of dead, hundreds of wounded.

Although the cognac had sunk deep into my brain with a burning sensation, I was completely sober immediately. It's hardly conceivable now, certainly not for the odd young reader that I have, but at the time there was no internet, no mobile phones, and the Soviet censorship — despite all the reforms set in motion by the Kremlin — was still fully intact.

During the breakfast of porridge, greasy omelettes and weak imitation coffee in the dining room, the professor of sociology looked at me with a contemptuous air, full of disbelief, after I told them about the horrors that had taken place in the capital the night before. A revolt? Why didn't I go and pull my granny's leg. But only half an hour later, we were officially informed: due to 'unexpected events' in the country, Intourist's excursion itinerary was being cancelled. What's more, a day of national mourning was announced. Everyone was to remain inside before we travelled on to Tashkent, by plane, the next morning.

'So we won't be seeing anything of Tbilisi?' asked someone, a

French teacher from Sneek, and also a former peace activist.

'I'm awfully sorry, my dear people, but I'm afraid not. All those dead and wounded!' I answered.

'Compensation!' someone shouted for good measure.


Timur is now a successful, well-off, not to say *puissant*, entrepreneur. I bump into him every now and then in Moscow, and he takes me to the roof garden of the Ritz Carlton on the Tverskaya Street for a drink. He's a waterfall of warmth, style, and charm. He declined a minister's post that was offered to him one day by the president of the now independent Georgia. He chose the business life. He has hundreds of hectares of vineyards in Kakheti, the Georgian Tuscany east of Tbilisi, a paradise of rural beauty where life is celebrated with wine and the adoration of women. There, they produce the costliest Caucasian grand crus from the Saperavi grape. And behind the mountains in the distance is Chechnya, where the death cult dominates, and women are degraded and oppressed. In Moscow, he owns villa villages, office blocks, apartment blocks; he can also pride himself on a real estate portfolio in Switzerland, where his two children went to school before finishing their studies in Oxford and Yale. With his now portly figure and grey film-star quiff, he is well-known as a solid family man, despite the rumours about his indestructible libido, whereby he accumulates blondes by the dozen (he's supposed to have them flown in by private jet from all over the world).

But at that moment, on that April evening in 1989, when he and a friend pulled up to the sanatorium in a Lada that rattled like a coffee grinder over the crunching mountain road, he was still a hustling, dirt-poor student with a pigeon chest and stubble: razor blades were more expensive than jewels. What I didn't know, what I only realised later, was that because of him I was witness to the first great revolt against Soviet authority; the first real rupture in the *craquelure* of the canvas of the USSR, after which it would quickly fall to pieces.

Chance is simply the dominant law in this existence.

# CHAPTER FOUR

My brother-in-law had been in possession of the sailing boat for a couple of months, and it was indeed an excellent boat, the *Nautilus*. The problem was that the investment he'd made together with his partner would only yield its first financial fruits in about five months at the earliest, when the last of the drift-ice had vanished from the Neva and the mouth of the Gulf of Finland, towards the end of April. He'd already prepared the teaching programme for his course participants. He'd start with the sextant and then move on to the latest digital navigation techniques. His dream was to give sailing lessons one day on a ship that was entirely his own, somewhere in the warm European waters. A person has to have dreams. In order to make a living in the meantime, he'd again picked up his glycerine business. The barrels he had in stock were stored somewhere on a factory site. He organised the sales from home. How he managed it all was a mystery. But the sanctions that the West had imposed as a retribution for Russia's annexation of Crimea were having a strange side-effect: internal production had increased, which had a tentatively positive effect on my brother-in-law's business activities. He's always upbeat, optimistic, full of energy and good humour, even though he also lost his father last year, and like my wife is now an orphan.

A month after he'd bought the boat, I was back in Saint Petersburg following a trip to the Crimea, of all places. After a few days, he wanted to show off his new acquisition. I had financed it after all.

The November weather was dry but bleak; a shrill wind was blowing beneath the grey clouds. I'd just returned home from the bakery, where a woman in a doctor's coat was selling the goods from a window in a side-wall, when my brother-in-law called. I felt like hitting the sack with the warm fruit buns, but my brother-in-law kept on, and half an hour later he was standing on our doorstep. As he no longer has a car — and neither do I — we took the metro all the way to the north-east of Vasilyevsky Island, where the boat was supposed to be kept in a boathouse for the winter. Although the first night frost had already fallen, the *Nautilus* was still moored alongside a jetty, bobbing between the other yachts in the leaden-grey water. In my mind were images of the blessed places I'd once visited — the marinas in Menton and Nice, and those in Spain and on the Canary Islands, where I'd lived for a while, the bright white sails of boats bobbing on the azure around the Peloponnese. The contrast with the scene here was almost grotesque. A factory chimney was pumping out iodine-coloured smoke a little further off; seagulls were circling around, screeching loudly. It made me think back to how in my twenties, an age ago, I'd first stood here on the waterside waiting for my illegal contraband bibles. A sort of duckweed was drifting on the waves between the washed-up rubbish, which made me wonder whether it had mutated: the green was slimy, almost transparent, as though it was of a synthetic genus.

'So, what do you think?' My brother-in-law nodded proudly towards the yacht, which I guessed was about seven metres in length.

I expressed my admiration and asked how long the boat would be moored here, with an eye to the winter that might arrive at any moment.

'It's a little devil, a polyester thoroughbred!' my brother-in-law went on in an animated fashion. 'Because of its superb rigging and the in-mast furling main, it's quick and very manoeuvrable. Fully battened sail, extra Blazer sail. Four sleeping berths, completely reconditioned 16 HP motor with folding propeller. Liquid compass, radio-telephone, navigation system, everything intact! Construction year 1988. I'd rather have had it a couple of years younger, but that didn't suit my budget. Anyway, another week, and it's going indoors ...' Alexei pointed to a dilapidated shed with a corrugated roof. 'That's why I called you. We're going to go for a nice little sail now. How shall we divvy up the tasks on board?'

My brother-in-law grinned when he heard that I not only couldn't sail, but had never actually been on board a sailing boat in my entire life — sailing, skiing, hockey to me were all aberrations of the rich. His grin was the somewhat obtuse specimen of someone who thinks you're taking the mickey, but isn't entirely sure, and is waiting for the approaching punchline. When he realised I was telling the truth, he couldn't get over it. I did actually come from the country of water, didn't I? God had created the earth and the Hollanders had created Holland — that's what he'd been taught as a child. How in God's name was it possible that I was ignorant of the pleasures of calmly rounding a buoy, the jibing of the mainsail, keeping an eye on the backstays, or the swift release of the luff? He continued on, as he led me by the arm to the gangplank, then we took a little spin with the motor. He wanted to let me feel how beautifully the *Nautilus* cleaved the waves, how well-defined she lay in the water.

A quarter of an hour after we'd entered the Gulf of Finland, a watery sun peeked from behind the clouds; the waves were splashing high, the dirty-white foam tasted vaguely of vinegar. I'd put on the same sort of poncho as my brother-in-law, which kept us good and dry. A couple of wondrously big seabirds flew along with us at first. I had no idea what they were, and asked Alexei, but because of the wailing of the elements, he evidently didn't hear me. Suddenly, the aerial escort disappeared. The water grew calmer; the sun gave off some warmth. As proudly as if he were the captain of an ocean steamer, Alexei stood at the wheel. He set course for the west, in the direction of Kronstadt, and after a while he seemed to have completely forgotten my presence. With his full, dark-black head of hair, he physically had little in common with his father, my father-in-law, who'd been as bald as a billiard ball. But they did share two characteristics: an amiable, kind-hearted nature and a passion for the technical.

After finishing his studies as an engineer, Alexei had spent quite a while sailing on international merchant vessels, which had become pretty common after the fall of the Soviet Union in 1991 — it was a so-called 'cheap' source of labour: ex-Soviet citizens were recruited for a few thousand dollars a year by shipping companies based in Cyprus, Malta, and the Philippines — until, one day, he'd had enough of the exploitation. His father and grandfather had sailed too: the old Boris Nikolayevich, my wife's favourite grandpa on her father's side, had been a captain on the White Sea Fleet during the war, leading the so-called 'Murmansk Convoys' with American aid supplies on board for the Soviets in their battle against Hitler. And my father too had sailed, in his turn. Not as a subject of the communist Soviet Union, but for a kingdom at sea where capitalism reigned and where, as a 17-year-old (having been injured in the war), he was forced to put to sea as a cook's mate to support his family who were financially totally destitute. That's how it was at the time if you loved your parents and there was no money: you supported the family. A smart, intensely shy, sweet man, thirsting for knowledge and books who, as a result, could never continue his studies. It was only me, I thought, who had no experience of the lures and dangers of the sea, as a wave struck the front of the boat with a ferocious whack, making my brother-in-law utter a triumphant cry in delight. I took up a position on the poop deck, where the water was splashing up the least. Alexei's contours were marked out sharply against the November sky. What a good and kind brother-in-law I had in him. He was almost the only family I had left. The rest had conked out at a rapid rate. The whole background of my youth had just about been entirely wiped out in a couple of years. Whenever I flew to the Netherlands, I could often just as well travel straight to the crematorium in Driehuis-Westerveld to say goodbye to an acquaintance, a loved one, or a family member. Death is like an infestation of fleas that takes possession of a house and can scarcely be combatted. Mostly it leaves other families alone, until it is their turn.

Julia's mother had actually been murdered six years earlier in a Saint Petersburg hospital. One autumn afternoon, my wife came home in a terrible state. Mama had been diagnosed with bladder cancer. Incurable. We immediately headed for the hospital with a bag of cash, knowing that without backhanders, a death sentence would be passed in any case. But there appeared to be little interest among the medical personnel and the doctors. What were we so worried about? The patient was almost seventy-four already, an ancient woman! They did take the cash, of course. Every day, Julia brought food to the hospital for her mother; nonetheless, her condition rapidly went downhill. One icy morning in February, it was all over. That afternoon we were standing in Dostoyevsky Street, at an undertaker's. The snow was piled up high in the streets. Icicles as big as people glittered in the zinc guttering.

'What have you come for?' A doorman with a swollen vodka face scanned us enquiringly.

'To arrange our mother's funeral,' my brother-in-law replied. 'To choose a coffin. She died this morning.'

'Luxury or ordinary service?'

'We don't know yet. First we want …'

'Queue at counter 3.' The gatekeeper irritably gestured towards the left. 'But first wipe your paws! Damn the devil, this isn't a station buffet!'

We bought a mahogany coffin. Consumed equally by grief and doubt, my wife and my brother-in-law decided on an autopsy. If only they hadn't. Because the results were appalling: there was no sign of cancer at all. Although we'd approached the best doctors and greased their palms with rubles and dollars, my mother-in-law had died of a common, untreated bladder infection. 'They've murdered her!' Julia screamed out. 'They've simply murdered Mama in that hospital!' In other parts of the world, there may perhaps have been the opportunity to appeal to a medical disciplinary board, or to a judge. But here there were roughly two options — either submit to your fate, or bugger off abroad.

Oh, didn't it all seem a long time ago now! Not just the burial of Julia's mother in the Jewish cemetery outside the city, but also her father's cremation last year in a sombre industrial estate in the north of Saint Petersburg one beautiful summer's day. It made me feel melancholy, so overcome that I wrote the following brief note:

*After the cremation of my father-in-law yesterday, the family, friends, and acquaintances of the deceased sat at a table in the open air for the 'pominki' — the traditional funeral meal. The sky above Saint Petersburg, which barely grows dark at this time of year, was now clear blue. There was salad, there was chicken, there was fish, there was vodka. Just as in many pages of Russian literature, some of the men present began to enthusiastically drink away the tension that followed the ceremony. In just the same way as a wedding in Russia frequently ends up in a fistfight because of drink, stories about the rows during the pominki are numerous. Read the stories of Chekhov, Tolstoy, and other Russian writers for proof.*

*In our case, everything proceeded calmly.*

*'Talking about Chekhov,' Uncle Viktor began telling my wife. 'You know that your mother's family originally came from the city of his birth, Taganrog. Before the revolution we had vineyards there. We did business with Chekhov's father, who was a small trader.'*

*For the first time, my wife was hearing the details of how her forefathers were transported to the camp by Stalin. The glass vodka pitchers were growing emptier, the voices louder. Then someone started talking about my mother-in-law's mother; in the thirties, she was an absolute Jewish beauty. One morning — as a 25-year-old — she was picked up from work in a black car. At the time this meant: the camp, rape by a party official, or a bullet in the neck. She was driven past the KGB headquarters in Leningrad, and was finally dropped off at the chic Hotel Astoria, where an old female friend greeted her in a room. 'Hello, are you pleased to see me?' Yes, she was. Her friend was married to a high-up Kremlin official and was by now so far removed from the world that she didn't realise what deathly fears my wife's grandmother had imagined. 'One day, all of these stories disappeared, just like our loved ones,' my wife sobbed. I said, just for once an optimist, that I didn't wish to believe that. At least, not while there are still people who write.*

While I stared at the figure of my brother-in-law, almost motionless at the helm of the growling boat, still on course for Kronstadt, I thought of one of the last times that I'd visited my father-in-law in his wooden dacha. 'Do you know what it is, boy?' he'd told me at the time, as he was kneading dough for the *pelmeni* — the Russian ravioli — in the dacha's little kitchen, which was enveloped in snow, like in a fairy-tale. 'For my whole life, I've been surrounded by lies. But I've still always wanted to make the best of things. I was good at learning, became an engineer. And later a Party member. You didn't believe in it, what's more, you *hated* it. As you know, in the war my father sailed on the White Sea, as a hydrographer and later as a captain. He was decorated for it. But every day, ev-e-ry day my mother was terrified that one day he wouldn't come home again. Not because of the icy waves, but because of the repression. When Stalin died in 1953, my mother ran to the shops for a bottle of Soviet champagne. "Finally, that bastard is dead!" Even as a child I knew all this. But, anyway, I became a Party member. After all, I had a wife, a family. And so the years passed. When you're young, life is wonderful. I was sent abroad twice for extended periods as a specialist — once to Romania, and later to Finland. I had to certify the ships that were being built there for the USSR. But even there, in your foreign post, they always kept an eye on you. You were obliged to attend readings at the embassy. About Marxism and that sort of nonsense. You were interrogated. By types like that president of ours now. At the time, he was responsible for exactly that kind of work as a spy in Dresden: following and interrogating people. Now he's once again a believer, namely a believer in the lie that he created himself. The lie that he's God — the 'czar' who can steal left and right without punishment. And hand out punishments.' My father-in-law walked over to the White Russian gas stove, a big brute that was crackling in the warping wooden passage. He had to get by on a pension of a €160 a month, and he now resumed his story. 'Anyway, we were happy in our own way. I was paid a percentage of my salary in foreign currency. A pittance, but nevertheless: *hard currency*! And I could buy my first car when I turned forty — a Volga. Everyone was envious, of course. In the summer, we always went on holiday to the Baltic Sea. We had nothing but wonderful summers at the time!'

At the end of the 1980s, when I'd visited my future in-laws for the first time in their cramped flat behind the Smolny Institute, the old Boris Nikolayevich was still alive. The 80-year-old hero of the White Sea, with his head like a calabash and his bristly grey eyebrows, was living with his only son and daughter-in-law, just as my grandmother on my mother's side and my grandpa from my father's side, had lived with us for a long while, a phenomenon that I was roundly ridiculed for at my grammar school in Haarlem. My wife's favourite grandpa shuffled through the little kitchen, humming, in his Tatar slippers with their red embroidery. Suddenly, he raised his head, looked at me with strikingly clear eyes, pinched my cheeks and said to his granddaughter, 'What were you saying, sweetheart? A Hollander? But he's a healthy guy! If he manages to keep going longer than number one ...' After I'd told the retired ship's captain that my father had also sailed in the 1950s, his aged seaman's chest swelled as big as a battleship with pride at his granddaughter's choice.

In the late 1980s, my father-in-law worked at the Shipping Register in the city, in a monumental building close to the Hermitage. His monthly salary was equivalent to six packs of Marlboro, or one and a half kilos of imitation coffee, or a pair of Polish jeans. I helped the family out a little. My father-in-law followed politics fanatically. He was in his fifties; the future was still somewhat open for him. There would now be a speedy end to the plague of communism. He was full of hope. On a misty autumn afternoon, just as I'd stepped into the flat, he drew me towards the flickering, dark-green eye of the Soviet TV. Gorbachev was speaking!

Only once did my father-in-law visit us, three years later in 1992, when Julia and I were by then living in a rented flat on the Dutch coast. His marriage to his wife was sadly in pieces by now; my mother-in-law never managed to pay us a visit.

My father-in-law spoke broken English, my parents just a few words. We went to dine with them. The ice was immediately broken when my father served up Dutch steaks, sautéed new potatoes, dishes with two sorts of vegetables — cauliflower and carrots — and took out something strong to toast with; I seem to remember it being a bottle of my mother's cherry brandy. Two men from two different worlds, with totally different lives. But they'd both sailed in their younger years. Anecdotes flew back and forth, simultaneously translated by me or Julia. Like the one about my father smuggling razor blades from South America. He was never busted because he stashed the contraband inside the carcasses of cows, which were then frozen. The customs officers in Hamburg, where the meat was unloaded to be defrosted and processed, never managed to nab him. They soon started calling each other by their Christian names, like two world leaders that got along well. Soon, not only would ideologies on earth be over, but their after-effects would be too. Hadn't the politicians of the last three-quarters of a century been nitwits! We were all people, we were all the same, with the same wishes. My father-in-law praised the steak: fried in precisely the right way, he'd never eaten meat of such quality in his entire life. My mother looked on the whole time, silently and gratefully, filled with pride and warmth. We said our goodbyes, with hugs. By now, my father had learned the words *spasiba* for 'thank you' and *do svidaniya* for 'goodbye', which my mother also muttered — tipsy from her half a glass — while no one knew that this would be their one and only meeting.

Walking along the beach at Zandvoort the next day, my father-in-law started telling me of the seven years he'd spent as a boy in Kaliningrad, the former East Prussian Königsberg. The sea here reminded him of his youthful years there. As a child, he'd seen how the Soviets had destroyed many of the buildings that had been spared in the almost all-consuming fiery hell of the Red Army advance on Berlin. Like the old city fortress. Out of a pure lust for destruction, hate! When we were halfway to Noordwijk, my father-in-law stood still for a moment, looked me right in the eyes and spoke solemnly. 'Boy, I have to talk to you. No, not about my daughter, that's all fine. I thank you for all of the Rembrandts, Frans Halses, and Van Goghs that you showed me, the canal houses, the wonderful shops. In five days, I'm going home. Can I confess something to you? I have a little savings left over from my years in Finland. Twelve hundred German marks. I'd really like to buy a second-hand Mercedes with it; I've dreamt about one all my life. A Mercedes! Could you help me out with that?'

The rest of his stay was dominated by this one quest: finding that car. We travelled all over the country by train. At the time, a Russian in the countryside was still a pretty exotic phenomenon. We ended up hiring a car because most second-hand dealers were based along the motorways. We were met with scorn everywhere we went. 'Twelve hundred marks? Tell that guy that a half-decent little runner would cost at least twice that.' Nevertheless, we did finally manage to find one: a brown Mercedes from 1980. 'This is my car!' When he saw it on a field in the Gooi region, my father-in-law beamed like freshly polished silverware. Just the right price. There was one small problem though: it was a classy second-hander, a rare golden opportunity, but the car wouldn't run. The head gasket had gone. My father-in-law, who scampered around the car excitedly, mumbled that he was an engineer. He'd fix the gasket in Russia! I kicked in three hundred guilders for the transport of the car to the harbour in Amsterdam, where my father-in-law — who'd already mapped everything out in advance — could drop off the car for transport to Russia. The next day, when the Mercedes was hoisted aboard the container ship, the *Maxim Gorky*, my father-in-law was determined to sit behind the wheel of his new acquisition. I can still see him in that car, dangling in the air in a gigantic net attached to a crane with chains, waving at me as happy as Larry. He was indeed able to fix the gasket. For nine years, my father-in-law drove as proud as a peacock past the palaces of the former czar's city that had now been re-christened

Saint Petersburg, watched by some of the inhabitants with envy. 'Look at that, a filthy capitalist!'


The imposing dome of Kronstadt Cathedral was snarling in the distance. My brother-in-law, who was still standing as straight as a rod at the wheel, turned his head to me, pointed forward with one hand free of the wheel, and cried, 'Kronstadt!'

Because that wretched revolution had been in my head for weeks, my thoughts drifted from my deceased father-in-law back to 1917, to the summer of that year. The sailors from the marine base for the Baltic Fleet on the island of Kronstadt — the most merciless, cruellest revolutionaries of all — left for the centre of Petrograd at the start of July to spread terror, to rob, to murder, to rape. The revolutionary days of February were in the past. The czar had abdicated and was spending his days as an ordinary citizen — under the name Mikhail Romanov — at one of his former country residences, the Alexander Palace in Tsarskoye Selo, in the bosom of his family, playing dominoes as of old, writing in his diary, smoking cigarettes and walking in the grounds. He was still ignorant of the fact that he would be taken by train to Siberia in August. First to the Governor-General's house in the provincial capital of Tobolsk, later to the city of Yekaterinburg in the Urals, where he'd be brutally butchered with his family in the cellar of a merchant's house by the soldiers of the revolution.

In those February days, ministers, high officials, and others in power in the old czarist regime were publicly lynched after manhunts, or went voluntarily to the lair of the revolution, the Tauride Palace, where they surrendered in terror, and, amid loud cries to murder them too, were conveyed to the cells in the Peter and Paul Fortress, where they had sent their opponents not long before. With a solemnity that the world had never seen, the martyrs of the revolution were buried on the city's old parade ground, the Field of Mars, in a sea of red flags and banners, to the strains of the *Marseillaise*, attended by half a million people. Because the ground was frozen, they had to use explosives to make the hole for the mass grave (just as dynamite would be used seven years later, after Lenin died, on the arctic-frozen ground of Red Square in Moscow, where at the command of Stalin a makeshift wooden mausoleum was erected to house for eternity the body of the leader, which was to be embalmed). By now, all army ranks had been abolished; ordinary soldiers no longer had to salute their former officers. In a wave of iconoclasm, the two-headed eagles and other czarist symbols in halls, passages, and on the façades of governmental buildings were hacked off with bayonet tips, pickaxes and army shovels. In the Mariinsky Theatre too, the superb imperial blue stage curtain was replaced with a red one, while the gold-braided men in their serving tailcoats, who'd previously guided the wealthy visitors to their seats with a calm solemnity, were suddenly wearing grubby, grey jackets. This was a harbinger of the egalitarian bleakness and greyness that for more than seven decades would cover the country from Murmansk to Vladivostok like a shroud. But Chaliapin, the legendary opera bass, continued to perform there. Fewer and fewer trams ran, and the number of horse-drawn cabs also declined. There was a fear that the city would be stormed and occupied by the Germans; there was the continual threat of attacks by aeroplanes and zeppelins. People suffered *en masse* from typhus, tuberculosis, scabies, and scurvy. The queues for bread and other foodstuffs were unceasingly long. Bandits and muggers skimmed the streets, where they were mostly on the hunt for people with a bourgeois appearance. Pretty soon, few dared to go out in expensive clothes, for fear of being molested by the children of the revolution — peasants, the city proletariat, deserter soldiers, and freed bandits who grabbed their chance.

Meanwhile, life on the volcano continued. The highest aristocrats remained beneath their crystal chandeliers in the city palaces, served by lackeys in livery, holding banquets with foodstuffs from their store-cellars, as though the smoke outside was only temporary and would soon die down. The Nevsky Prospect teemed with whores, just as it would in the turbulent days during the collapse of the Soviet Union, and just like today. The dual power in the country had fallen into the hands of the Provisional Government and the Soviet, with the *trait d'union* between the two rival blocs being the young former lawyer and socialist Alexander Kerensky, who — hysterical by nature, and sickly, but at the same time filled with an ever-growing megalomania — had experienced a lightning promotion to Minister of War and finally premier. Like a Napoleon, he moved into the Winter Palace, adopted an operatic voice while alone among the golden mirrors in the ballroom, enjoying his sudden omnipotence, like a big kid that can't actually believe its tempestuous success. He wrote his *ukases* at the czar's desk, slept in Alexander III's four-poster bed, under the silk sheets with the double eagle, to be chased off shortly afterwards by Lenin's Bolshevik gang (he was able to escape, lived for a while in France and Germany, and would hold out as an inhabitant of the United States until 1970; the man who'd breathed in the scent of three hundred years of the Romanov dynasty in the czar's bed would live to hear the Stones and the Beatles). Lenin, after more than sixteen years in exile, returned from Switzerland through Germany in a sealed train, travelling via Sweden and Finland to Petrograd in April 1917, where a reception was organised by his Bolshevik followers at the Finland station as though he were the Messiah. Again, an orchestra played the *Marseillaise*. The Bolsheviks, with their feel for propaganda and spectacle, had drummed up the flashing brass of tubas and trumpets, red banners and an honour guard of sailors. Lenin was ushered out into the frenzied chaos of the masses, their heads lit up dramatically by silver searchlights, and then he was hoisted onto the turret of an armoured car, where he promised to bring an end to the shameless lies of predatory capitalism for good.

What few realised, and still don't realise, is that at that moment Russian democracy was still in with a chance. Czarist Russia could have become a democratic Russia, with a constitution — just as elsewhere on the old continent. But Lenin wouldn't brook any cooperation at all with the Provisional Government. He was an apostle of death, arriving to destroy. He dreamt of a regime that would carry out a reign of terror, like the one after the French Revolution in 1789; he wanted to unleash a civil war in Russia and elsewhere in Europe, to cast off the twin yoke of capitalism and imperialism worldwide. Because Russia was officially at war with Germany — the British and French ambassadors in Petrograd, as representatives of the Allies, had tirelessly tried to encourage the czar and later the Provisional Government not to give up the fight — Lenin was seen by many as a plain traitor to his country. With German help, he and his comrades were conducted through hostile Germany in that special train, and through business and other arrangements he was well supplied with D-mark banknotes and even gold from the Kaiser. He was reputed to have come home as a spy to bring down holy Russia, so that the Germans would have their hands free to fight the French on the Western Front. After his arrival, he pitched his tents in the mansion that had been taken shortly before by the Bolsheviks, which belonged to Mathilde Kschessinska, the former mistress of the czar Nicholas II; it is a fine art-deco building not far from my house, right next to the city's mosque, with its always imposing dome of azure-blue stones. The ballerina had danced *Sleeping Beauty* in the Mariinsky Theatre only two months earlier at a special gala performance for a visiting delegation of the allies. Now she was invaded by soldiers, sailors, and other Bolsheviks, with mud on their boots, waving their bayonets and rifles, and driven from her sumptuous accommodation, which boasted a large auditorium for private performances, a winter garden with citrus fruits and palms, and another salon with a domed roof and balcony. Here, in this fairy-tale environment, where art and sophistication had flourished under the crystal chandeliers and silk draperies, Lenin commenced the death drill, with his shrill voice, his neurotic movements, and his murderer's eyes. He provoked the soldiers who still hadn't deserted into doing so, to overthrow the current Provisional Government, and to kill those with money and fortune who didn't want to share. With his intimidating demagoguery, he was able to engineer it for women to march over the Nevsky Prospect, singing the melody of an old Russian hymn: 'We will plunder! We will slit throats! We will rip open bellies!' The Kronstadt sailors revolted in the first week of July, after having already butchered their officers *en masse* in their island fortress during the February days. They now moored their boats on the granite quays of the city, stoked up by Lenin and his adjutant Leon Trotsky to take over the revolution — in a new wave of violence and plunder. But when the time came, and it was clear that the revolt wouldn't succeed, the great revolutionary Lenin took flight in terror to Finland disguised as a woman, with his beard shaved off.

Lenin was first and foremost a coward.

'Go to the devil!' My brother-in-law's voice roused me from my ponderings about the revolution. '*Blyat*, all whores!'

We'd just rounded a buoy and were about to start on the return journey to the harbour when the motor fell still after a vacuum-cleaner blast and a pervasive smell of singeing. Alexei rushed back to the poop deck, cast a glance at the water, and vanished into the cabin.

With my back craned, I peered from the deck down the white metal steps, asking what was the matter.

'An obstruction! Unbelievable! The seller swore to me that everything was reconditioned this summer.'

Alexei made a few fruitless efforts to get the thing going. Finally, he climbed back up and raised the mainsail. The wind flapped frightfully above our heads. For the first time in my life, I was sailing. A sea haze had risen. My brother-in-law flew back and forth over the deck, pulling straps and rigging.

I asked if I could help.

He said I'd be better off going below; if I stayed up here on deck, I'd have to watch out for the boom.

'What do you mean?'

'The boom! A potential guillotine!'

I slunk down to the cabin of the *Nautilus*, a third of which had been paid for with the phantom money from my still-unwritten book.

———

There'd already been frost a couple of times that week when it had been minus thirty; the winter had been exceptionally harsh in spells that year, not only in Saint Petersburg, but elsewhere in the country too.

A month after the sailing trip with my brother-in-law, I was caught in a snowstorm on a walk in the woods near the town of Sergiyiev Posad, forty kilometres outside Moscow. I suddenly found myself in a wind turbine of chicken down. It was the first snow of the year. I'd been to much more inhospitable places in Russia; nevertheless, I was overcome by panic. It was as though I was being pursued by a pack of wolves, in a sort of feverish horror, in a blizzard that swept through the bare branches of the trees and back to the town. Once back in Moscow, I had the feeling that I'd eluded some vague disaster.

That evening I wanted to drink, so called up two friends. Gerbrand, a pale-blond Frisian with a Ukrainian mother, a performer with a panther act, who'd come to Russia a year and a half previously to look for work, now that taming wild animals in Dutch circuses was over. And Igor, an art dealer and professional bachelor. Both twenty years younger than me. Excellent guys. We arranged to meet in Zhan-Zhak, an eatery on one of the boulevards. The place was once the lair of another revolution; namely, the one four years before, in the winter of 2012 to 2013, when the people of Moscow went out onto the streets *en masse* to protest against the rigged elections, the repression, the press restraints, the state censorship, the fraud, and the corruption.

As of old, swarms of young women were seated at the round marble tables with carafes of wine, between the silver wall-mirrors, which simplified all of the looking and being looked at, the assessing, the smiling, the flirting, and the reeling in of their prey. A Russian with the hollow-eyed, bearded face of an icon saint was playing an accordion, lending the establishment the allure of a Paris bistro. But through the vicissitudes of time, the character of Zhan-Zhak had changed in a bizarre way. The ladies à la Pussy Riot, who had often taken up residence here with their noisy entourage — the artistic, intellectual, socially-engaged types — had left the country, gone underground, or apparently thrown in the towel.

The revolutionary fire had been snuffed out with an iron fist, without one spark appearing to remain.

'What were you doing in those woods?' After I'd told them about the snowstorm that I'd been caught up in that afternoon, Gerbrand looked at me and chuckled. 'You weren't planning to hang yourself, were you?'

Igor stared with incomprehension at the animal-tamer, who'd only been making a joke. The half-Frisian, who I'd given all my books to one day, quickly began telling him about my account of my search for a fellow countryman, an organ-maker, whose body was found dangling in a tree one morning by ice-fishermen, in a winter forest close to the Volga.

'What strange stories you write,' said Igor.

'It's a true story,' I replied.


I can't remember exactly what time it was, or the circumstances in which it happened, but infused with the aniseed taste of the sambuca that we started drinking after the beer and wine, I now found myself in a car. What am I saying? It was a limousine, just like the kind usually used for weddings, and always available to the two girls who'd joined us. I sat between my friends opposite the girls, both dark-haired; one was wearing a blue fur coat with a white collar and the other a white coat lined with blue fur. The coats hung open. They were hot. I was really feeling the strong liqueur; I was suffering from a blackout. A series of details were already missing: the conversation at the table, the moment that the girls had sat down with us, when apparently we'd collectively decided to adjourn.

It was only in the freezing cold outside that I recovered my senses. The four of us floated through the city, past the pistachio-green, lit-up, tall buildings, the jungle of light at the White House, over the similarly excessively lit bridge, to the Hotel Ukraina, where the brunettes were staying and had invited us.

'Two plus two is four,' I said. 'Guys, please drop me off here. I'll take a taxi home. But do have fun!'

But the girls, who'd both started smoking like crazy, commanded me to stay.

'What are you doing here, actually?' It was the Russian in the blue mink coat, who I guessed was in her late twenties. The limousine had stopped at the hotel, the doors opened; we walked up a crimson carpet, which was rolled as straight as a die from the revolving door and out over the snow.

'I asked what you do …' The girl in the blue fur coat took me by the arm boldly. Her predator's profile, which was steaming through the mascara, now came very close to me.

'He's a writer,' Gerbrand said.

'And you?' emanated from the lipsticked mouth of the other girl, who Igor was leading to the entrance.

'Animal-tamer.'

'Yes, and my father is the king of Siam!'

'Panthers,' Gerbrand explained, deadly serious.

In the late eighties, I'd housed large groups of tourists in the

Hotel Ukraina, when Intourist or Cosmos, the then futuristic hotel colossi in the north of the city, were full. I'd also stayed there a couple of times myself. Now it was called the Radisson Collection Moscow. The imposing entrance with tall ceilings and marble pillars had, of course, been left intact, but the handsome interior of superb Stalin baroque had been partially demolished and replaced with a flashy luxuriousness that was valued by both Russians and cosmopolitan foreigners.

'Where are you going?' The doorman had stopped Gerbrand in his tracks.

'He's with us!' the ladies cried in unison.

In the lift, the white fur-lined coat immediately wormed her tongue into Igor's mouth. Lithe, moaning. We rose to the sound of violin music. The ladies' names had slipped my mind. Half dizzy, and with a parched throat, I stood beside the young Russian in her blue fur coat, who was nuzzling up to me like a cat … Olga … Of course, the sweet child was called Olga. And the other one Anastasia. But there seemed to be a misunderstanding. I cast an imploring glance at Gerbrand, with his pale-blond, handsome Frisian head leaning against the padded lift wall. I begged him wordlessly to free me of the girl, so that I could quickly go downstairs to get a taxi home.

'And so we're going to live here for a few months,' said Anastasia, as we hurried down the passage, where the threadbare Soviet parquet had been replaced with royal blue carpeting with yellow stars.

'Why?' asked Igor.

'Our husbands want us to amuse ourselves. They're on a special mission, to the United States. We aren't allowed to come. Rotten politics! We're from Siberia, from Krasnoyarsk. Have you ever been to Krasnoyarsk? Luckily, we have a house there with an indoor swimming pool. We swim in the warm water under the palms, while the Siberian cold rages outside. But everything else is really boring there! We want to do yoga here. And learn vegetarian cooking.'

We went into a suite that consisted of three rooms that merged into each other, immense in size, again with the high Stalinist ceilings, each different in style, colour scheme and furniture.

'What sort of books do you write? Detective stories, I bet?' Olga had tossed her fur coat onto a blue-and-pink striped sofa in imitation of her friend, after which we walked into a modern room, where just about an entire wall consisted of a flat-screen television.

'Sometimes there are corpses in them,' I mumbled.

'Oh, do you hear that, Nastja? There are corpses in his books … What did you say? No, *no* champagne! Whisky, I want Irish whisky!'

Without asking, she pressed a sizeable bulb of whisky into my hand, with tinkling ice cubes. I took a couple of hot sips, it reacted well with the beer, the wine and the sambuca. A crystalline acquiescence overcame me, while I considered how I could extricate myself from this company as quickly as possible.

'You remind me of my father!' After she'd daringly kicked off her pumps, Olga crawled onto my lap. 'He was bald too. He left us when I was seven — my mother, my sister and me … The bastard … Come on, give me a kiss! Hey, don't you hear me? Kiss!'

Gerbrand was sitting slumped in a white-leather bucket seat. He was staring, with a can of beer in his hand, out of the panoramic window, over the skyscraper décor of the city that sparkled like Manhattan.

'Well, this is going nowhere ...' Olga freed herself from me, crawled on hands and knees to my Frisian friend, with a grimace on her face, teasingly taming: 'Hey, you there! You're supposed to be an animal-tamer, aren't you?'

Her disbelief about his profession turned to shrieking admiration when Gerbrand showed her the photos on his smartphone of his performances with his three black panthers in famous circuses all over Europe. But those bastards in his fatherland had banned his act. The girls were wearing necklaces of sparkling imitation diamonds. Olga called to her girlfriend to attract her attention to the miracle, but Anastasia had long since disappeared with Igor.

I quietly slipped off; I could already hear the clattering of a shower behind a padded door in the last room, with cooing and the calm brassy groans of Igor in the background.

Just before I stepped into the passage, my iPhone vibrated, and I answered without a sound. It was Julia, my wife. Calling from Saint Petersburg.

'Where are you?' she asked.

'I'm excellent! I'm just heading out.'

'I didn't ask how you were doing, but where you are ...'

I started to tell her about my crazy adventure earlier that day in the woods, close to the town of Sergiyiev Posad. I got caught up in a snowstorm. It was as if I was inside a white tornado.

'What were you doing in the woods?' My wife's voice sounded far away. 'Eh, what were you in the woods for?! Where are you now?'

'Just, you know ...' A commotion came from behind the bathroom door.

'What was that?'

'I don't know …'

'Where are you?'

'I've been writing again for three weeks straight. It's making me dead sick. I wanted to stop. I'm doing it all for your brother …'

'You're dead drunk …'

'A couple of glasses of wine … I'm just stepping out now …'

'Where are you?'

'Hotel Ukraina …'

'Where?'

'Don't you remember? That time with that Swindleman …'

I stepped out into the lobby of the hotel that at the end of the eighties had reeked of overcooked green cabbage — the scent of crisis, of scarcity, of the start of banditry and currency speculation — but which had now metamorphosed into fairy-tale luxury.

'You hear, Jul? I'm outside now …'

My wife began to sob, to cry. I stood there motionless in trepidation on the royal blue carpet with its golden stars. It was Ljòlja. Our middle cat was still sick, or rather, she'd got sick again. Julia had kept me informed every day by WhatsApp; she told me about her visits to the vet behind the Vitebsky Station, about the medicines, the injections that she was supposed to administer to her now.

'You have to come home … It doesn't matter what you're doing or where you are … For all I care, you could be in a hotel in Moscow with a couple of whores … but you have to come home quickly … Are you coming home?'

At three o'clock the next afternoon, I took the Sapsan Express, the Russian high-speed train, and arrived in Saint Petersburg three hours and fifty minutes later. Julia was waiting for me in a fur coat, a tatty thing that she'd bought second-hand off an old lady some place the year before.

'How's it going?' I asked her.

She fell into my arms; her face was warm and wet, swollen with sorrow. 'I'm trying everything, really everything …'

The newly arrived passengers were fiercely lugging their cases; porters on flat trolleys were driving through, bawling, a frosty breeze blowing kilos of snow onto the rails. Young sailors in long black coats, with black fur hats, disappeared into the diesel-powered train on the opposite side of the tracks. It was already dark. But everything under the wrought-iron roof was bathed in a warm yellow glow.

'We have to go to Dostoyevsky Street,' said Julia.

'What do you mean?'

'Ampoules, I've ordered ampoules …'

Because of the boycott, the medicines that Ljòlja needed were nowhere to be found. After a long search, Julia had come across a company on the internet that still had them in stock. We went there by metro right away. When we were above ground again, I had trouble dragging my suitcase on wheels through the stiffened snow. The company turned out to be a private apartment, housed in a portico that stank of rotten fish *colatura*. We rang the bell. A grey steel door opened, an androgynous bird's head snatched the money, the door closed again, and a few moments later re-opened, a package was handed over and everything was again closed up.

The building was directly opposite the funeral parlour where we'd bought Julia's mother's coffin a couple of years before. Then, too, there were icicles hanging from the guttering.

'We'll take a taxi,' I said, when we were standing outside and my wife began to head towards the metro. 'I'm gradually getting dead tired of public transport …'

'Not because of anything else?' Julia remarked softly.

The Christmas lights were twinkling on the Nevsky Prospect, as though a jewellery box as big as an ocean steamer had been emptied out over the city from the sky. The shop windows majestically radiated an occidental prosperity in an almost imperial manner. In a park, there was a Christmas tree as big as a house, made of Swarovski crystal, the snow around it coloured light blue. We drove along the bank of the Neva. We curved to the right at the level of the red-brick monster of the Kresty Prison, on the far side of the frozen white river, and then we entered our blessed neighbourhood. I could smell the sweet scent of bread through the car windows; they were already baking for the following day.

The area between Shpalernaya Street and ours was covered in thick snow. The taxi's tyres churned through it. I thought of the diary entry that I happened to have read that afternoon by Louis de Robien, a young French count who'd been a military attaché in the city from 1914 to 1918. It was precisely on this stretch of less than a hundred metres — in this artery of the revolution — that he'd seen twelve dead horses scattered among the puddles, many of which were coloured red, following the heavy fighting in July 1917 between the Bolshevik soldiers and the Cossacks who still supported the Provisional Government. The hides of the dead animals were taut and glistening from the rain.

So that my wife didn't have the chance to start talking about the telephone conversation of the night before, even though I had nothing to fear, I told her about the book that I'd now started. A sort of chronicle. I usually kept my literary plans to myself — out of fear of failure. But she knew about the advance, and the ten grand that I'd lent her brother for the sailing boat. I couldn't keep quiet any longer.

'It's about the Russian Revolution?' As we inched slowly past the drinks kiosks, teeming with the figures of drunken bums and professional alcoholics, she snorted, 'A rotten subject.'

'We're there!' the driver announced. Tchaikovsky Street 40.

Just as in Western Europe and elsewhere around the world, people in Russia were getting ready for the holidays. There wasn't much going on in the country; I wrote my pieces for the paper and finished off some other writing assignments, in the hope of making some decent progress with the book I had on my hands.

The frost persisted; the snow on the street outside was scarcely cleared away. One morning, an elderly lady in a dull pink coat — the dull pink of old-fashioned powder boxes — was pulled down near a drinks kiosk by her *bouvier*, which had seen another dog a little further off and started to run out of pure enthusiasm. The colossally strong barking beast dragged her a few metres over the bumpy ice. I helped her up. Her wrist was excruciatingly painful; I got a taxi and took her to a clinic on the Liteyny Prospect. The *bouvier's* warm, wet panting on the back of my neck gave me the creeps. The doctor was a maternal woman of about 50. She treated the heavy bruising for free. Not everything in the country was rotten.

Every evening, Julia lit candles and tea-lights in the living room of our opulent two-room apartment. I'd fetch fresh, dry, good wood for the open hearth from a forester who lived like a lonely gnome in a forest close to the Finnish border. The first Christmas trees were being sold in front of the metro station a hundred and twenty metres from our house, just past the bakery. An orchestra of war veterans was standing around playing music and singing, freezing in their faded-blue, padded battledresses, with weathered faces marked by the suffering borne in Afghanistan, Chechnya and elsewhere; this was in addition to the usual grannies who were selling potatoes, apples, and garlic from crates, to supplement their meagre pensions, which worked out to be €100 in a city where a coffee now cost €3. A century after the revolution, the difference between rich and poor, not just in the city but all over the country, was again as great.

Our metro station — Chernyshevskaya — was named after the utopian socialist philosopher and writer Nikolay Chernyshevsky, who was condemned to death after the publication in 1863 of his novel *What is to be done?* After a mock execution, as in the case of Dostoyevsky, he was exiled to Siberia. The main protagonist in his story, the ascetic, weight-lifting, raw-meat-eating Rakhmetov, who spent his nights on a bed of nails to harden himself for the coming revolution, was a hero in his time for the youthful populists, students and other principally well-off young folk who had gone to 'the people', to the countryside, to the peasants — who sometimes lived less well than pigs — to offer proof of their goodness, founding communes, dreaming of the idyllic and just society that the writer had presented to his readers. But just as later in history, few were genuinely prepared to make sacrifices for a better life for the poor. People became members of the right groups, read the right papers, but in the meantime, they arrogantly strode past the people in the street, for whom they usually felt only an abstract warmth. *What is to be done?* was a great source of inspiration for Lenin too, who as the reader now knows, lived for some time in Tchaikovsky Street, just as the writer Ivan Goncharov lived a little further off — in

Mokhovaya Street — where he finished his novel *Oblomov*, and another five minutes further on Joseph Brodsky wrote his mythical poetry in his communal flat, before he was exiled by the Soviet regime. To say nothing of Zinaida Gippius in her *bel étage* at the end of our street. All things considered, I was living in the midst of literature, though by now I was no longer able to write.

However charmingly the candles burned in the evening, however deliciously my wife cooked, however the hearth crackled when we were sitting by the fire with a book at around nine, a feeling of doom had settled over everything because of Ljòlja's recurrent illness.

'Oh, my princess, my sweetheart, my lovely,' Julia sang to our middle cat reassuringly when we had to give her an injection twice a day — afternoons and evenings.

Ljòlja wasn't only our middle cat, she was the smallest too. Our tomcat Peach was the charmer in the household, the Don Juan who was able to win over every lady immediately with his thick, sandy fur, and the motley Moesha was Buddha's lazy ambassador. But Ljòlja still possessed the energetic innocence of a child, even at the age of eleven, with her blue-grey fur and marine-blue, emerald eyes. She approached everyone inquisitively. But as soon as Julia began to prepare the ampoules, accompanied by the rustling of the plastic on the sterile needles, Ljòlja would disappear like a streak of lightning — under our antique desk, behind the heavy drapes by the heating, or dextrously concealed in the wall-closet in the bedroom, under the sweaters, socks, dresses and other clothes of my wife, whose wardrobe was an eternal jumble.

While I was travelling through the country for my work, or staying in Moscow, Julia kept me informed via a tide of messages: Ljólja's appetite was good, the swelling in her intestines stable, but according to the vet behind the Vitebsky Station there'd been something wrong with her blood for the last week and a half. It was as if I was hearing my mother talking about my father again, in the last months of his life. 'Don't you worry, boy. The doctor is very able. He says that everything's all right, except for the blood ...'

One morning, I was just about to walk out of the door to buy a Christmas tree at the metro station; I always associated the scent of pine needles in the house with ultimate happiness. My wife begged me not to: suppose our cat got its drip tangled up in the branches. That afternoon, Julia made a Christmas tree out of green cardboard and red mica paper. She put it on the mantelpiece, with a lit tea-light behind it. We spent the evenings reading by the hearth. After every glass of wine that I poured, my wife mumbled that this really was my last. Although I actually wanted to anaesthetise myself, I used the justification that I needed the drink, that without the alcohol I didn't have any clarity of thought, let alone the original insights and brainwaves that I needed for the book that largely still had to be written.

I'd been avoiding the question, but a week after I'd started helping my wife with the injections, I asked her if our cat had a chance. That day, she'd visited the vet behind the Vitebsky Station for the umpteenth time.

'Of course she has a chance! Sixty per cent, the vet told me again today ... But the blood's still not completely right. And she saw something new on the scan ... It doesn't necessarily have to be something serious ... Oh, Natalia Grigorievna is such a fantastic woman ... She has three cats herself; she knows how it is. Did you know that her family owned a gigantic estate outside the city before the revolution? Only her grandmother was able to escape that dance … The rest were finished off … It is true that Ljòlja has lost quite a bit of weight over the last few days … We weighed her again today … But that's supposed to be normal with these medications … Ljòlja, sweetie, where are you?'

Despite the medication, our cat deteriorated. She lost a lot of weight. She no longer crawled up onto my wife's lap so naturally; she more often kept herself to herself, nestling among the clothes in the bedroom closet. Her eyes were still clear, but her thin, brittle bones poked through her greyish-blue fur. Apparently, Julia didn't see it, or didn't want to. The cats were everything to her. She was a cat lady, but a married one.

'Well, look here!' When Ljòlja grandly walked into the room a day later, the white tuft of her bandage comically curling around her left back paw, my wife beamed. 'She's almost back to herself again! She's slowly beating it! Oh, my princess, my sweetheart, my beauty! Come over here quick, my sweet little treasure!'

The next evening it took a bad turn.

I'd written up something for the paper; we'd had a late dinner. After her injection, Ljòlja had slunk off to the bedroom closet. Outside it was snowing. At about twelve, I was just about to head to bed when Ljòlja made her appearance in the living room, trembling violently and stumbling. It was as though our sick cat had drunk a saucer of pure alcohol. Then she fell over, to her left. My wife uttered a cry of panic. She hurried to the cat, lifted her up, pressed the animal to her chest, kissed the blue fur, all the while whispering sweet things to her. Call the vet! Right now! Natalia Grigorievna had given my wife her mobile number. Julia could disturb her at any moment of the day, even if it was the middle of the night. Where was her damned phone? The vet's number was in her mobile. I called my wife: her smartphone had slipped down the gap between the cushion and the arm of the chair that she'd just got up from.

A little while later, I was walking through the lashing snow. I was on my way to Kirochnaya Street, a little under two hundred metres from our house, to the chemist that was open day and night. In my trouser pocket I had the piece of paper on which my wife had written the prescription for some sedative that the vet had given her. The next morning at quarter past eight, Julia had the first appointment at the clinic behind the Vitebsky Station. A temporary deterioration in cats that were on heavy medication was not uncommon.

Despite the late hour, it was full to bursting at the chemist. So full that I had to stand outside with a woman whose full-moon face was enveloped in marten's fur. The tiny pharmacy was a place where the nightlife gathered together bizarrely; drug addicts bought their medicines here, half-illegal preparations for the cocktails they were addicted to. Cars stopped all night long in front of the display case that was specially kitted out with condoms, intimate gels and Viagra. But there was evidently also a great nocturnal demand for run-of-the-mill aspirins, powders and pick-me-ups, which were also sold here. The figures of customers moved behind the steamed-up windows, with their red faces, most of them wrapped in fur. As I watched how the snowflakes recoiled from the tall dark house-fronts in the dim sheen of the streetlamps, I was overcome by a rising restlessness.

There was scarcely any movement inside the chemist; the woman beside me with the full-moon face mumbled that at night they still worked like they did under the communists. Between filling prescriptions, they popped out for a cup of tea. Meanwhile, her husband was at home dying of a severe bout of bronchitis!

Right next to the chemist there was an Art Nouveau building, a dilapidated, slate-coloured colossus with a bright-green, illuminated modern doorbell, which struck you right away. Two taxis had already pulled up there, and each time a man had got out, and after ringing the bell had gone inside.

'A whorehouse, the whole city is just one big brothel!' That's what the driver of a taxi had said when I'd stopped him on the street the day before. 'You see all those houses, all those façades? Some of them look like they've been nicely refurbished. But behind them it's a rubbish dump. I've got two daughters, sixteen and seventeen. When they get a job later — *if* they get a job — they'll have to work for three months just to get one of those mobile phones. I've been driving for twenty years already. There isn't a single street in the city where there isn't a whorehouse. I'm worried about my daughters. I've completely had it with that capitalism. They once called the tune in the Winter Palace, now it's the Kremlin. The masses keep quiet, do nothing. And meanwhile, this country is an unending brothel!'

*What's keeping you?* Julia had sent me a WhatsApp.

I answered that it was insanely busy at the chemist, but that I'd be home as quick as I could.

A boy with Jesus hair came out. Hollow eyes, totally emaciated. Krokodil is what they call that junk that they sell the ingredients for here. Then one day, the skin just falls from the addict's bones, like braising steak from an *osso buco* shank. The wretched creature pulled down a balaclava, lit up a cigarette and disappeared. The lady with the full-moon face went inside, and I was left behind alone.

The snow was being driven further by the fierce wind.

On the train from Moscow, when I was reading a chronicle of the years immediately after the revolution, I discovered that Rasputin had also lived in my neighbourhood for a long while. To be precise, here on Kirochnaya Street, at number 12, a hundred metres along. The Siberian peasant was already right at home at Tsarskoye Selo with the czar's family. A fine family, with four splendid daughters and one boy. Rasputin was addressed by the czar and czarina as 'our friend', and in turn, he was allowed to call them 'Mama' and 'Papa'. That the holy fool, with his unmistakeable supernatural gifts, had a few times saved the life of the little son who was suffering from haemophilia was incontrovertible – even when he did it by telegram or over the phone. Oh, I've always understood the czarina in that respect, despite her hysterical, egotistical and inflexible Teutonic character, and her living in her country palace as a sort of hermit, in an atmosphere of icons, holy relics, faith healers, and miracle workers. What mother with a sick child wouldn't go to the furthest extremity? Meanwhile, when the miracle-monk with his deeply set, hypnotic eyes wasn't in the palace or at home receiving his admirers of both sexes with tea and biscuits, he was behaving like a debauched beast. He took girls, high-ranking ladies and others of the female sex to bathhouses to 'make glad' with them in orgies. He saw them as the necessary tools of sin; sin that was actually essential in this sub-lunar realm in the eyes of God, because without sin he believed that no salvation was possible.

The taxi driver from the day before was right. The city, indeed the whole country, was a brothel, or rather, just as big a brothel as a century ago. The czarist secret police had followed Rasputin because of his sexual scavenging; his escapades were recorded in their reports with the precision of a totalitarian state. From here in Kirochnaya Street, he'd transported himself countless times by automobile or *droshky* — a carriage with one horse — to places in the city, like the Haymarket or the Nevsky, where the whores were ripe for the picking. He was a terrible fairy-tale figure with his scraggy beard and his patent leather boots.

'What's keeping you?' said my wife, who'd now phoned me. 'Why is it all taking so goddamned long?'

A quarter of an hour later, when I was finally standing in our living room with the sedative, I found Julia in her chair, with the sick cat clutched tightly to her chest, beside the marble fireplace, where the fire was no longer raging and crackling, but only smouldering.

The following morning, Ljòlja had to be put on a drip in the clinic behind Vitebsky Station; the vet recommended a procedure that would last seven hours. After four hours, Julia came home downcast and exhausted. She didn't want to eat, only have a cup of tea. She'd left Ljòlja the lavender-blue cashmere shawl that I'd given her one spring day in honour of the publication of my seventh novel. Because of her scent. So that the cat would feel a little more at home there in the clinic, and not entirely abandoned and alone.

My wife headed back after half an hour.

The next day, there was a second drip. Meanwhile, I was sitting at my desk, writing pieces for the paper; I wasn't getting to grips with my book at all. A person has to be happy to write prose, to be able to look ahead to an extended period without too many obligations, and be in a state of complete harmony and rest; it was a mystery how I'd managed to write ten other books.

When Julia phoned me on my mobile towards evening, I immediately knew that it was over, before I'd even answered. 'Please come to the clinic quickly. Ljòlja has died. In the end, we put her to sleep ... There was nothing else to do ... There was no more hope ... Oh, what am I to do now?'

'I'm coming ...' I said.

An hour later, we took our middle cat home in a taxi. The lavender blue shawl with Ljòlja wrapped in it was lying on Julia's lap. The clinic had offered to dispose of her — it was part of the service. Dispose? How could they even utter that awful word?

But as soon as we were home, Julia was overcome with doubt. What were we to do with Ljòlja? We didn't have a dacha or a garden. Then my wife decided we'd bury her that very evening in the Tauride Gardens. 'What time is it now? Seven o'clock? I'm going to sleep with Ljòlja for a few hours first. Wake me up at ten. Make sure you have a shovel for the grave ... Then we'll go ...'

I'd often seen all sorts of tools on the landing of the communal flat under us — crowbars, hatchets, buckets, and also cement shovels. I went down the stairs. After I'd pressed one of the seven bells at random, which were pathetically held together with cables, bits of plastic and even plasters, Gennady Nikolaevich's bright red, sea-dog's head appeared almost immediately. I hadn't seen him since he'd smashed up a dresser with an axe.

'A shovel? Why?'

I made up the first thing that sprang to mind.

'What's in it for me?'

I said I had a bottle of whisky upstairs, scotch. It was a present that I'd once been given after a reading.

We set out shortly after ten. While my wife heaved herself into her fur coat, and draped a black woollen shawl around her head, she asked me to take Ljòlja off her for a moment. It was the first time that I'd held the dead body. You could feel the stiffness, the infamous *rigor mortis*; it felt awful through the cashmere.

A savage arctic wind was blowing up the tall, broad, straight Tchaikovsky Street. The top layer of snow was frozen; it crackled under our soles as though we were crushing icing sugar. I half dragged the shovel behind me. The leaden thing's blade was caked with dried-up remains of cement. Julia walked beside me in silence, once again pressing the shawl containing the cat tightly to her chest, as though she were trying to protect the dead animal from the biting wind. There were hardly any people walking on the street. Most of the windows were black. The only place there was a little life was in the Chinese restaurant, two buildings before the florist with the stone-dead bouquets. It was housed on the cellar floor that had been empty for years. The lamps beside the steps cast flecks like red wax seals over the snow.

We passed the building where Lenin had once lived. Since I'd delved into the Russian Revolution, the images of those years that had accumulated in my mind from writings, diaries, and other materials now constantly flitted through my head. Twenty-four years later, the blockade would follow, the almost nine hundred days that the city would be besieged by the Germans, when a million people would die of hunger, cold, exhaustion, disease, and bombardment. A million dead, in *one* city. How many of them had lived in our street? In our portico? In our apartment maybe? And how many of them at the time had trekked through Tchaikovsky Street in this bitter cold, along the house-fronts darkened against air attacks, not bearing a dead cat like us now, but with a sleigh conveying the body of a family member, a husband, a wife, a child or another loved one, to take them to the collection point? Though many bodies were left behind in the snow because the living no longer had the strength to carry them — in fact, they sometimes fell dead themselves beside the sleighs. They were the survivors of the civil war that had swept over the country like a murderous scythe in the preceding years, initiated and encouraged by the

Satan whose former residence we'd just passed, the bastard who must have once walked here, precisely on this stretch of pavement, where I now advanced with my wife, the cement shovel scraping behind me. We were approaching the home of Zinaida Gippius, who one day in 1917 had noted dryly someone's words: 'They're shooting dead officers who are stuck with their wives. Some ten, or eleven a day. They take them to the courtyard. The commandant, with a cigarette between his lips, counts them — and then they're taken away.' The same day, she wrote about one Professor Nikolski whose wife had gone insane after her husband had been shot by a Bolshevik firing squad and his magnificent library was confiscated. Shortly after, the son had to report for military training. His commandant, a Bolshevik joker, laughingly said to him, 'So do you know where your pappy's body is? We fed it to the animals.' Everyone knew that the animals in the zoological gardens were fed fresh bodies from the firing squads at the gaol in the Peter and Paul Fortification a little further on, all with Lenin's approval.

The gate to the Tauride Gardens was often closed at night, but this time it was open, fortunately enough. We entered the enclosed desert of snow that was surrounded on four sides by fine nineteenth century buildings, with *bel étages* and little towers, palaces and other buildings from the time of the czars; the shadows of the trees were marked out purple against the sheen of the street lamps. The low sky was the colour of slate. I put an arm around my wife. She sighed that she would rather walk alone. We slowly traipsed across the snow, which crunched stiffly, as far as the frozen pond where I'd seen children skating earlier that week and whizzing down the slopes around it on sleighs. Fathers and mothers were standing around proudly, uttering cries of joy in the thin, freezing air. My wife abruptly stopped just beyond the pavilion, where bridal couples were photographed in the summer, and the local *Mafiosi* drank champagne with their sweethearts. She nodded, 'You see that group of birches? Past the chestnut trees? Nobody ever goes there ...'

We left the path, ploughed our way through the snow, which was half a metre deep here, as far as the seven birches that stood close together. In the summer, this part of the park was a sunbathing field; even before the revolution it had been a meeting place for gay men. After my wife had pointed out the exact spot, in the middle of the fairy ring of trees, I began shovelling away the snow. A gust of wind from the Neva blew through the bare branches above us; white powder filtered down. After I'd cleared a layer of the snow, the ground turned out to be as hard as granite. And however much strength I put into it, everything was frozen solid. I began to hack at the earth with the pointy edges of the shovel; the remains of the cement spattered off. My wife looked on in silence the entire time. In spite of the frost, I was dripping with sweat; the droplets on my nose froze instantly. After about ten minutes, I managed to dig a hole. I nodded to my wife in silence. Julia stepped forwards with the dead cat in her arms. What happened next exactly escaped me; maybe she was suddenly overcome with dizziness, or stumbled over a clump of earth, but my wife slipped and fell backwards. Ljòlja came loose for a moment but landed safely in her lap. I wasn't able to reach out a hand to my wife in time to stop her falling — not even that.

When we walked back home through Tchaikovsky Street, she said, 'Did you know that Dostoyevsky's widow also lived in our street? Maybe that'd be nice for your book. I don't know what number exactly, but shall I look it up for you sometime?'

In my mind, I could see the lavender-blue shawl disappearing beneath the clumps of frozen black earth that I'd shovelled on top, while my wife stood there softly sobbing beside me. Finally, I'd levelled everything out with the cement shovel as best as I could.

After one night of snow, there was nothing left to be seen.

# CHAPTER FIVE

But let's get back to the late eighties, to Moscow, the capital of the Soviet Union where, after my bible-smuggling mission to Leningrad, I was now running the Russian branch of a Dutch travel agency with Swindleman. Energising times! My work as a coordinator, hotel room booker, and group guide hadn't only worn me out completely after just a year, it had also gradually started to repel me. The black market that I'd eagerly delved into had now reached surreal proportions. Because the officers in the barracks were no longer afraid of their superiors, everything was being flogged under the counter. Armoured cars, tanks and other military paraphernalia still in mint condition were being disassembled and sold as scrap for export abroad – a practice that kept Pozorski busy in Leningrad. This yielded foreign currency. And whoever was in possession of foreign currency was king in this country of the 'wooden' ruble, which was actually worth a hundred times less than the rate set by the state. Almost everything was rationed, but even if you had ration coupons, *talony*, you could still often get nothing at all. For seventy years, communist law had forbidden profit-making, property ownership and the functioning of the market. But now barter ruled everything, together with the brand-new phenomenon of cooperative companies, a cover used to hollow out the legislation with the speed of a heath fire.

In the meantime, I'd been home only once, for a week. I'd spent hours in the shops in Haarlem and Amsterdam buying the things that my Russian contacts had asked for: the usual medicines, coffee, tea, underwear, jeans, videotapes, tampons, toothpaste, blouses and dresses, shoes, winter boots — everything specified by colour, form and size — together with an espresso machine, a video game console, a laptop and a fax machine, as well as things that I needed myself — liquorice, cheese, condoms — and lastly, at Schiphol airport, as many bottles of Johnny Walker (Black Label) as possible, because they could open just about any door in the country in which I'd taken up residence, even in the gulags and the prison cells.

Three months after the revolt in Tbilisi, a disturbance broke out in Siberia, and very soon in other parts of the country. The army of mineworkers — wretches with diseased lungs who crept, digging like human moles through the layers of coal, hacking at it with their picks, and risking their own lives — didn't even have any soap to wash the dust from their cracked hands, from their pores, and from their eyes that were often scarred with conjunctivitis and cataracts. On my last trip, I'd seen desperate mineworkers in Novosibirsk, sitting in the middle of a scorching square, ramming their helmets against the asphalt, which was almost molten beneath the hot Siberian summer sun. They'd travelled by slow train to the city to force the local authorities to give their families soap, but also extra bread, sausage, and other provisions. The Soviet house of cards was on the verge of collapse — you could feel it and smell it. People on the eve of a cataclysm are the first whose animal instincts are aroused. I was always pleased as Punch to be back in Moscow after a trip, once again in my Intourist room on Gorky Street. When Swindleman also returned from a trip to Siberia at the start of October he said, 'We have to have a serious talk.'

My partner once again took me to a bathhouse. This time, not to an establishment in a distant suburb, but to the first-class section of Sanduny, close to the Blacksmith's Bridge. Here and there in my novels I've described this superb place, with its entrance like a Venetian palazzo; the wooden benches in the central relaxation room, covered with Moroccan leather; the Tatar serving personnel who handed you slippers; the sheets in which you could wrap yourself like a Roman senator, to be served in curtained alcoves with beer, vodka, tea, and hot prawns; the sweat sessions in a hellish cabin, where the temperature could reach as much as ninety degrees when fresh water has just been flung on the stone oven; the men on the wooden tribunes thrashing each other with wet bundles of birch twigs; the medieval-looking white felt caps above their fiery red faces; the cold immersion baths at the end of each session in the sauna; the smooth granite tables, on which masseurs with the muscles of gladiators got to work on the steaming bodies. But on that autumn day in 1989, I was sitting there for the first time and couldn't believe the naked and mostly tattooed bodies around me, the majority of which were remarkably wiry, with only the odd paunch. Entire torsos, thighs, arms and even heads were transformed by the tattoo into canvases — Mothers of God with child, cathedrals with onion-shaped domes, death's heads, fire-spewing dragons, portraits of Lenin, Stalin and, in lascivious poses, half-naked girls, dollar signs, swords, knives and stars.

Some guys gave Swindleman a nod from the distance with a look of recognition; he loosely shook the hands of others, or embraced them, even kissed them. He'd brought me along on this Tuesday afternoon on purpose — it was the time of day when the *banya* was traditionally frequented by ex-cons, fraudsters, small and big-time criminals, members of the Soviet mafia who, on account of the fresh wind that was blowing across the nation, no longer kept themselves concealed, and appeared with an astonishingly arrogant self-confidence in their second-hand Mercedes. The Tatars skittered out of their way, bent double like flick knives, or were given a dressing down if they didn't carry out an order fast enough, or were buried under tips, grubby wads of rubles that quickly vanished into the deep, slit pockets of their baggy grey trousers. Swindleman had learned to read the tattoos; he knew the symbolic meaning of most of the images that had been applied in cells, camp barracks and God-knows-where with specially converted electric razors, using pigment mixtures consisting of urine and burned rubber. He was able to tell precisely how long and for what reason someone had been in prison, and what position the criminal occupied in the hierarchy. The two-headed eagle sported by many was an expression of their total contempt for the Soviet Union. A rose on the chest indicated that someone had turned eighteen in the cells; a dicky bow around the neck with a dollar sign meant a conviction for theft involving state property; a knife through the throat indicated that the bearer had murdered another prisoner and was ready to do that again to order.

After we'd nestled into an alcove, spent two rounds steaming with the damp sheets wrapped around us, and a gaunt Tatar had fetched us two big jugs of beer, Swindleman said that I was looking pretty depressed. Ignoring his remark, or rather talking over it, I began to tell him that a couple of weeks earlier I'd been able to wangle thirty theatre tickets for *Swan Lake* from a new ticket lady at the Bolshoi Theatre, in exchange for an Atari games console that I'd brought back from Amsterdam. The console hadn't even cost two hundred guilders; the tickets fetched more than twelve hundred US dollars. I'd turned a tidy profit. But more and more small-time hustlers were beginning to encroach on our turf.

'The party's almost over ...' After Swindleman had taken a swig of beer, he curled his plump, childlike lips in an almost burlesque fashion. 'By which I mean we're on the cusp of something new. I met two interesting guys in Novosibirsk, highly educated, members of the Academy of Sciences ...'

We needed to branch out on our own as soon as possible, my partner continued. Who else had the right contacts and the expertise to buy up hotel rooms in this mishmash of new cooperative companies that had sprouted up? In Moscow, we were practically the only people, but our current job paid peanuts, small beer. He was past thirty now. Time was pressing. Beside the travelling life, our future mostly lay in imports — that's where the big money was to be made, the fortune that was beckoning to us. For the time being, we'd carry on with our present activities. But from now on, we needed to focus on setting up an infrastructure. He gave us three months, until the new year. Then everything would be more or less on the rails. 'But what's the matter with you anyway? Ah, I can see it, our guy's in love! Eaten up with hormones and serotonin ... Well, out with it! Who is it?'

I blushed, caught out, but kept silent.


I had indeed met a girl three weeks earlier, during a trip that I'd made with this collective of art historians from Leiden around the archipelago of age-old towns that surround Moscow: Zagorsk, Vladimir, Suzdal, and Kostroma. She was a brunette from

Leningrad. A German teacher at a high school near the Hermitage, who did a bit of work on the side as a tour guide to supplement her meagre, worse than meagre, salary of a hundred and twenty rubles a month — a sum that wouldn't buy her three beers in the foreign-currency bar of the hotel where I lived. The organisation that had hired her had added her to our group. She'd been given a second-class train ticket from Leningrad to Moscow, where the bus was waiting to ferry the group around the so-called 'Golden Ring' for ten days — in the summers, Arcadian scenes of monasteries, woods, and onion-shaped domed churches and merchant houses, with geese, cherry orchards, and the buzzing of bees, and in the winters, everything buried under fairy-tale-like snow.

Luckily, it turned out that German wasn't a problem for the art historians from the fatherland. Within two days, she'd enchanted everyone with her dark, elegant looks and inexhaustible knowledge of the history and architecture of the places we visited.

Each morning, the sun beamed in the unblemished blue sky. During the day, the temperature rose above twenty-five degrees. Everyone was enjoying the Indian summer to the maximum, but the September nights were already cold. I'd fallen prey to despair in Zagorsk, the centre of the Russian Orthodox Church, which was gradually waking up from its communist hibernation, where we spent the first night. The presence of the fragile Russian lady with her greyish-green eyes had captivated me from the first moment. But the wedding ring sparkling on her left hand when she gesticulated with a ballerina's grace as she told us about a painting, an icon, or a sculpture, immediately crushed all my hopes.

The entire nation was in the grip of a reading fever. Everywhere in the country there was the scent of cheap printer's ink from pamphlets and papers that turned the fingers black and reported on the most recent turbulent political developments in Moscow. Here, in the provinces too, where the country folk still mostly worked for the state farms, there were daily struggles with the humiliating scarcities of foodstuffs, the total collapse of the infrastructure, the social and economic degradation. A bustling congregation around the black-and-white TV in the hotel lobby, consisting of cleaners, serving staff, porters and cooks who had slipped out of the kitchen, watched the reports from the capital. In their eyes glittered astonishment, disbelief, and hope.

But, in contrast to millions of her fellow countrymen, our guide appeared to be scarcely interested in politics. She always slunk off to bed with a book after the frugal dinner that almost invariably consisted of pork or chicken and mash, while the art historians would go for a drink in the hotel bar, full of local *Mafiosi* and whores who did a decent trade with the Russians on their business trips. During the communal meals, she always sat by someone different in the group, and never by me. She was friendly to me, but at the same time distant, formal.

On the fourth day, we arrived in Kostroma. After lunch, we travelled in the blazing sun from the hotel to the Ipatiev Monastery, built on the spot where the river that's named after the city flows into the Volga. Larks swooped from every side, displaying their aerial acrobatics. In some parts of the former merchant city, the wooden pavements from the old days had been miraculously preserved. On our way to the hotel, Julia stopped and pointed out the nineteenth-century fire brigade training tower, a little masterpiece with a pillared gallery, now so dilapidated that the red bricks peeped out everywhere through the yellow plaster. She told us how the city had historically been closely connected to her place of birth. In the spring of 1913, after an orgy of festivities, the Nevsky Prospect, in what was still then called Saint Petersburg, had been the scene of numerous celebrations full of splendour, with banners reading GOD SAVE THE CZAR and garlands of coloured lights strung above the streets. The bond between the czar and the people seemed closer, and revolution farther off than ever, so Nicholas II and his wife Alexandra made a pilgrimage to Kostroma, to commemorate the founding of the imperial dynasty three hundred years previously, when Mikhail Romanov had been crowned as the first czar in the Ipatiev Monastery. The aristocrats had indulged in lustrous balls, while the poor were given little gifts and free meals from the soup kitchen. This was the cradle of the Romanovs, who four years later would meet their downfall.

After she'd told us all about the frescoes around us with her customary waterfall of details, she flung me a special glance for the first time, in a corridor of the centuries-old monastery.

That evening I knocked on the door of her room at about nine. She didn't respond. I knocked a couple more times. In vain. So then I went outside. I lit a cigarette and began to stroll through the park around the hotel, beneath an absurdly starry sky. I came across Julia on a bench with a black shawl wrapped around her shoulders.

'Why did you knock on my door just now?' she asked.

With my heart pounding, I asked her how she knew.

'I just know …' Julia gazed up at me with the expression of a wounded deer. She gestured for me to sit down, took my hand, squeezed it, said she knew everything, that she hadn't been able to talk to me because it simply wasn't possible.

'You're married,' I said.

'How do you know that?'

I nodded towards the ring on her finger.

But that wasn't it, or rather, it was only part of it.

Oh, it was all so rotten, so confusing, so hopeless, Julia began to sob. She hated this country, which was still the biggest prison on earth. She hated her life, the total lack of prospects, because when all the bastards who were now in power had been overthrown, other bastards would come, she was convinced of that, and they'd be followed by new ones in their turn. Things would never be normal in this country. Suddenly, she let go of my hand, looked at me aghast with her wide-open, teary eyes, and said, 'Leave me, do you hear me? I'll only bring you bad luck. Leave me!'

Six days later, she again took the train from Moscow to Leningrad, second-class. At the end of the trip the group of art historians had given her an envelope with thirty guilders — one and a half guilders per man for ten days. But of course, that was a fortune for a girl like this, as the lady from Leiden whispered to me after giving a thank you speech on the bus in a snooty voice.

Julia didn't have a telephone at home. When we said goodbye at the station, she handed me a scrap of paper with her address on.

'Will you come to visit me soon?' she asked.

I nodded gravely.

The next day, I travelled after her, making use of the half a week off I had before my next trip. My whole being was filled with the night that I'd ultimately spent with her, in one of the little wooden houses on the grounds within the tall, whitewashed walls of a medieval cloister in Suzdal, kitted out as a lodging for tourists. We were woken at 5 am by the airy chiming of bells: the nuns who had returned to the abbey in dribs and drabs were being summoned to morning prayer.

The poverty in which I found Julia struck me like a sledgehammer. She lived in a *kommunalka* on Vasilyevsky Island —

a tiny space of ten square metres, two and a half by four, with just one double-glazed window that faced out onto a courtyard like a refuse chute, which the daylight barely entered. The rats that calmly crept around slid their greasy bodies from the guttering onto the metal bins, fighting and shrieking loudly. She lived amid a clutter of furniture. Up against one wall was an antique sideboard, with all sorts of drawers and wonderful bevelled windows. Beside it was a black-lacquered piano, covered in scratches and dents, bearing the trademark Odessa. Printed above on the red-striped wallpaper in black felt was *Ich bin frei!* As for the rest, the apartment was filled to the brim with books, books, books. The collected works in Russian of Flaubert, Stendhal, and Maupassant, standing fraternally next to the brown-leather volumes of Goethe, Schiller, and Thomas Mann in German. There was an entire shelf that consisted only of dictionaries, with just about all of the languages of old Europe. There was no space for a table or chairs. The central area was a sofa covered with a saddle blanket; it could be folded out and used as a bed. From the corridor, you could always hear footsteps, mumbling, swearing, howling, coughing or sneezing. The door almost seemed suspended in the unpainted doorframe, and through the crannies came an unremitting hideous stench. A mixture of cooking smells, people relieving themselves, garlic and sweat, the dank and stuffy exhalation of an old damp building, as well as gas seeping from the communal kitchen, where six rickety cookers leaked continuously and were covered with thick crusts like lepers. There was a mad jumble of pots and pans, and a sink that was forever full of grease and baked-on filth; there was a soup bowl on the window, full of cigarette butts (it was the only place where you were allowed to smoke), and a battery of little fridges and store cupboards pasted with threatening messages from *Don't touch the milk!* and *The flour in this tin has been weighed,* to *I'll kill you if I hear your paws have touched my sugar!*

The first night that I spent at Julia's, I stepped into the communal bathroom with revulsion. There, the white enamel tub had been turned almost completely brown because of the rusty water, and there was washing hanging to dry on a myriad of lines; cockroaches skittered off in every direction, and both the walls and the ceiling resembled the landscape of a nuclear disaster with damp stains, paint pockmarks, and orange fungi. I brushed my teeth with mineral water, which I'd brought with me in a bottle, breathing through my nose, attempting to touch as little as possible, when someone pounded on the door, and in a gravelly male voice yelled that I — and all the whores for crying out loud — should get my skates on, that he'd figured out I was a foreigner, that I didn't come from here, that maybe he'd call the militia, because this wasn't a brothel, and then he started to bawl that I should beat it because he was about to burst.

The toilet for the sixteen occupants was also in the bathroom; there was no toilet seat and the ballcock was chronically defective.

When I got back, Julia had already unfolded the couch with the saddle blanket on it, and was making up the bed with fresh linen. She spoke hoarsely, 'I'm so ashamed. I wanted to give the bathroom a good clean one time, but they called me a bitch and yelled, "Do you think you're better than us? With your piano and your books!"'

From the very first moment I saw her, it was as though I'd known her all my life, but we'd been living for all that time in a sort of parallel universe; as though a mysterious, magical osmosis of time and place had now finally brought us together. My questing travels around the world so far had inevitably led to our meeting.

Of course, this was all a complete delusion on my part, I initially thought, until it turned out that the feeling was entirely mutual.

'Where is your husband?' When I entered her crammed apartment for the first time, where I found a kettle and two blue cups waiting on the piano, I resolved to ask her straight out.

'Dead,' Julia answered.

She'd been separated from him for the last year. They'd got married much too young — it had all gone too fast. They didn't suit each other, and were planning to divorce. That winter he'd left for the southern Soviet Union with a group of mountain climbers, for the Pamir range on the border with Afghanistan, where the entire twelve-man mountain expedition was involved in an accident. None of the bodies were recovered.

'So, you're a widow?'

'It's as though it never happened to me, but to someone else.' Julia unfolded a pillowcase with a sigh; it crackled from the starch. 'Hey, come here! You always smell so nice!'

Once back in Moscow, preparing for the next trip, I had the sense that I'd been amputated. I felt entirely lost. I was tormented by the idea that my Russian lover was all alone in that awful pigeon coop, working in that school from early in the morning till late at night for a monthly salary that wouldn't buy you a pair of jeans on the black market. Once again, I was gripped by the desire to leave the Soviet Union, to take Julia with me, to save her, even if I had no idea how. At the same time, Swindleman was nagging me to get a move on with our plan: we were supposed to be independent within three months. And shouldn't I be thinking about the legal structure? I had studied law in Amsterdam, hadn't I? I was a lawyer, right?

Just a week later everything was different.

I was in the right place at the right time. With a high-pitched whine, the tectonic plates were shifting under the Soviet Empire, at least for those who wanted to hear it, like the ice chunks on the Neva when the floes were forced over each other in the spring and floated off on the current to the Gulf of Finland.

A day after my return from Julia's apartment in Leningrad, a group of hoteliers from my fatherland arrived in Moscow. Twice a year, they took a trip together. In the preceding fifteen years, they'd just about travelled the entire globe, and the secretary of the club had suggested the Soviet Union as the next destination for a bit of fun — the country that there'd been such a to-do about recently, with the new openness and reforms. The majority had initially protested, but the secretary had persevered, dug up some more information, and booked a six-day trip with the organisation for which Swindleman and I worked — three days in Moscow, three days in Leningrad — observing that money was no problem, that there needn't be any scrimping with the food, and that they wanted to stay in the very best hotels. In Moscow, that was the Metropol. Because the hotel sections of both the Astoria and the Europe were being refurbished, they were lodged at the Hotel Moskva in Leningrad, an architectural monstrosity from the 1970s, at the head of the Old Nevsky, a tourist factory where one of the first illegal casinos was housed; the lobby was crowded with riff-raff, and it had already been the scene of some of the first liquidations in the criminal underworld but, with the other two shut, it still counted as the best in the city.

While I left for the airport to pick up the group, Swindleman flew to Novosibirsk at the expense of the two members of the Academy of Sciences that he'd got to know and who had now come back with a very concrete proposal for future collaboration.

I remember vividly how the twenty hoteliers, mostly couples, with a few travelling on their own, had come walking towards me in the terminal, lugging a load of suitcases as though for a trip around the world. Even though the Indian summer had only just ended, and the first snow was still a month and a half away at least, and the trees on the Moscow boulevards were radiant in their brocade and ruby adornment, they all emerged in thick fur coats. The next day, after they'd figured out their erroneous climatological calculations, the furs were replaced with camel-hair and cashmere overcoats. The women were draped in jewels, the men wore flashy watches — everything teetering on the edge of good taste.

I organised the welcome dinner in the dining room of the Metropol, beneath the glass Art Nouveau ceiling, beside the burbling fountain, a location that I would also use later for my novels and stories. After I'd ordered Crimean champagne and black caviar in dishes of two hundred grams per person — items that were officially unobtainable, but after greasing the palm of the administrator with a hundred dollars, were delivered in whatever quantities you liked — I told the group that I happened to have been brought up in a hotel, that my parents were also hoteliers, after which I was treated like one of their own. Then I took a stroll through the drizzle, past the demonstrators at the granite bust of Marx on the square next to the Metropol, who were screaming until they were hoarse against the communist junta in the Kremlin which still refused to give up its autocracy. But once I was back in my Intourist room, I was gripped by remorse. At that moment, my father was in hospital, being treated for cancer for the second time. That morning, I'd called my mother; she was optimistic as usual, and said that everything would turn out all right in the end.

The hoteliers were very different from my parents, who'd slaved all their lives from early morning till late at night, my father behind the stove, or doing the bookkeeping at a table in the storeroom, my mother serving dinner, washing plates, changing sheets, all the while looking after my two brothers and me – until we were also able to work in a business doomed to ruin, which I did until my last year as a student. But these people were a sort of hotel aristocracy, and the carefully manicured fingers of both the sun-bronzed ladies and the gentlemen suggested that in recent decades they hadn't touched a dirty cup, scrubbed a wooden worktop, or changed a pillow case. They were investors, property millionaires who, as well as owning hotels in the Netherlands, had others in France, Italy, and Switzerland, while their children followed in their footsteps at the hotel school in Lausanne, and they spoke about their employees like the Russian aristocracy once spoke about their serfs. The wages and the social security payments for their receptionists, cooks, and chambermaids had risen far too high in the last few years, they declared. All because of the socialists.

From the outset, there was a school-trip atmosphere among the hoteliers. Their mirth was continuous: new jokes, witty remarks, and references to previous outings, all of which prompted bubbling fits of laughter among the group. The next day on the bus, they wiped little circles on the steamed-up windows with handkerchiefs, tweed sleeves or their fingertips, and peered out through these portholes. They commentated on everything: the buildings, the greyness, the barren streets quivering in the drizzle. Never before had they seen a city quite so ugly. We drove past a ruin with PRODUKTI (foodstuffs) written on the façade. Out front, hundreds of mostly older men and women were waiting patiently, in the formless aubergine-coloured or tobacco-brown raincoats that everyone wore in those late Soviet years, and they

153

were greeted with scornful laughter. It was a source of amusement: the massed queues of desperate people in front of the shops, like the unemployed outside job centres, which took you back to the crisis years just before World War II, and swarms of beggars by the steps of the metro stations. I thought of Julia, and how overjoyed she'd been with the jar of instant coffee and a box of French chocolates that I'd bought her from the foreign-currency shop. The hoteliers were talking about the people around us as if they were animals. I managed to control myself, but eventually I could hold it in no longer. I struggled to the front of the bus, grabbed the microphone from the tour guide — a middle-aged Russian woman on autopilot, who was dishing out the customary lists of years, production figures and communist heroes — and began to tell them what was really going on in the country. About my many travels through the USSR over the past year and a half, and about the fire now smouldering that might one day rage, whose scorching heat would sooner or later be felt in Western Europe and the rest of the world — even if that took twenty-five, or fifty years.

When we boarded the night-train to Leningrad two days later, everyone was already tipsy after their early dinner at the Metropol. Their suitcases were bulging with souvenirs — sable hats, beluga caviar by the kilo, antique and Soviet watches, czarist pottery, even hunks of gold. They showed me their trophies, telling me the price they'd paid for them, then asked if it wasn't too much. I answered that they'd bought everything for a song, which was largely true. There are few things that make a person with alcohol in their veins as happy as the realisation that they've got a bargain. I was sharing my two-person compartment with a handsome blond guy in his late thirties from The Hague. The club secretary had invited him as a token of gratitude because as an economist, organisational specialist and consultant, he'd successfully advised a number of the hoteliers over the last year about more efficient management practice. And by now, he'd got the rest of the hotel owners under contract too to advise them on running their businesses more efficiently. The magic words were cost savings and cheap personnel of African origin. As the night passed, while we were drinking Armenian cognac on our plank beds, the consultant harked back to the talk that I'd given two days earlier on the bus. He expressed his astonishment that a university graduate like me earned his living through such a pitiful activity as being a glorified tour guide.

'You're a lawyer, aren't you?'

I told him that was correct.

'You're not even thirty, you speak fluent Russian, and what's more you're a law graduate. Man, what are you doing? Damn it, you're sitting on a golden egg! And I'm going to help you to hatch it!'

He made me a proposition. It was so enticing that as soon as we arrived in Leningrad, I called Swindleman in Novosibirsk. I had to keep this guy warm, he told me. If we really wanted to get to grips with things, then we needed an office in the Netherlands as well as one in Moscow. And that was precisely what this consultant, whose name was Baldwin Borger, had proposed.


Three days after taking the hoteliers to the Leningrad airport, I finally flew to Holland to visit my father, who'd been operated on two weeks before.

For the first time in six months, I found myself walking through the windy streets of my youth. More old buildings in the seaside village had been knocked down. The last chestnut trees, which used to filter the amber sunlight in the summer, had been felled. The sea was grey and raging beneath a sky filled with ink-blue clouds. While I had been travelling the world, I saw those with whom I'd been to primary school, moving very naturally through the withering décor, now grown into men and women. This one had become a plumber, that one a baker or a house-painter, like their fathers. As many as three were working in the post office. Most of them were married and had kids. Only two out of my class had gone to the grammar school in Haarlem — I was one of them, the other was dead. In our third year, this notary's son, with big army boots on his feet and an orange Mohican, had slit his wrists in an attic, ravaged by drugs.

I landed at Schiphol at three. By six, I was sitting at the table opposite my mother. She'd made my favourite dinner — boiled endives and mashed potato, a meatball floating in the gravy, then chocolate custard and whipped cream for afters. My brothers had left for Brussels for a couple of days, to get away from the tension, and would be coming back the next evening. Because of my visit, and as a great exception, my mother had been allowed to visit my father in the morning rather than in the afternoon, just after the doctors had made their rounds. My father meanwhile had been told about my presence in the country. He asked my mother to pass on his warmest wishes to me, but also asked if I'd wait before visiting.

I looked at my mother quizzically when I heard these words, and the ribs in my body seemed to crack. There was something not right about this. I stared into the almost 60-year-old face of the woman who'd given birth to me, red veins on otherwise strikingly flawless cheeks, with the kind-hearted, watery-blue eyes of someone who'd never lived for themselves, but always been there for others; she, with her three classes of domestic science, who'd never lied in her life, who I'd walk through fire for, was now trying to keep something from me; she'd fallen prey to a grief that she could clearly barely suppress.

'Do you want some more custard?' She'd already got up and poured the last bit out of the brown carton into my bowl.

I'd spent the three days before I left Leningrad with Julia, in her tiny apartment. She was mad about any kind of chocolate. She would have loved the thick custard that my mother was now pouring from the upturned carton, bending over like Vermeer's Milkmaid. At the same time as my soul was being eaten up by the distress and silent despair in my mother's eyes, the feeling of being in love was glowing in mine, which made my feelings of confusion and betrayal all the stronger.

'Mama, what else is wrong with Papa?'

'Well, my boy ...' My mother swiftly licked a last drip that was clinging to the spout. 'Shall I get some nice cream from the kitchen for you?'

I shook my head. My mother sat down and started to tell me how the operation had been successful — the stomach wound had already just about healed — but that sadly something else had been found. A tumour had been discovered in my father's throat, which they'd also removed immediately.

'In his throat?'

'Something wasn't right ...' My mother's cracked fingers slowly moved across the tablecloth, as though she wanted to smooth out all the pleats and air bubbles. 'Your father can't talk at the moment ... We do everything with notes ... Even me sending you his regards ... I can show you ...' Nervously she delved into the pocket of her sky-blue work apron, which she always wore at the table too. 'Dash it, where is that note? I could have shown you ...'

Only later did I realise that my father was no longer in Haarlem, but nine days after the intestinal operation, he'd been transferred to the VU in Amsterdam, because that was where the good throat specialists were. The procedure on his uvula had been performed just two days before. My father was having quite a tough time.

As I walked into the lobby of the VU hospital at ten the next morning, I had my excuse ready: I was the son of a patient who'd been operated on recently, I lived abroad, and I was only in the Netherlands briefly. I more or less begged to visit my father. They phoned. It was impossible. When I persisted, they phoned again, and the girl behind the counter said, 'Okay, but not until a quarter past eleven. After the doctor's been.'

Just like everyone, I suspect, I've had my own visions of hell over the years. The old people's home in the distant suburb of Leningrad, where I'd handed out bibles the year before and taken Madam Pokrovskaya out for the afternoon in her wheelchair, had come close to an earthly inferno. But when I entered the ward where my father was lying, I realised I hadn't seen it all by a long shot. I felt the blood leeching from my face as I turned pale from shock and dismay.

My father wasn't lying in bed, but sitting up straight on a metal chair in a fluffy purple-brown robe; his milky, bluish-white calves and feet were peeping out from under it, stuffed into his leather slippers. The ward was full of other male and female patients, in various stages of human degradation. In the case of one, the whole lower part of the head had been surgically removed, another was missing a lower lip, while the throat of yet another was bound in blood-sodden bandages. Some had the feral look of beasts. Exhaustion and defeatism floated in their eyes, which were swollen from the medication. It was a ward full of grenade victims from a filthy war, although here the filthy war was cancer. Almost without exception, there was a plastic tube for air sticking out beside the Adam's apple of each sufferer, and you could hear their choked and wheezy breaths.

My father had one of these tubes too. When I came in, his 59-year-old face was staring fixedly outside, at the pale-green, mist-clouded motorway to Amsterdam. The remains of his barely greying black curls, which he'd had since a boy and which had made him look like a Sephardic Jew all his life — the secret deep within the genes — were now soaked with sweat.

Gingerly, he turned towards me and smiled sadly with his intense dark eyes.

'Hello, Papa,' I said.

A watery rattle escaped from the breathing tube.

My father's hands dropped to the pockets of his robe, which I didn't even know he had. The hands that he'd earned his bread with for forty years, first as a cook's mate in the merchant navy and later behind the stove (that he always called 'the fireplace') in his own business. His fingers had that groping, quivering, uncertain quality of a blind man's.

He took out the stub of a pencil and a writing pad.

'Hello, lad …' They were the scribblings of a child.

I cautiously leant over him and carefully and in silence gave him a gentle kiss on his forehead; it was burning up and clammy with sweat.

'How's everything going in Russia?' my father wrote.

I quickly whispered to him that everything was going well.

He raised the stub to the paper again.

'That's great … And the Russian girls?'

He gave me a conspiratorial look.

'I may be going into business, with a partner,' I said, without getting into any details. 'Hey, look, the sun's coming out …'

My father was already writing again, with airy wheezes and muffled moans coming through the tube. 'Have you been thinking about your mother? I'm doing all right, but she's having a hard time …'

At that moment, he began coughing convulsively, from deep within his bronchioles. His body, which was quite emaciated because of the earlier intestinal operation, was now trembling and quivering in such an awful way that I cried out in panic that I'd fetch the doctor, but my father made a dismissive gesture. Apparently, this wasn't the first time it had happened, and he knew how to calm himself back down again, which he did. He'd coughed up some phlegm, and quickly wiped it away with the tissue that was lying on his lap.

'Dry, it's all dry now …' he said with difficulty, in a completely shattered voice. He nodded towards the night-stand beside him. There was a glass of water, and beside it were pistachio-coloured mini-sponges on white sticks, like children's lollies. He was on a drip, and was absolutely forbidden to drink — the nurse who'd finally let me in unwillingly had expressly said so — and now his lips above his battered throat were as wrinkled as the neck of an iguana. After I'd dipped the sponges in the glass of water, and smeared them all around my father's mouth, he tried to illegally slurp a couple of droplets, by stiffly pursing his mouth and swivelling his tongue; all the while looking up at me intensely grateful, like a child that had done something wrong.

'What were you saying just now, in business?' When his body had again settled down a little, he picked up his pencil and notebook from his lap. 'That's great, my boy, but be careful. The people in this world are sons of bitches.'

# CHAPTER SIX

When I returned from visiting my father in the Netherlands, the Moscow pavements had been transformed into deep trenches of piled-up snow. It was freezing dismally; streams of ghostly cars drifted by in pearl-grey clouds of condensed frost. God existed, without question. And I had scolded him as a brute, a sadist. Not only the times that I'd stood helplessly beside my father in his metal hospital chair, but also silently in the weeks that followed.

But then a miracle took place: both the second intestinal operation and the throat operation were a success. The doctors expected a complete recovery. After waiting for an hour and a half for a connection to home, I got to hear it from my father's own mouth, and my cocoon of fear, grief, suppressed rage and depression disappeared, after having enveloped me for months.

I could be happy again, abandon myself to my usual carefree thoughtlessness, even if by now I'd realised that happiness is a concept that is determined by the negative, namely the absence of unhappiness.

Because of the hospital visits, and because I wanted to support my mother as much as I could, I'd only popped by to see Baldwin Borger a day before my return to Moscow. The consultant had an office on Javastraat in The Hague, in a white, former patrician's home, by coincidence a stone's throw from the Soviet consulate.

There were a number of girls there in their twenties, wearing grey-blue pleated skirts, who all pronounced the letter 'r' in just the right way; they were not just in the marble reception area, but also in the grand gentlemen's rooms, which had been transformed into offices. They'd been taken on as interns from the secretarial training course at a chic institute nearby. In addition to two male employees — a recent law graduate and an economist — Borger always had unpaid personnel, with this inexhaustible reservoir of ladies to answer the telephone, receive guests, type up reports, research things for him, look after the archive, make coffee, and occasionally accompany him to meetings with clients outside the office, when he always took along the prettiest specimens, the ones who contributed to his status and his success. Two out of three were always ready to give him a blow job when he fancied it, and on a Friday afternoon after staff drinks there was usually one who stayed behind, to give herself to him on the floor or on a desk — the snootier and more reserved their manner, the more they would come out of their shell. He'd confided all the details to me with all the braggadocio of an American frat boy on the train to Leningrad, as we moved on from cognac to beer.

'Am I glad to see you!' He'd greeted me in his blue-and-white striped shirt, bronzed from the sunbed, sitting behind an immaculately white plastic desk, to which one of his harem had guided me. 'My first question, when are you going back?'

When I told him I would be on the plane to Moscow the next morning, and I urgently needed to speak to Swindleman who'd just got back from Novosibirsk, his handsome face winced.

'Why didn't you come sooner? Did you have to pop by the ladies or something?' As he sneered, he exhaled compressed air through his fine white teeth. 'Anyway, I want to meet this Swindleman myself, as soon as he's in the Netherlands. There's money just lying on the streets in Russia. I could see it right away, even if I don't particularly want to go there again in person ... You see this?' He gestured around proudly with a Bic pen. 'It's all mine. I paid off the building in ten years ... The best mortgage is no mortgage. That's the first piece of wisdom that I share with my clients.'

Borger knew that Swindleman and I were planning to organise trips ourselves, as the basis for other possible activities. He was happy to offer us the office space we'd need in the Netherlands for free. The upper floor was almost entirely empty. He already had the rooms, the phones, the ladies, the whole damned infrastructure.

'What are you going to call your business?'

I told him I still didn't have the faintest idea.

He began telling me about the project he wanted to do with us: organising specialised business trips. In recent years, he'd had some tentative experience of this; if you handled things well, it was a potential goldmine. A six-day trip to London wouldn't usually cost more than a thousand guilders; if you organised it for certain financially well-heeled target groups — lawyers, doctors, bankers, industrialists, investors, whatever — you could easily ask three, or even four times as much. It actually didn't make any difference how much you asked. Most of it was promptly paid by the companies, and in the case of private citizens, could be deducted from tax as a work expense. Wealthy professionals were eager to be away from their work for a change, from their partners, their children, their families. To finally have a fling abroad with a long-desired colleague or a chance encounter. They were prepared to shell out capital, as long as everything was officially presented and formulated in the right way — you dressed up the itinerary with a local programme that was especially tailored to the target group:

visits to hospitals, factories, meetings with professional or branch colleagues, influential figures or politicians. He would provide us with groups via his European network; we were to organise the trip and the programme on site. The split of the net profits would be fifty-fifty. The Soviet Union was still *terra incognita*, but things were developing at lightning speed, the course of the rivers would be rapidly diverted. 'As I said to you in Moscow, you're sitting on a golden egg! Picture it: we have a group of thirty bankers, who'd already like to come and take a sniff of their future hunting grounds. We add three thousand guilders extra to each one. Then you're talking about a hundred grand. Ten groups and we're talking about a million. Are you starting to understand?'

I nodded, and said of course I understood.

When writing this little chronicle, I've noticed how difficult it is to present the character of Ragnar Swindleman.

My keyboard cursor instantly goes on the blink, like an eyelid afflicted with a tic. He did exist, and although many of those depicted behind the scenes or in front of them, or who are yet to make their appearance on stage, are now long dead and have disappeared from the face of the earth, my former business partner is still alive as far as I know. But it isn't that fact that makes it difficult for me to write about him, it's shame. The shame that in this life, which will ultimately prove to be a bloody battlefield for everyone, we lose friends and loved ones, because of misunderstanding, greed, lust, stupidity, cowardice, vanity, hate, betrayal, the desire to be glorified, the hunger for status, fame, power, and money, and sometimes love.

———

At the start of December 1989, we definitively ceased our work for the travel agency. And one morning, I thought up a name for our new company. I still have one of the ivory-white calling cards:

## INTERSOVIET CONSULTANCY
*Advisors in Business and Tourism*

'That's a great name,' Swindleman said. 'I couldn't have thought of a better one myself, let's go with that.'

In the week and a half of my stay in the Netherlands, commuting between the VU hospital and my family home, and the visit to Baldwin Borger in The Hague, Julia wasn't out of my thoughts for a second. I was overwhelmed by a nagging sense of guilt that weighed on my whole being, as I walked through the charming, lamp-lit centre of Haarlem or of Amsterdam, in the midst of what then was the almost embarrassing wealth in which old Europe bathed, with its perverse butter mountains and skewed farming subsidies; this was especially so when I bought something in a shop, or when I devoured a chocolate éclair with a coffee on the top floor of Bijenkorf department store.

I thought of the tiny apartment inhabited by my girlfriend at that moment, of the mould in the communal bathroom, of the sickening thuds of the rats dropping from the guttering to the bins on the courtyard below. And also of the empty shelves in the shops, scarcity, the queues, the musty-smelling mass of people, largely clad in rags, with disillusioned faces. The faces of the deceived, over whom the filth of history was washing afresh. The revelations kept coming — the Kremlin even confessed that the

Molotov-Ribbentrop Pact between Hitler and Stalin in 1939 had been paired with the so-called 'secret protocols', whereby Poland and the Baltic States were divided up between them like pieces of cake — but by now barely anyone had faith in the future, they feared war, and further impoverishment. They seemed to have lost all of their illusions, retaining only the slenderest vague hope for their children and grandchildren, but nonetheless they continued to go to work. To their offices, hospitals, ministries, and factories, through their pontifical portrait gallery of socialist heroes; they had largely ceased their senseless production because of the absence of orders from above, or sabotage or sheer lethargy, but the work canteens did at least guarantee a served meal of soup, cold peas, mash, and sometimes some unidentifiable stewed meat. Towards evening, under a summer sky that reached as far as the pale moon, with its dull pink and green veins, a pistachio green that you will only find in Russia, and then only in the cast-iron vault of the autumn, these people crowded the pavements like dense streams of actors, amid the insanely high Stalin-cake buildings, storming onto rusty trams and trolley buses, descending escalators into the metro, the belly of the city, where it's always nice and warm. Real life still mostly took place at home, behind the doors of cramped flats, in damp rented rooms, in tiny kitchens. A world of unremitting want, fear, silence, and lies, even if it was true that everything had now begun to shift, in the halls where meetings were held, in the papers, and more and more often on the radio and TV. A universe that only a few elsewhere on the globe had any idea of, any real understanding.

So, in that year, the myth of the creation of the Soviet Union was being sullied by the day, but at the same time the red banners with party slogans still hung over the streets, while the reaction, the counter-revolution, was an ever-present threat. There was fear of spontaneous combustion in the barracks, of the whims of the generals, of conspiracies and secret deals behind the scenes, just as in the revolutionary year of 1917. Most of officialdom kept quiet. The apparatchiks consulted feverishly among themselves about what to do, what orders to carry out, who to pal up with, who to ignore. Life in this mud-bound Russia had once again been reduced to a game of chance, in which the stake was sometimes your own life.

'Intersoviet Consultancy …' Swindleman had taken me to a cellar café on Pushkin Square to drink Chechen beer. 'It really is a great name. You've done some good work. Of course, I want to meet Baldwin Borger as soon as possible. We're in business, man! The day after tomorrow, we're supposed to be welcoming the Siberian delegation. Our Russian partners. Get ready for some heavy days!'

But the delegation from Novosibirsk, consisting of the gents Khinshtein and Trofimov, arrived the very next day. Swindleman called me in bed at nine in the morning in a panic. They were at the airport and were supposed to be travelling to the city in an official car.

I asked him where we were meeting.

'In the Akademicheskaya Hotel.'

'There are two of those, aren't there?'

'That's right, I'll expect you in an hour in the lobby of Akademicheskaya Hotel 2. By the way, you do speak Spanish, don't you? Anyway, I'll come and pick you up by taxi.'

It had been days since I'd seen Swindleman in the room that we shared in Hotel Intourist. Our salaried work had come to an end for good. Before we began our own business, he decided to marinate for a week, as he called it. I kept quiet about Julia, apprehensive that my brand-new romance would be sullied by his sexual perversity, which bordered on the grotesque, and by his self-interested gossiping. His women and girls came and went by the wagonload, his libido inversely proportionate to the state of the country. The worse things got, the more he was able to get away with. Fortunately, I didn't know the half of it. I mostly avoided his perverse confessions, his attempts to involve me, not only mentally but also physically, in his excesses in bathhouses, rendezvous hotels and underground casinos, where the names and telephone numbers of women were written on chips in felt pen, before raising the stake for an extra card at blackjack, or the *rien ne va plus* of roulette — French was once more in vogue, just as the surviving aristocrats had continued to speak it well into the twenties under Stalin. Sometimes a guy would leave with a handful of chips, a handful of available women on call. From the start, my attitude towards Swindleman was businesslike. There was never any question of a real friendship between us.

But at the same time, his company was entertaining. He had life experience, an astounding knowledge that he could call on when needed; he was smart and energetic, in spite of a certain sluggish indolence. I understood why girls didn't just fall for his money, for his suitcase of mirrors and beads from the West, but would also fall under the spell of his natural charm, his dark-brown eyes, with fanning creases in their corners, which gave him the authority to continually laugh at life.

One day, his dark-haired 18-year-old, who was fresh from high school, was suddenly out of the picture. In the meantime, he'd hooked up with a ballerina from Archangelsk, a Russian girl made of pure porcelain, sixteen years old, nothing but fragility, with opal, almost transparent hands — you could see the blood streaming through them. She'd only once deigned to give me a glance. She'd been allocated a room close to the Patriarch Ponds by her institute because of her great promise. It was a cavern of pure delight, where Swindleman nestled like a Turkish pasha, to partake of the physical pleasures of this girl when she came back from the academy, dead tired but freshly showered, all in exchange for a certain sum. Russia is, was, and will always be the country of the sugar daddy. The most attractive characteristic of female beings, Swindleman once said, is their uncertainty. As soon as he detected a hint of feminism, he was gone.

Khinshtein and Trofimov were sitting smoking in the lobby of the Akademicheskaya Hotel 2 when we entered.

In the taxi on the way, Swindleman had divulged to me the details of how and where he'd met the two members of the Academy of Sciences. One free afternoon, when he was taking a walk in the woods outside Novosibirsk, they'd stormed naked out of a wooden hut and into the snow, uttering primal screams, followed by two equally naked young blonde women, whose skin, like the men's, was as red as boiled crabs from the *banya* that they'd just fled from. None of the four took offence at Swindleman's unexpected presence. On the contrary. They began to roll through the snow with extra daredevilry, then stood up roaring with laughter, and pushed each other over again into the cold mass, riotously bawling with the abandon of young animals, or as children are wont to do when they play and know their parents are secretly watching.

Swindleman was invited inside by the four of them. There were bottles of beer at the ready, vodka, beside a dish of boiled river crabs, which were still warm and indeed the same colour as the skin of their devourers. First, they squeezed half a lemon over the delicacy, a lemon that in those days was as great a rarity in Siberia as a cassocked pastor on a nudist beach.

'I see you've got a strange look on your face? Did you think we didn't have any lemons here?' One of the men laughed raucously. 'Ha ha, we've got everything here, everything! I could even have French grapes sent to you!'

His unexpected hosts and the young Russian women, who were by now in bathrobes, began feasting and drinking by the open fire, which was crackling in a corner. Both men were professors, the blondes their former students, and now their personal assistants. From the start, they treated Swindleman like an extra-terrestrial. They hadn't seen a westerner for years in this Siberian industrial backwater. The men were married, the women too. All four of them had children. This gathering was taking place entirely beyond their private lives. The dacha was officially university property.

As a gifted young student in 1961, Khinshtein had been involved as an observer in the hydrogen bomb test on Nova Zembla. A great scientific success, whose blast shattered windows almost a thousand kilometres away. In the years following, he'd met Sakharov a couple of times, but he didn't have much appreciation for the way that the Nobel Prize winner — at the end of his exile — hadn't just repented but had grown into a fanatical critic of Soviet values. In fact, he considered him a traitor. Also, his colleague, Trofimov, a dermatologist who'd specialised in medical technology, was of the opinion that they'd gone mad in the capital. A little longer, and the nation would be lost! They were law-abiding Soviet citizens, Communist Party members, and what's more they were members of the Academy of Sciences. They were part of the absolute Soviet aristocracy. Each one of the men had been assigned a splendid wooden country lodge by the authorities. They both had an apartment in the city, while they and their assistants flew to Moscow every other week for a long weekend — four hours there, four hours back — where they took up residence in one of the hotels of the Academy of Sciences, which had health spas, hostels, dachas, and apartments throughout the entire USSR for their members, which they could freely make use of. The guys were natural Soviet profiteers, parasites of the system, and these blonde girls were no less than hookers, Swindleman continued, as we approached the towering statue of Lenin behind a curtain of raging snow at the head of the Leninsky Avenue. They were opportunists, but at some point, Swindleman had realised that these guys sitting there were people we could work with in our future business.

'They've been rushing things politically in Moscow,' Khinshtein said to my business partner. 'I'm a scientist, what scientist doesn't want to make an advance? But what we're seeing now is pure sabotage.'

Although morally faithful to the conservative red rulers in the Kremlin, there was one thing that aggrieved him: that it was still almost impossible for decent Soviet citizens to travel abroad. As a Jew, he could perhaps hand in an emigration request — many had already disappeared to Israel, to Western Europe, often as a springboard to the ultimate destination: the United States. But it wasn't his plan to leave the Soviet Union at all. This was his fatherland. He had it good here. What's more, he possessed certain state secrets that would make travelling abroad formally impossible. In the meantime, he'd found a solution for this: a new domestic passport that listed his profession not as 'scientist' but as 'joiner'.

And by now, this was also printed in his international travel permit, while a friend in a high position in customs had provided him with a document that was valid as a passe-partout. But this only solved half the problem: those wretched foreign consulates continued to be difficult with issuing visas.

'We'd really like to go on holiday to Spain,' his academic colleague Trofimov explained. 'With the girls here.'

The foursome began to dream out loud about the pleasures of the Mediterranean, the palms, the culinary delights that they'd learned about in western glossies. Then Swindleman had let slip that he had this friend who spoke fluent Spanish, with good contacts at the consulate in Moscow, and who could undoubtedly arrange something.

In euphoria, Khinshtein uttered something incomprehensible.

'Quid pro quo,' Trofimov said. 'As good communists, we are of course open to a quid pro quo.'

Swindleman immediately let them know what he wanted in exchange for arranging things: cooperation from the academics in finding inexpensive space in Moscow to set up our office. We would soon have to leave our hotel room in Intourist, and because of the streams of tourists, space elsewhere was pretty unaffordable.

'Comrade, that can be arranged with just a signature,' Khinshtein said cheerfully. 'One signature and a round rubber stamp!'

When we were standing in front of the hotel, I asked Swindleman who he had in mind with a knowledge of Spanish and good contacts at the Spanish consulate. He answered, 'You, of course. Man, don't give me such a strange look. Don't worry. We'll work it out. But behave yourself around these guys. They're our partners …'

The two academics looked almost exactly the way I'd pictured them from Swindleman's descriptions. They were both in their early fifties, and wore grey Soviet suits, White Russian footwear with heels and soles made of pressed cardboard, shirts the colour of old-fashioned suspender belts — a fleshy dull-pink — and collars that exposed the albino-white stubble (Trofimov) and neck-hair like black stiches (Khinshtein) that was sprouting around their Adam's apples. They may have belonged to the Soviet aristocracy, but razor blades were still worth their weight in gold. There was a subtle distinction between those who had fully profited from the new age and those who had been left behind after all: you could tell this with men by whether or not they had smooth chins, and with women, it was judged by the shade of their lipstick, their perfume, or the cut and colour of their clothes.

Khinshtein's chiselled bird's head was topped with a helmet of blue-black hair. The boyishness of it clashed somewhat with his tortoiseshell glasses, behind which two frightful bright eyes flitted back and forth. He also had chicken legs and the pear-shaped belly of a glutton. Trofimov, in contrast, was skinny, and within his frame there was still the athlete that he'd been in his sporty youth, as would later become apparent. As soon as Swindleman and I entered the sombre lobby of the hotel, the men got up. They shook our hands formally, after which Khinshtein — who seemed to be the leader in everything — proposed an early lunch in the little restaurant on the third floor, although we shouldn't expect too much.

'We've had the revolution, the civil war, the great war for the fatherland, and now our poor people are again being ravaged by catastrophe,' the physicist said, and only now I spotted a gleaming gold watch on his wrist. 'Do you know what I saw outside on the street today? Handing out bread. The soldiers to the people. From trucks. These scarcities are due to the reformers in the Kremlin. As a scientist and as a person, I want to get on, of course. Reforms, agreed. But what's happening now is pure sabotage!'

We went to a dimly lit, empty salon on the third floor, with a gold metal ceiling. There, the gentlemen called for a table to be laid with delicacies that were almost unobtainable at that time, except with a lot of money and the right connections on the black market. It was the traditional festive spread of dishes of fruit, dark-green bottles of Soviet champagne, with necks of striated silver foil, pitchers of vodka, Georgian mineral water that smelt of the dentist, and *zakuski* — cold *hors d'oeuvres* — like pork pâté in jelly, slices of foal's meat, red salmon sliced paper-thin, white fish, eggs dripping in mayonnaise, cubes of beetroot with pickled onions, vinegar and dill, white and black bread. Before the main course arrived, two pouncing waiters in green sweater-jackets rapidly supplemented these delights with Julienne, the age-old, warm Russian dish, despite having a French name, which consisted of chicken or mushrooms in ragout, hot from the oven, with a layer of melted cheese and crème fraiche, served in doll's house skillets, with white cardboard sheathes on the handles to stop you burning your fingers during the gratifying, palate-filling, creamy ladling. Then butterfat blinis of red and black caviar, the latter of which was hawked in kilos back then, scooped by hand from the bellies of the sturgeon that were nonchalantly sliced open with a sharp knife by nocturnal poachers in wormy fishing boats on the head waters of the Volga. The blood that came with the costly fish eggs was rinsed out as far as possible through a sieve and the eggs were salted and swiftly tinned, to continue their illicit journey by road, boat, and air, courtesy of a network of smugglers, to the lounge bars of Paris, Milan, and New York, with the epicentre being the old market of Astrakhan, riven with corrupt police officials, with their bigoted purple drinker's faces that looked like poppies. There, torpedo-shaped, deliciously sweet melons were also sold, and occasionally there was even a lost camel, masticating its stupid face and lopsided jaw, stinking, plagued by huge flies, tied to a pole among the feral dogs and cats, and the open white sacks of spices from Central Asia, including the gold-dust of saffron, beneath the rays of sunlight that pierced the market's canvas, shining and sparkling, and the black caviar, edible black gold. Its consumption reached its zenith in the latter days of the Soviet Union: a final flourish before the almost total collapse, Dionysian, because in the next decade, during the rollercoaster years after the collapse of the USSR, water pollution became apocalyptic, state supervision of the over-fishing and poaching of sturgeon stopped, and the hunt for these miracle-fish that had survived on earth for hundreds of millions of years with their stumpy heads was no longer conducted merely by poor sods in rickety sloops, trying to earn a bit on the side. War was literally declared on the last beluga, sevruga and ossetra by warlords in Dagestan, residing in marble palaces with gold taps behind high walls, guarded by slaves with Kalashnikovs, who looked from their bedroom windows over the steel sheet of the Caspian Sea. There, their private armies with ships from the former Soviet fleet and supersonic speedboats imported from the west, kitted out with the most modern, satellite-guided detection equipment, tracked down the last sturgeon under water, even before they'd reached their dizzyingly old spawning grounds on the Volga. They hauled up the fish and with their knives like scimitars roughly gouged open their bellies, a jihad against the sea-animals, and then they scraped out all the still unripe eggs with soup spoons and tossed them into plastic containers, and the bodies of the fish were flung into the waves, for a moment colouring the white foam like raspberry-red soda, amid the wild cries of the seabirds. These things I saw myself, experienced myself, in a capacity that I wouldn't have thought possible at that moment, and would even have passionately despised, because later my life would again take a direction that only a fool could suspect beforehand. Lastly, to return to the black caviar: to me, the tragedy of the sturgeon, their slow but steady and irreversible disappearance from the wild, was the symbol of the demise of Russia, which leads to the question of what one day would be the symbol of the resurgence, even if by then I'll probably have long followed the sad fate of the sturgeon.

*'Prosit, meine Herrschaften!'* Khinshtein said a couple of times in German. *'Cheers, gentlemen!'*

We drank. The two academy members, Swindleman, and I made toasts in turn. It soon turned out that not just Khinshtein, but his colleague Trofimov too had started studying German a few months before. They insisted that we speak as much German with them as possible. Then they could finally get some good practice. Their interest in the language was dictated purely by pragmatic motives. A year before, they'd set up the first semi-private tomographic institute in Russia, using the legislation that the new age offered them. The tomograph, which created advanced two-dimensional representations of three-dimensional objects — people, plants, animals, and also 'dead material' such as mammoth remains or chocolate bonbons — was expected to have a flourishing future in Siberia too, especially in medical analyses. The duo had already moved into a building in the town of Akademgorodok, beautifully situated in the woods around Novosibirsk, and they'd also taken on some employees from the inexhaustible reservoir that they had access to almost for free, as university bigwigs. In short, the infrastructure of the company was already complete by that winter of 1989. Only one thing was missing: a tomograph.

The Soviet Union lagged fifty years behind the west in the field of micro-electronics and medical equipment. And this was the reason for Khinshtein and Trofimov's sudden Teutonic linguistic interest: Germany. Bonn's policy towards the east had been coloured for decades by a collective sense of guilt, a secret national penance for the millions of deaths that the Nazis had caused in the USSR, from Smolensk to the Crimean Peninsula to Baku. A fate that was not only suffered by Jewish and Slavic *Untermenschen*, such as Russians, White Russians, and Ukrainians, but also Tatars, Kazakhs, and Uzbeks. A sense of guilt among an entire people can be viewed decades later as capital with a nice bond attached — at least that was how pragmatically Khinshtein and Trofimov saw the support of the Federal Republic, which had started piecemeal aid programmes for the needy Soviet Union, involving funds being made available for precisely the sector they were aiming for. Somewhere in the land of Goethe, Mercedes-Benz, and Hitler, there were a million German Deutschmarks waiting for them, which could easily flow into their tomograph project, with no strings attached.

'Just imagine, a million marks!' Khinshtein's tongue was quivering, as if his mouth was a fissure in a rock which was home to a fiery-red reptile. 'That means that we need to hand in an application in the next few months, write letters, maybe even travel to Germany. We need reliable foreign partners to assist us. And thank God we've found them in you. Cheers!'

But first another issue would have to be dealt with, preferably this very afternoon: the application for a visa for the two scholars and their mistresses for their pleasure trip to Spain.

No problem, Swindleman said; squinting his eyes, he took a bite of the boar's meat that had now been served.

# CHAPTER SEVEN

The Siberian academics' request turned out to be a piece of cake. After the extravagant dinner, I immediately took a taxi to the Spanish consulate at around four, just as it was about to close. I was a bit the worse for wear. A bleached-blonde girl in her mid-twenties opened the mahogany door. She was clearly quite pleased, almost thrilled, to meet a westerner who spoke her own language.

'You have a southern accent,' she said, after she'd let me into the almost deserted building. 'Where did you learn Spanish?'

'On Tenerife,' I answered.

'What were you doing there?'

'Recreation leader,' I said.

'Oh, one of those pool boys that picks out the prettiest girl from every new batch of tourists and whips her off to bed.' Her eyes had an almost insane gleam. 'So you're here to apply for a visa for Russian friends? Do they have enough money to spend on the trip? Ah, you already have the photocopies of their papers. I can't promise anything, but maybe I'll be able to arrange something.'

She was a history grad-student doing her internship in the visa section. Marta, from Madrid. Her grandfather had been a communist sympathiser during the Spanish Civil War, and had even been to Moscow twice in the 1930s as part of a secret military delegation. She'd chosen Russian as her minor, then she'd finally decided to write her thesis on the Spanish community in Moscow. She was going to do her archive research on location. The six-month job at the consulate was a stroke of luck.

That same evening, she invited me to her home, a flat on the twelfth floor of an apartment block that was specially reserved for diplomats and other foreigners, with Soviet guards and a red-and-white checked barrier gate out front. The windows had been almost entirely darkened by the icy snowflakes from the storm that had hit that afternoon. Among the imported western furniture were three lit, green, dripping candles. Marta had sliced up a chorizo sausage and put green olives in a bowl, along with other Spanish delicacies that were delivered every other week by diplomatic post from Madrid. We finished the first bottle of rioja within half an hour. She opened a second. When she'd emptied out the last dregs of that one, she got up and with her octopus-like arms deftly plucked a bottle of whisky from a bookshelf and poured some into her wine glass. She had the figure of a diva.

I'd already gathered that she'd been terribly unhappy for the last four months. Things had all gone wrong. She'd barely managed to get any of her archive research done because of the flood of visa applications, work that she was nearly drowning in. In the meantime, she no longer cared about the history of the Spanish community here. Academic research was not for her. The only reason she'd done it was for her grandfather. By now, she hated the Russians, she hated this country. Once back in Spain, she'd switch studies, do Italian, German and English, and then go and work in tourism. She had a strong Madrilenian accent. The way she pronounced her saliva-rich consonants moistened her curvy, red lips. There were only old guys working at the consulate. One by one, they'd gotten hitched to Russian wives — the girls who stamped documents, typed things up, did the administrative work. They were all whores, whores the whole lot of them.

'Yes, filthy putas!' The Spanish woman got up again, a bit wobbly, and then plonked herself down on the couch beside me. She slipped her hand into my crotch in one fluid motion, while she placed the other on my mouth in a choking clamp. 'Callate! Shut up!'

Then she deftly unbuttoned my flies.

After I'd visited Marta a couple of times, the visas were sorted. By the time the two Siberian academics and their sweethearts were finally able to travel to Spain three weeks later, my new life had already begun. The initial plan was that I would go back to the Netherlands for six months and set up the office on Javastraat. And Swindleman would do the same in Moscow.

Arranging a Dutch residence visa would be a hellish task, but I'd cautiously sounded out Julia to ask if she'd like to come with me. She immediately began to learn Dutch with the earnestness, dedication and thoroughness of the Russian intellectual, using a textbook from 1923 that she'd picked up in a library somewhere.

But things would work out differently. A week before my departure, Swindleman caught jaundice. The whites of his eyes turned the colour of stale beer. His already chubby face now took on a permanent puffiness. He panted and sweated, as though he was working off a hangover from a heavy night's drinking. He'd had a rushed blood test done in a clinic for generals from the Red Army, for a bribe of three hundred dollars. The clinic turned out to be just as primitive and miserable as the hospitals elsewhere in the country. He was diagnosed with a definite hepatitis B infection. He was furious. As he swore and gave his 16-year-old ballerina from Archangelsk what for, he took greedy slugs from a bottle of carbonated Caucasian mineral water, because there was no question of any alcohol for the time being. He wouldn't surrender himself again to the Soviet healthcare system, not for any price. And that's how it came about that I, rather than Swindleman, would man the Moscow branch. While he was being treated for his condition in the Netherlands, he'd set up our branch in the fatherland, in the building that belonged to Baldwin Borger on Javastraat.

My new office-cum-home was a *chambre en suite* on the sixth floor of the Akademicheskaya Hotel 2, with a view of October Square and the mighty statue of Lenin. Although the country was now in complete chaos, even teetering on the brink of anarchy in some places, the Soviet bureaucracy still continued doggedly. To be able to stay in the Academy of Sciences hotel, I needed to have an official academic title. Before the two Siberian partners had even got on the plane to Las Palmas, they'd arranged everything impeccably. I received an identity document with a passport photo and a stamp, contained in a fold-out booklet with a red leather cover, just like the agents of the KGB had – which they quickly flipped open before they arrested anyone, just for the form, because most suspects would never know who their assailants were. It stated that I, Doctor P. A. J. Waterdrinker, had been appointed to carry out research in the territory of the USSR into the operation of the tomograph for the period of a year. Reference: Professor Khinshtein, Lev Abramovich, University of Novosibirsk.

And so my apartment cost me a pittance, because in my new capacity I never had to pay for anything in foreign currency, but in rubles that I'd bought on the black market.

———

I'd met Julia for the first time exactly six months earlier. It was a given that I now wanted to whisk her away from her Leningrad dive, from the depressing neighbourhood on Vasilyevsky Island, which had been a hotbed of resistance during the revolution of 1917, and where people still lived among rats and mildewed walls.

'My God,' she'd sighed, when we stepped into the double hotel room one February afternoon; she'd never lived in so much space in her entire life. 'Just look at this lovely furniture. And that big bath!'

She'd made the Dutch language her own at an astonishing rate. Our conversation was soon made up of a mishmash of German, Dutch and Russian. Naturally, she'd been looking forward to staying in the Netherlands, but she'd accepted the change to my initial plan with complete equanimity. She didn't even ask why. Although she had a deep dislike of Moscow, she'd follow me and help to arrange things, make calls and set up meetings. She'd met Swindleman shortly before he'd left, among the marble pillars of the dining room in Hotel Ukraina, where he was having lunch between an orgy of bottles of mineral water, with a corpulent Russian who I absolutely had to get to know. It was only in the taxi back when Julia commented that Swindleman's face was like an over-ripe lemon that I told her about the jaundice. She hissed like a kitten, kept silent for a while, then said, 'Did I understand right that the fat Russian wants to deal in butter with you? Why butter of all things?'

I told her about the butter mountain, about the warehouses all over Europe that were full of agricultural surpluses, how in Europe they gave farmers subsidies to encourage them to produce less.

'*Stjo?* What?' Julia looked at me as though she'd seen water burning, as we drove through the streets where the people were still standing in queues outside almost empty shops, beaten down, crushed. 'I thought that I'd been born in a madhouse here in the Soviet Union. Giving farmers money to produce *less*? Swear to me it isn't true!'

As I've said, these were dynamic times! In the first weeks of 1990, Swindleman began to pelt me with faxes from The Hague, constantly making new proposals for our business. He had impressive letter paper printed in two languages — English and Russian — and signed all the letters and other documents as 'general director'; for me, he'd thought up the title of 'senior advisor'.

He'd appeared to hit it off with Baldwin Borger from the start. They'd already arranged the first business sector trip for the second week of March. Six days in Moscow-Leningrad for thirty bankers. From the start, they were charging three thousand guilders per person above cost price. Almost a hundred grand. It looked like everything would be just as Baldwin Borger had indicated.

Because of the unchecked and rising flow of visitors to the Soviet Union, it became increasingly hard to find good hotel accommodation, particularly in Moscow. The fall of the Berlin wall before Christmas had brought a new euphoria to Europe. Swindleman and I had sat in the lobby of the Hotel National, open-mouthed and astonished, staring at the TV pictures of the Ossis jubilantly crossing to the west. My partner sighed that this new development could turn out badly for our business. We'd have to trade on our unique knowledge, our exclusivity. He felt things were moving too fast. But the reverse turned out to be true.

The vibrations that were felt elsewhere in the Eastern Bloc mostly popped like soap bubbles in just a few weeks, but they could be felt on every street corner in Moscow. Despite the reforms, the Communist Party and the KGB still had a firm grip on power. There was always the threat of counter-revolution. There were increasing rumours about conservatives thirsting for revenge, who accused Gorbachev of treachery and saw the country rapidly falling apart, sliding into a bourgeois state, and abandoning the dogma of Lenin.

During the day, there were public disturbances and riots everywhere, where men and women were manhandled away. I resumed my regular visits to the political meetings in Dom Kino. Andrei Sakharov, the conscience of the nation, had died shortly before, but once again among the intellectuals, artists, and representatives of bohemian Russia, I saw the self-confident masculine woman with the short-cropped, straw hairstyle that I'd seen appear there before — a sort of Angela Merkel *avant la lettre* — who took to the stage with a raised fist, warning about the ethnic cocktail that was ready to explode.

The agitation in the city only seemed to settle down again in the late evening; once the metro was no longer running, no ordinary folk dared to go out on the streets, and foreign cars huddled together outside nightclubs that weren't festooned with neon lights — that would only come later — but were quite dark. On the pavements that had been cleared of snow, you could hear the clacking of heels, the screams, sometimes a pistol shot somewhere in the distance.

By seven thirty in the morning, I was sitting at my desk, working on the first few things. Julia was a night-person and a late sleeper, and she would usually still be snoozing like a cat in the next room. I shut the padded door as quietly as possible on my way to the bathroom with its rose-pink bath tub. I had a typewriter with Cyrillic letters. The fax machine's green light was always on. I stamped every document that I drew up with the round logo of our new company.

At nine o'clock, the first human forms appeared in the pitch darkness of October Square near the Lenin statue. Within a few minutes, this had grown into a throng, from which steam was rising. In the glow of a single lamppost, I saw the following scene every morning: a middle-aged woman in a fur hat and a white doctor's coat with more fur bulging out from under it standing in the back of an army truck with an open canopy, handing out bread, or rather, tossing it into the mass of raised arms and hands. When I opened the window, I could hear the airy cries of men and women for *khleb*, bread. This would degenerate into protesting screams when the load on the truck had run out and not everybody had been provided for; when groups of newcomers arrived, scuffles would sometimes break out. People were literally fighting for bread. On seeing this pitiful sea of poverty, I always thought of my father and how, as a 17-year-old in the 1950s, he'd gone off to sail in the Dutch merchant navy out of sheer necessity. They had often anchored in the harbours of Buenos Aires and Montevideo and seen the penniless young men on the quay, crying in Spanish — *Por favor! Por favor!* — to be given the chance to empty the ship's hold as human beasts of burden.

'I always thought that was so awful …' he often confided to me. 'Those poor buggers with their arms raised, begging for work. And how as a simple cook's mate, there's nothing you can do for them.'

Once again, a revolution was taking place in this country. And just like in every other fomenting Russian revolution, the outcome was entirely uncertain.

———

Swindleman's abstention from alcohol gave him the energy of a nuclear reactor. One morning, he devised a plan to do sublicensed trips as well: others would sell the tours in the Netherlands and in the USSR while we middlemen would provide the complete hotel and excursion package through one of the new cooperatives, entirely independent of Intourist.

It all went awry as early as the second trip. I'd handed everything over to the director of the brand-new company Wonder Travels, which was operating in an entire wing of an artists' hotel for the Russian State Circus in the centre of Moscow, near the Blacksmith's Bridge. The director of the hotel was in on the plan. They divided up the loot, while they took on girls from the universities to be tour guides in museums, churches, cloisters, and the city. A day before the group of twenty-five from Amsterdam was due to arrive in Moscow, I learned that the Russian I'd concluded the contract with had slipped through the ice in his car during an ice-fishing trip to Siberia. Two other passengers had died, local girls. The hotel director let me know that he'd gone into business with someone else now, and that the agreements the deceased man had made were no longer valid — 'A signature? Are you trying to tell me that the signature of a corpse has some value in the West?' He couldn't accommodate the people coming; I'd have to sort it out for myself.

The next day, I quickly managed to find accommodation for the group in a city barracks close to Sokolniki Park, when the soldiers were out on manoeuvres in the woods around Moscow. This was via an old contact, a colonel who I'd come across a year earlier on a bench, all alone and blind drunk, and who I'd continued drinking with. Once, we went driving crisscross and singing through the city in the black service Volga. He'd fallen in love with an actress from Tomsk who was six years older, and he was planning on getting divorced. He believes that I saved his life because when he was finally lying semi-unconscious on the back seat, I had his driver take him to Hotel Intourist rather than his home, where I found him the next morning, a deathly-sick, big kid in the breakfast room with a weak cup of tea and an untouched plate of scrambled eggs in front of him. He gave me his telephone number, solemnly promising that I could always call on him for a favour, as long as there wasn't a war on. He gave me his word of honour. His word of honour as a Russian who, as a sergeant had saved the lives of three comrades in Afghanistan, which he'd invaded with the Soviet Army ten years before. Some of his legion had been captured and flayed alive. He'd rather not say any more. Now, a year later, I successfully managed to call in the favour.

The corpulent Russian who'd initially been interested in making profitable use of part of the European butter mountain with our intercession never showed up again. This is often how things went: five out of six contacts ended up in nothing, many were blabbers, scavengers, chancers, portraying themselves as something that they weren't. It was an age of the big personal lie, while the monopoly of state lies about the bloody Soviet past was swiftly coming to a conclusion because of the continuous stream of new revelations.

The work piled up. Pretty soon, Julia and I were in our hotel room every day making phone calls, sending faxes, typing letters and requests on a typewriter that had been produced by the Blithe Birds company from Minsk in 1981. We'd only done three commissioned trips — the first profitable business sector trip for the bankers was still to come — but Swindleman felt that this arm of our company was actually just a sideline. The real capital was to be earned through trade: exports and primarily imports. I had to send him requests from Moscow to deliver items and goods, so that he could approach the right parties in The Hague.

'No more messing around,' he stressed to me one afternoon from the office on Javastraat. 'The time for buggering about with military watches, caviar and theatre tickets is over. We're going to do this big time! I'll send you a fax in a while with the names and addresses that I've been given by our Siberian chums. They'll be coming to Moscow again soon. Make a big deal of their welcome, they're our friends.'

Food supply in the city was getting worse by the day. Even the foreign-currency shops were growing empty. In our double room, we had a machine for making tea and coffee, but we couldn't cook there. From late afternoon, there were already academics sitting in the restaurant of our hotel, drinking mostly, either together or with their sweethearts. Khinshtein and Trofimov were certainly not the only ones who enjoyed their privileged status to the full. There was only one dish on the menu: *boeuf stroganoff*. After Julia had been harassed a couple of times by drunk guys, she no longer showed her face in the dining room. And so every day at around eight in the evening, our *boeuf stroganoff* was delivered to our room on a serving trolley. Always by the same waiter in a white jacket — a thin, intense, dark man of around forty, with a sunken, rather Spanish face, with big, tragic eyes, and pale like a character in a painting by Goya. After some time had passed, he told me that he was indeed the descendant of a Spaniard, a peasant from the region around Segovia who'd converted to communism and come to Moscow in the 1930s with his wife and three teenage sons, and then stayed. His speech was shy, almost whispering, 'My grandfather, and almost everyone in my family, died in the gulag.' You only had to scratch the surface of any random person and the bloodshed of recent history spurted out as though from the severed artery of a calf. The waiter would have been excellent study material for Marta, but I kept quiet about this. Julia was standing next to me, listening to the man attentively. It struck me as better that she remain ignorant of the voluptuous Spanish girl at the consulate, with her light, crazy eyes.

The *boeuf stroganoff* was dirt-cheap in black rubles, less than thirty Dutch cents. Despite the first word of the dish's name, the beef was barely edible. It seemed to consist of strips of boot leather and the beige sauce with moribund slivers of red onion and mushrooms floating in it, mostly stank of charred garlic, with a hint of the dash of vodka that it had evidently been deglazed with. But we scarcely had any choice. I heard a professor with a goatee sneeringly remark to a colleague in the lift that the hotel kitchen had managed to get its hands on a couple of cows from the stalls of the Academy of Sciences outside the city, which were used for trialling new medicines. I wasn't sure if it was a joke. The Russian gutter press — miraculously resurrected after almost seventy years, often with anti-Semitic, neo-czarist, and of course half-pornographic content — reported frequent horror stories of cannibalism in the provinces, while in the Urals a couple was recently arrested for selling the flesh of sick butchered animals on the free market for years, from the zoo where they worked.

However much the food scarcities in the countryside affected the Moscow departmental hotel of the Academy of Sciences, there was one thing that there was no shortage of: Soviet champagne. A bottle of sweet or dry sparkling wine of the Sovetskoye or Kornet brands cost less than thirty cents. My later alcohol addiction began at this time. Oh, how often did Julia and I shoot corks at the wall as evening fell. And the slogan on the front of the metro station opposite us — THE PARTY IS THE MIND, THE HONOUR AND THE CONSCIENCE OF OUR AGE! — was buffeted by the freezing winds, as the Mercedes of the first ruble millionaires whipped by like torpedoes in the darkness!

We soon swore off the *boeuf stroganoff*. We made do with bread, the odd piece of fruit, some conserves and other things that we could find in the shops among the unhealthy smelling human swarm. We drank away our relative sense of hunger with champagne. When I was offered first-class poacher's caviar one day, I bought seven kilo tins and put them in the fridge next to my desk. I wasn't particularly a fan, but often at around noon, Julia would snack on half an ounce with a wooden spoon, with her eyes half closed, radiant in silent happiness. I also bear some guilt for the swansong of the beluga. The vitamin pills that my mother gave me soon ran out because I insisted that Julia take them too.

More and more often, I went out for appointments, meetings with potential partners that I'd arranged myself, or Swindleman had passed on to me from The Hague. And more and more often, I had to travel outside the city, to Julia's immense dislike because she was left behind in our little office to deal with any business at hand. The groups of tourists kept coming; by now, with everything more or less running smoothly, I'd delegated everything to others. But nothing could be certain, contracts were worth even less than the ever-falling ruble, and if anything happened again, as with the State Circus hotel, then I'd have to be able to intervene quickly.

Can current and future generations imagine those times before the mobile phone? But even the ordinary telephone, the analogue version accessible by cable, was also a constant source of annoyance, and an inconceivable loss of time. Swindleman was able to call or fax me from The Hague with no problem. But if I needed to reach him quickly for a consultation, I first had to request an international line, which usually meant waiting half an hour, or sometimes a whole hour. The same was true for sending international faxes.

One afternoon, when the sun was hanging over the city like a mighty copper pan, I was sitting facing a Russian, a potential client who was interested in the delivery of sixty second-hand Audis. His office was housed in a building on the Clean Ponds. The dripping icicles on the window frame heralded the first shoots of spring.

The man was around sixty. A year earlier, he'd still been the director of a department of the Ministry of Transport, his son was on the board of the communist youth organisation Komsomol, but the new times hadn't been too unkind to them. They'd slipped into the space that had been vacated by the command system of the Soviet economy, which had more or less collapsed. As badly as things may have been going in the country, a society never entirely ground to a halt — just as in times of war, the fighting isn't constant. This is something that I would realise years later when I found myself in a warzone for the first time. Life generally carries on. The state shops were empty, but an entire underground system had sprung up, or rather, a parallel system in which bricks were made and traded, pipes, carpenter's wood, petrol, commodities such as clothes, shoes, toys, plugs, plasters, TV sets, fridges, radios and foodstuffs, even though the last of these was the Achilles heel of the market, and was also un-sexy for most roguish traders because of the laboriousness and likeliness to spoil.

The son of this former apparatchik, who I'd met a week earlier by chance, had trained as a dentist, but at a record speed he'd made the tricks of capitalism his own, using an American textbook about marketing and economics, with the Russian translation circulating as a smudged photocopy, held together with paperclips and sellotape, sold in markets everywhere. He was now on an official trip to Perm, but he'd sworn to me that I could do good business with his father, and we could immediately strike a deal as long as I made the right proposal. The father and son already owned a semi-private transport company on the railways. The transportation of raw materials, such as nickel and even old scrap, to the ports in Leningrad, Vladivostok and Murmansk earned them millions of rubles a day. They were almost literally swimming in money, and trying to convert as much as possible to foreign currency, buying real estate and transferable property, but they were also on the lookout for other investments for the longer term. The plan was to set up the first private taxi company in the city, aimed at the segment of customers that could pay in dollars, just as you could only pay in foreign currency in most restaurants then. The dollar, the currency of the United States, which so many in the Kremlin were deeply suspicious of, or even hated, had overrun the country like a fungus. The maximum term for a return on an investment in the latter days of the USSR was only six months, and in the rollercoaster years that would follow, it was only three months with most deals. In order to earn back their investment in six months, and at the same time not compromise on the luxury, comfort, and quality that they wished to provide as a business, the Audis couldn't be more than three years old, and certainly cost no more than a certain sum either, the amount of which I can no longer remember.

A few days before, after I'd passed on the son's first requests about the cars to Swindleman, he called me back jubilantly within an hour. He'd been asking around; a dealer in North Brabant had the cars ready and waiting, exactly sixty in number and all sprayed metallic white. We'd make three thousand dollars profit on each car, including the transport via Lithuania that he'd already more or less arranged.

I knew that I'd succeeded when I walked out of the Russian's office and into the corridor of the building that used to be a school and had now been transformed into a beehive for all sorts of little commercial enterprises, businesses, small traders. The man had talked about a letter of credit in dollars via a German bank. I now found myself in a sea of Russians, Georgians, Armenians, and other Soviet citizens with grand plans, visions for the future, and stories. But when it came down to paying upfront, cash on the barrel, the majority soon dropped out.

The winter sun was gleaming through the high windows onto the glazed, tiled floor and falling in precise lines. I'd more or less sorted out the first deal outside of our tourist business. And now I'd been overcome by an almost intoxicating exaltation. In the preceding weeks, Swindleman had sometimes bawled me out impatiently, warning me to hurry up with other things. But now he would be satisfied. The first few hundred thousand were on the way.

All around me, I could hear voices, telephones ringing, footsteps, mumbling, nervous commands. Some of the doors to the former classrooms were open and you could see inside the rooms, crammed with desks like billiard tables, where men and women were feverishly working. In one of them, Lenin was looking down angrily with a thoughtful pose on the neo-capitalist throng beneath him. If he could have stepped out of the wooden frame and off the wall, he'd have slated everyone here as whores and cockroaches, and then ordered the scum to be summarily executed on the spot.

But most of the classrooms were locked, as though doing business was something furtive, clandestine, and indecent, an activity that ought not to see the light of day. I passed the doors with their enamel business plates. On one of them was written: FROZEN PORK; while the next stated: IVANOV BROTHERS, DEALERS IN BEE VENOM. Followed by: VIDEO RECORDERS DIRECT FROM THE FACTORY, TAIWAN — SECOND-HAND PIPES, METAL ROOF-SUPPORTS AND CABLE TROUGHS — YURI BEYLIN, MUNITIONS AND RIFLES FOR HUNTING — AKHMEDOV, CHECHEN OIL — BERNSTEIN, LAWYER — ROMANOV, ARCTIC FOX AND OPOSSUM FUR — SIDOROV, RAPID MEDICAL LABORATORY TESTS — THE RAINBOW COMPANY, SPORTS COSTUMES AND TRAINERS (ADIDAS) — KOGAN, FILM AGENCY — NATASHA VOLKOVA, HABERDASHERY — DAVID SMIRNOV, MODELLING AGENCY — THE CHARMS OF ASTRAKHAN COMPANY, RED AND BLACK CAVIAR/DELICACIES — BLUE JEANS, POLISH AND AMERICAN DENIM — SOLDATOV & COHEN, LAWYERS — SAKHALIN, FROZEN RED SALMON — KARPOV & KARPOV, IMPORTED WINDSCREEN WIPERS AND CAR COMPONENTS — SAUER, COMMUNICATIONS — NICKLE, COPPER TELEPHONE CABLES & SCRAP — NIKOLAYEV, SIBERIAN BEER — DOCTOR L. FEINSTEIN, INTIMATE MEDICAL HYGIENE, and so it continued in this cloister-like corridor that was at least ninety metres long. As I walked past OLGA & OLGA, SEXUAL LADIES LINGERIE, the door swung open. A blonde with stiletto heels clacked outside, passing me with her fluttering fake eyelashes. I was about to turn around when I was more or less stormed by the figure of a man whose face I couldn't see because of the blinding, radiant, penetrating sun, who said, 'No, how many summers, how many winters?' (The Russian greeting for 'long time no see'.) I immediately fell into a clammy-coated embrace, still freezing from the street, and only after I'd half turned around did I recognise the face of Pozorski.

'Good grief ...' He shoved me away, looked at me in disbelief and beaming at the same time. 'What are you doing here? My old bible delivery man! I thought you'd left the country for good.'

Since our meeting a year and a half before in Hotel Europe with the hysterical Madam Pokrovskaya, I hadn't seen him again. I'd gone back to Holland from Leningrad without speaking to him again. But he seemed to have forgotten.

I simply had to wait for him, he continued brightly. He had a couple of things to arrange here. It would take ten minutes, a quarter of an hour at most. He disappeared into NICKLE, COPPER TELEPHONE CABLES & SCRAP, then five minutes later he popped into SOLDATOV & COHEN, LAWYERS, and when he was back in the corridor, he explained that he was really almost ready now, and then he disappeared for about ten minutes through the door of OLGA & OLGA, SEXUAL LADIES LINGERIE, where the blonde with the high heels had now returned, with a glass pot of tea that she'd fetched from God-knows-where.

It turned out that Pozorski had his own office a bit further off, in a spinach-green building just behind Lubyanka Square. It was in a street that ran downwards at a slant, where the KGB used to have torture and execution spaces in the 1930s at the highpoint of the purges and the terror. This difference in elevation in the old neighbourhood had come in handy: the blood could easily be hosed away into the drains of the Moscow sewers, and then the bodies could be taken by lorry to the crematoria and mass graves outside the city.

'Good God, am I glad to see you again!' Pozorski swiftly whipped a bottle of whisky out of a drawer, poured out a couple of measures and shoved a glass towards me unasked. 'Cheers! And how are you doing?'

I nodded cheerfully, a sign that I was doing well. I still had an instinctive aversion to this man, but I also realised that in my new position, I could no longer avoid him.

He was a potential partner.

His office was teeming with attractive girls. Now and then, one would come in, lay a paper in front of him and ask him to sign, and then disappear again. OLGA & OLGA, SEXUAL LADIES LINGERIE was a side-line, which had been thought up by one of his mistresses. It had been started more or less as a joke, but the business had grown like a weed and was now bringing in a fortune.

During a three-month stay in Budapest, a year and a half before, Pozorski had made contact with the Hungarian partners with whom he was now importing video recorders and other electronic equipment from Japan. The Soviet market seemed to be insatiable. This was a golden business, even though he'd still continued his original scrap trade. He was not on good terms with his old mate Nikolai Borodin, the harbour director in Leningrad. In fact, the man was no longer among the living. Following a mega-deal with a shipload of copper and nickel, Borodin had slipped off with the money. Pozorski had tracked him down to Murmansk, managed to get back his share of the profit, forgiven his partner for everything, but a week later something terrible had happened. One morning,

Borodin was found dangling from a tree upside down, naked in the frost, twenty below. He'd been strung up with a rope by his left ankle. His skin was blue and white. It must have been a slow, hideous death.

'I lay awake for a whole night! But these are the times, dear friend …' By now, Pozorski was wearing glasses with dark-orange lenses that obstructed any view of his eyes, and there was a sickly orange glow to his cheeks. 'Come on, tell me a little about yourself.'

He took me to Aragvi, the Georgian restaurant on Gorky Street that had once been the scene for the excesses of Stalin's youngest son. You couldn't get in without an invitation, but Pozorski appeared to know everyone by name, the manager, the waiters, the waitress, even the members of the orchestra that were playing on a dais. He began to tell me about the pleasures of the Caucasian country, about the sumptuous beauty of Tbilisi, about the delicious dishes that would soon be brought in, in the belief that I'd never been to Georgia. Meanwhile, I could see the images before me of the men, women, students, and priests, some of whom would be chased away, knocked down, or beaten to death by the army a couple of hours after I'd seen them demonstrating on the Rustaveli Avenue in April of the year before.

Suddenly, Pozorski started talking about our trade in bibles, in that melancholy tone of an old man confessing a youthful sin. His orange-coloured face was beaming. He roared with laughter over the warm cheese-bread that had just been brought in. He'd really taken everyone for a ride back then! Right after the arrival of the first load of holy scriptures from Rotterdam, he'd heard that a Protestant association in Denmark wanted to satisfy the spiritual needs of their fellow believers in the USSR with Russian bibles. And so, a week later, the next shipment of another 80,000 bibles was ferried to Denmark by boat. There, he sold them to a clerical organisation until they once again began their journey by sea to Leningrad, where they were distributed to the faithful.

Pozorski had been putting on an act for me.

'What do you think of the war in Nagorno-Karabakh?' he said, to abruptly change the subject. 'Our Armenian and Azerbaijani friends are at each other's throats! Socialist brothers! Where's it all going to end? Awful, awful ... But at the same time, we're living through great times. Do you know what, comrade? We're finally going to do some business! You get ready, I'm going to make you rich!'

# CHAPTER EIGHT

One morning, a few months after our cat Ljólja's death, I decided to skip my daily walk to Gorky Park and take a ride on the tram that stops close to my rented flat in Moscow. There was still snow on the ground, with the glazed blue gleam that is a sign of the first thaw. As I walked towards the stop, I could hear the excitable tweeting of birds in the black poplars. I could smell the ammoniacal scent of the coming spring, as I always smell the humus of autumn in July (at the height of summer).

I bought a ticket for a few rubles and sat down, then we drove off. We rumbled over the bridge across the Moskva River, with the Stalin-cake on the left where Paustovsky wrote a section of his memoirs, and the silhouette of the Kremlin beyond it in the distance with its gleaming golden dome, all beneath a cast-iron sky. There was a man sitting in front of me with a thoroughly purple nose, staring out from under his damp beaver hat. I guessed he was around seventy. Old men in public are rare in Russia. Most of them die early. Those that are still alive tend to lie low, or are hidden away, frequently among the warped icons and candlelight of churches.

Was the pensioner a born Muscovite? If so, the shadowplay that was probably taking place in his mind would partly match mine.

That shadowplay that comes with the years, where what you see around you is in a constant dialogue with images from the past. I'd linked my fate to this country, to the literature, to my Russian wife, even if there was no bow of flesh between us to underline this to the cruel outside world.

When we reached the inner boulevard ring, the old tram crawled and ground with a high-pitched metallic shriek at every curve, past a building where in my twenties I'd seen girls with just a dot of white fur in their arses, dancing on stage beneath strobe lights. Now the clandestine restaurant had been transformed into a luxurious bank, with glass doors and a marble entrance. The city looked hyper-modern in many places. Nowhere were there as many expensive cars driving around as here. When I'd lived here, some shops had been repurposed as many as four times. Where once stinking chunks of Soviet beef had been sold, and later imported textiles, and later still the first mobile phones, there was now a lounge café populated by the Moscow youth, drinking their cappuccinos and latte macchiatos while scrolling on their iPhones and iPads. Should I tell them that when I was around their age, I had to wait an hour in this city just to get someone on the line elsewhere in Europe; maybe they'd glance up at me in astonishment, but I suspect they'd be more likely to turn their heads away, bored by this bald spectre who'd emerged from pre-history. The generations are succeeding each other more and more quickly, and they don't even realise that they're prematurely signing their own death warrant.

In 1929 (the year of my father's birth), Curzio Malaparte, the contentious Italian author with a fascist vibe, made a visit to Moscow and Leningrad. He found himself among the last human remnants of the czarist empire that had collapsed twelve years earlier, but most of all among the newly formed Bolshevik elite.

The highest echelon of communism: the greedy, cruel, dissolute clan of Marxist aristocrats surrounding Stalin's throne, their wives, daughters, mistresses, the profiteers, the dandies, the pederasts, the proletarian merveilleuses, the actresses, the ballerinas — and this sentence is an almost literal quote — those who had taken the place of the aristocracy of the old regime and would, quite soon — following terrible secret trials — die in front of execution squads on the courtyard of the Lubyanka.

History doesn't repeat itself, it rhymes.

And sometimes it forms its own mirror image.

Malaparte had witnessed the rise of the Soviet Union, the first five-year plan, and more than half a century later, I would witness its slow but steady decline.

I managed to get hold of *The Kremlin Ball*, Malaparte's literary account of his time in Moscow just before the start of The Great Terror, which he would only write many years afterwards. The writing in this stunning Proustian novel totally bowled me over. Through his eyes he showed me what I would later see with my own — in the same place, but at a different time. He described the Moscow where entire neighbourhoods were demolished, literally, to make way for the wide roads that would hasten Stalin from the Kremlin to his dacha in the woods. After the Napoleonic fire of 1812, the majority of wooden houses, merchant houses, and city palaces had been replaced with stone buildings. Charming boulevards had risen up, following the example set by Paris; yet the city still possessed a rustic, almost Arcadian character with its gilt and colourfully gleaming tiled church domes, cloisters with fields full of pullets, goats and cows, carriages for hire and farm carts. This quickly disappeared with that spiteful destruction and the socialist concrete clamour for new buildings. I also saw houses and neighbourhoods that had grown dear to me in my almost twenty-five years in Moscow disappear, by and large because of the actions of greedy bureaucrats and villains.

An insane metamorphosis. Not only literally, but politically and socially too.

Even before the collapse of the Soviet Union, I'd witnessed the first moves towards the massive kleptocracy of the 1990s by a clique of cynical and clever people that the world would soon come to know as the oligarchs. The usurpers of oil and gas fields, and mines that spewed gold, copper, tin, aluminium, nickel, and rough diamonds. The heroes of both the international serious broadsheets and gossip press, with their scrabbled together fairy-tale fortunes of billions of dollars, their castles and country houses, their flashy motor yachts, art collections, wives, mistresses, sons, and daughters who now made up the new Russian aristocracy. They no longer live in Saint Petersburg around the Winter Palace of the Romanovs, residing in imperial lustre, nor in special buildings with their own well-stocked shops, cinemas, and other facilities which Stalin had built in Moscow for his hangers-on, paladins and thugs who would later become the victims, as Malaparte reported. Now, they reside in their megalomaniac quarters, charmingly situated in the woods half an hour's distance from Moscow, in a circle close to the new 'czar' in the Kremlin. They are once again cradled by servants, nannies, cooks, bodyguards, chauffeurs, gardeners, yoga and sports instructors; they are as focused on their earthly pleasures, status and fleeting fame as their predecessors were, and their lives are perhaps once again being threatened by an uprising.

The pensioner with the purple nose and the beaver-fur hat had stepped off. A grimy, powdery snow had begun to fall as the tram was picking up speed over the boulevard in the direction of the Clean Ponds. I thought of what I suspected was an invented, but wonderful passage in which the war correspondent, diplomat and novelist Malaparte — in the company of the genius Mikhail Bulgakov—had come across the extremely elderly and impoverished Prince Lvov on the street in Moscow near the Arbat. He'd been the first premier of the Provisional Government and he was carrying a golden chair on his grey side-burned head, aiming to hawk it on the flea market under the green trees on the Smolensky Boulevard, where his fellow aristocratic partners in misfortune (amazingly still alive, not having been murdered or fled) were selling the remnants of their previously privileged lives — rings, icons, porcelain, bound books, coloured silk ties, Cossacks' daggers; there was even a girl holding up her underwear — to diplomats, foreigners, the profiteers of communism, their spouses, daughters, and lovers.

In the first days of the February Revolution in Petrograd in 1917, Prince Lvov had driven his service car down Tchaikovsky Street every day, on his way to the chaos in the Tauride Palace, which was suddenly swamped with workers, soldiers, and sailors, and the garden where my wife and I had secretly buried our cat a couple of months before.

I thought of Julia, of how she was doing, six hundred kilometres away, of how the cats were doing. Just as I was about to call her, my iPhone started ringing in my trouser pocket.

'Hi, where are you?'

'In the tram,' I said.

'Why?'

I told her that I was on my way to see a politician that I had to interview for the paper; our appointment was in half an hour.

'And how is everything going?'

'Shitty weather … And there?'

'Hail,' my wife replied. 'Oh, I so long for the spring. Are we going to take a real holiday this year? There's always that writing of yours. When are we finally going to get around to life?'

She asked how things were going with my book. Just the week before, I'd told her that the project I had on my hands was threatening to turn into a sort of chronicle of our own Russian life together.

'We've just moved into the Akademicheskaya Hotel 2, winter 1989 …'

'God almighty, Jesus …' She was speaking Dutch, and it was pretty plain at that, '… have you only got that far? You still have to cover a quarter of a century!'

I promised my wife that I'd get a move on. The tram curved around a slight bend; it drove stiff and gnashing along the Clean Ponds, where there was a hive of activity on the ice under the strings of white lights. On the other side was a pavilion. The café rested partly on poles in the pond, and in the summer was surrounded by pleasure boats, and now by swarms of skaters. There were a lot of people inside. I'd often eaten and drunk there myself, in the company of Russian friends and colleagues from the fatherland gutter press that I no longer associated with. There were few people left who I trusted. In the event of emergency, I had no one I could call on. I'd have to get by on my own, together with my wife. That thought was liberating.

'You sound a bit down,' Julia sighed.

'Oh, no, everything's going fine!'

The conversation that I'd have a little later with the descendant of a pre-revolutionary statesman actually turned out to be material for a novella. I could only use five hundred words of it in the paper.

I sent the interview to Amsterdam, and that afternoon continued with my book, contrary to my custom — I can actually only write early in the morning, whether I have a hangover or not.

But I had to get my skates on and cover some distance.

When I look back on my years as a businessman now, in what was still communist Moscow, I mostly feel overwhelmed by a sense of guilt. Guilt towards my wife.

I was always travelling, leaving Julia behind in the miserable double hotel room with its view over the square that was wrapped almost every day in a bleak wintry mist, with the towering statue of Lenin; abandoned to the restaurant with the awful *boeuf stroganoff* on the menu, and conmen constantly in the lobby, as well as women for sale and suspect characters. At the Intersoviet Consultancy, she took care of the faxes that came in, as well as telephone calls and other business that needed to be dealt with. After a while, she had Swindleman on the line from The Hague more often than me. Meanwhile, I was travelling around a Soviet Empire that was shaking to its foundations, in search of possible lucrative deals, which took me to every corner of the country.

In Kazan, I was introduced by a Moscow contact to a Tatar in an impeccable black suit, with a purple calotte on his bald head, a grey goatee, and emerald eyes that seemed to spew fire. He was the import king of the Tatar capital and seemed to be interested in everything. Full of pride, he talked of how the first mosques were slowly beginning to reclaim their old role. Just like many orthodox Russian churches, they had served for seventy years as storage barns for grain or tractors, or simply remained empty. The beads of his rosary ticked with each word. As soon as the conversation turned to hard cash, he opened his flaccid mouth with an obtuse smile, and showed off his completely rotten teeth, with one golden canine, then burred the magic word of those times: *barter*. Hard cash? He only did business on the basis of trade. For ten thousand pairs of American jeans, he was prepared to deliver tons of locally sourced crude oil, lumber, copper, scrap, whatever I wanted. When he asked if I could transport a container full of French red and white wine to Kazan each month, in exchange for an unlimited supply of tender Tatar beauties to work as dancers in the Amsterdam nightlife circuit, I got out of there as fast as I could.

Most of my efforts came to nothing. I tried to dismiss as best I could the thought of the pointlessness of my gruelling activities — pointless except that they were focused on earning money. I hardly ever read a book, had no time to go to the theatre, was more often away from Julia and for longer periods. The deal with the Audis went ahead, even though the number dropped from sixty to forty at the last moment. The cars were delivered to a factory site somewhere outside Moscow on three trailers with Polish licence plates. Swindleman faxed me a couple of hours before to say that the money had been deposited in his bank account via letter of credit. We'd made more than a hundred grand profit in US dollars. To celebrate, he immediately went off to Paris for three days with one of the receptionists from the office on Javastraat.

The treatment for his jaundice was going well.

The licensed trips were earning us a few thousand dollars a month, but the real money was coming increasingly via incidental trade. I resumed my association with Pozorski, who took me out for dinner twice a week, and our future collaboration began to take shape.

'Flowers!' he suddenly said one evening over a glass of beer. 'Do you know how crazy Russian women are for flowers? People in this country will go on spending their last rubles on flowers, chocolate, and sex.'

We were going to set up an import line between the Dutch bulb fields and Russia for freshly cut flowers; as early as next spring, the first tulips were to leave for Moscow in specially refrigerated vehicles.

I kept my partner abreast of the plan. Swindleman was ecstatic.

Meanwhile, ominous rumblings went on behind the scenes. The immense poverty and the constant scarcities that I came across in Moscow, and on my trips, sometimes literally made me sick. The number of *bomzhi*, homeless, drunks, the mentally ill, wretches who no longer had any shelter because of the collapsed bureaucracy, increased by the day. They were moved on by the militia like beasts. By night, they crept like vermin away from the freezing cold towards the hot-water pipes that ran across the street in many places. Their mournful appearance was the contemporary echo of the *Bezprizorni*, familiar to Moscow in the 1920s and 30s, the clusters of street children whose parents were caught up in the terror and the collectivisation of agriculture by Stalin, and who had come to the city hidden in train carriages, on ships, or simply by walking. There, dressed in rags and often literally black with filth, the children formed street gangs, lived by begging, theft, armed muggings, and even murder, while they prostituted themselves *en masse* — there were child brothels then — until in 1936, they suddenly disappeared, into homes where, according to some, the conditions were better than if their parents had remained alive, but according to others, they were mistreated, exploited, raped or murdered by thugs.

———

The first business group — the thirty bankers, which Baldwin Borger had arranged for the start of March — was an unparalleled success. Although the Soviet Union still didn't have bankers in the literal sense, I'd organised activities like a meeting with high officials from a number of Soviet ministries that Pozorski had arranged for me. These officials had already long been secretly in business for themselves behind their desks and literally hurled themselves around my neck in gratitude because I had brought them into direct contact with key figures from the world that they one day hoped to belong to: the international banking class. There was also a meeting with students of economics and history, as well as a visit to a bathhouse, where all the gentlemen got so drunk that when the parade of half-naked girls began, they surrendered themselves one after another, led by quivering pinkies to alcoves behind greasy red curtains.

The four grand per person that Swindleman and Borger had added to the cost of the trip didn't pose a problem at all; the employers paid the sum for each participant and deducted it as a business expense. By and large, the tax office paid. Of the hundred and twenty thousand guilders gross profit, half went to Baldwin Borger. The golden egg that he'd once promised me was now starting to hatch. A couple of days after the trip, I had to listen to Swindleman cursing our Hague business partner over the phone for fifteen minutes. In his eyes, Borger had done nothing for that 50 per cent; in essence, we'd done all the work.

'But he does let us have a free office in his building in return, right?' I said in reply. 'What's more, that's what we agreed.'

'That's not the point!' Swindleman sputtered. 'Anyway, let's just goddamned leave it. What do you even know about business?'

For several weeks, the money had been pouring into The Hague, but I hadn't actually seen any of it myself yet. I was living off what I'd earned in the year and a half before, from my activities as a glorified tour guide. And we didn't need much. The hotel of the Academy of Sciences was almost free, there wasn't anything to buy in the city, and what's more, we didn't have any time to spend any money anyway.

When it was Julia's birthday at the end of April 1990, I took her to the one and only pizza restaurant in Russia, which had only been open in the city for a little while. I'd just closed a deal to export Russian lumber to Antwerp, which would yield our business at least another hundred thousand guilders. Among the newspaper reports of the threat of war in the Caucasus, and the growing disharmony in the Communist Party, there was also widespread attention for the western phenomenon of this very first pizzeria.

The restaurant was located at the head of Kutuzovsky Prospect, not far from the town house of the former Party leader Leonid Brezhnev. Because you could only pay in dollars, a visit to the pizzeria was a fantasy for the more than twelve million inhabitants of the city, apart from a wafer-thin sliver of corrupt officials, black market dealers, and Mafiosi, who set the tone with the always-heavily-made-up girls around them. There was a whole platoon of security guards at the door. The hyper-capitalist establishment, where Coca-Cola 'flowed from the tap like water' (as an astonished journalist from *Pravda* wrote), was chock-a-block day and night.

In that cold spring of 1990, Julia ate pizza for the first time in her life, and for the first time drank foreign wine. She got so tipsy from those two glasses of *pinot grigio* that at one point she began quoting a poem by Slauerhoff in Dutch, which she'd found in a book she'd picked up somewhere a little while before and then learned word for word by heart. Proud and full of glowing love, I looked on adoringly as she spooned up her tiramisu.

Everything was fleeting. This exhausting, crazy life here was temporary too. Should I tell her now? The secret that I was carrying, but which I'd never spoken about? How I couldn't care less about business, about earning money? That in essence I wasn't suited for it, and I'd only ended up in this business by chance, but that I had an absolute aversion to the telephone calls, the faxes, the travelling, and the negotiating of contracts. That there was always one thing in the background that really grabbed at me: literature, the urge to create something. Meanwhile, I was already twenty-eight and not only had I not published a single word but I had never actually written anything either. I decided to continue my work for Intersoviet Consultancy for the time being, just long enough to save the money to be able to live freely with Julia somewhere, for at least a couple of years. I'd write my first novel in peace and quiet, then a stream of books would follow, even if I had no idea what they'd be about.

'I'd like another glass of that lovely wine ...' Julia said, with a mischief that I'd never seen before.

Just then, a group of proles invaded: the lowest rung of the capital's extortion guild, in sky-blue tracksuits, the bulges from their knuckledusters and pistols next to the bulges from their dicks.

I quickly asked for the bill, paid, and as we were driving back to the hotel in a Volga that had been waiting outside the door, Julia whispered that she definitely wanted to have some champagne in a little while.

'What kind?'

'Sweet! So delicious with the taste of the tiramisu in my mouth!'

'Of course, sweetheart, *dorogaya*, even if you want a bath full.'

Julia took the lift upstairs right away. I went up to the restaurant manager and placed an order: ten cases of sweet Kornet. That would have cost thirty-six old Dutch guilders, converted from black rubles. To speed things up, I slipped the Russian a twenty-dollar bill. Two men in overalls delivered ten cases of twelve bottles of Soviet champagne to our room a little later, as though it was the most normal thing in the world. When I told Julia what I was planning, she pulled me under the shower with a whoop of joy. Then she carefully cleaned the bathtub with scalding water, and wiped the pink enamel dry with a pillow case. Meanwhile, I'd begun getting our blowout ready in the smaller room. Slowly but steadily, the bathtub filled with the sparkling gold liquid. As it did, my girlfriend and I took slugs of the sweet Soviet bubbles, before lowering ourselves into the bath one at a time, hooting and naked.

The next morning, I was woken by the phone at around ten; it was the receptionist downstairs in the lobby, who told me that something had been delivered for me. It turned out to be a letter from my mother, in an envelope that was covered with photos of our queen.

*Zandvoort, 11 March 1990*

*My dear boy,*
*This is a letter from your mother. How are you, my son, over there in faraway Russia? Is it still as cold there? I*

*think of you so often and I always think, why does our boy have to live in that filthy, faraway country, why doesn't he just get a nice job in an office here? That's what you studied for? I really don't understand it.*

*Your father's doing well now. How is that possible? I think God heard my prayers, because even if I only still go to church at Christmas, Our Dear Lord most certainly exists and He wants the best for us, even if I don't understand why there's still so much rottenness in the world. But Papa's almost back to his old self, who'd have thought it? He only has to go to the hospital once a month now for a check-up, on the bus and the train because they won't pay for the taxi any more. I always go with him, and afterwards we have a coffee in the lobby downstairs with a chocolate éclair or a sausage roll. We make a real outing of it. He does often have trouble with a dry mouth — he has this stuff in a syringe for it — and swallowing is still a bit difficult too, because they've cut out one thing and another. I'm actually writing to you about the following though: you'll see that I've put a one-hundred guilder note in the envelope, and I hope it gets to you okay and isn't lost or stolen on the way.*

*Why the money? This is why: You'll remember Theo Veen, yes? He was in service with us, just after the war. He and your grandfather delivered newspapers together during the war, and when he still hadn't found any work two years after those terrible times, your grandfather took him into his service. First in the auction room, and later in the restaurant too, as a jack-of-all-trades, so to speak. It was a long time before you were born. I see him in the village almost every day passing by on the bike, but I had no idea that he'd been married to this Russian woman for a while, one Sima. When I bumped into them together earlier this week and told them (the wife already speaks decent Dutch) that I have a son in Russia, in Moscow, she looked at me shocked, and her face turned pale. They walked straight on. But later in the week, Theo rang the doorbell. He told me that his wife was still afraid, that she naturally didn't know me and she was startled by what I'd said. Even here in a little Dutch coastal town, Theo said, it appeared that the Soviet Union wasn't far away! Then he gave me that hundred guilders and asked me to send it to you by signed delivery, because Sima apparently has a sister in Moscow, or a half-sister — I didn't quite understand it. I'll write her address in Moscow at the bottom of the letter in a moment. Could you give the money to her? Sending it to her directly isn't possible for some reason, or it's too dangerous for her. It seems the sister is having a hard time of it. I see pictures of Russia on the TV every now and then, and I think, what an awful world this is and why must my son stay in that filthy land so far away, of all places. Maybe you'd like to give a little extra to that woman yourself, a hundred guilders maybe, and you'll get the money back later from your father and mother.*

*When will you give us a call again, my boy? We always appreciate it so much every time you phone. I know it's expensive, but it means so much to us. It's nearly mid-March again, the bulldozers on the beach have done their work and the pavilions are open again. It was warm*

217

*weather last Sunday; the terraces were full. We're getting*
*towards summer, which is always a good sign in life. Will*
*you phone again soon? A big kiss from me, and from your*
*father too.*

    *Your mother*


*P.S.: Oh yes, I've also put a photo in of Theo and his wife.*
*Could you give that to her sister in Moscow too?*


It had taken a month and a half for that epistle to get here. The fact
that the money had arrived at all was a miracle: in the bureaucratic
anarchy that had broken out, postal workers opened international
letters and packages wholesale, to see if there was anything inside
worth stealing.

    That same afternoon, Julia and I took the metro to the Riga
Station; the street that my mother had given me the address for was
just behind it. Over these last few days, the cold had disappeared
from the air, and nature had exploded. It was beautiful, mild
Russian spring weather.

    The person we were looking for was called Rena. My mother
hadn't written down a telephone number, but perhaps this
woman didn't have a phone, like many Russians at that time. The
courtyard where she lived, with its three Khrushchev flats, looked
as though a heavy battle had just been fought there. The brick walls
were blackened. The drainpipes and gutters were hanging loose
and rusted, totally buckled. Two homeless men with bags were
grubbing around in search of empty bottles for the deposits, under
the chestnut trees that were already adorned with soft, green leaves.
On the way, we'd passed a state shop for MEAT, with the usual
long queue outside with people swearing loudly and shoving each

other, until a Russian woman in a bloody white blouse stormed out and began to yell like a dockworker that everyone should clear off, that the stock of pork had run out, that maybe a shipment of mince would be delivered next Tuesday from Belarus. But everyone stayed standing there out of fatalistic exhaustion, or simply because they didn't believe her.

We didn't have the door code either. I just pressed 4, the apartment number written in the letter. We heard a weak, faint voice through the intercom, '*Kto tam?* Who's there?'

We told her who we were.

'How do I know you're telling the truth?'

Julia took over the conversation, and a moment later the lock of the steel front door opened with a dry click. We climbed the stairs of a remarkably clean portico. Everywhere, there was the penetrating scent of recently sprayed insecticide — spring was the time to attack vermin. On the third floor was a woman over sixty years of age, with a flushed face, short grey hair, and kindly greyish-blue eyes, waiting for us in the doorway. 'Did Sima send you? Oh, I'm so happy ... I haven't heard anything from her for ages. I haven't any idea how she's doing. Come in, come in ... Here are the slippers, I have them in all sorts and sizes ... Sima is afraid that she'll cause me trouble if she writes or phones me here ... I don't think she has any idea of how fast things are changing ... Come in, dear children ... My goodness, I suddenly have youngsters in my home ... Julia, you said? And Pieter? What lovely names, sit down, my treasures, I'll make tea ... I even have a little sugar ... You can't get anything in the shops around here anymore ... nothing at all, but I always have sugar ... Without sugar, I wouldn't want to live ...'

We put on our slippers and went in.

'Doesn't she look lovely …' Shaking her head in amazement, the Russian woman looked at the photo that I'd given her of her sister and her husband, taken through the hollow tree outside the *Kraantje Lek* restaurant in Overveen. 'That dress makes her look like a young girl!'

Then from one moment to the next, the woman grew unwell. She turned entirely pale, began to sweat and to tremble, mumbling that there was something the matter, that she often had this, but asked us to leave quickly, she had to lie down straight away. Before we knew it, we were standing outside again and I'd plumb forgotten to give her the money we'd brought. We did leave our telephone number though.

Two days later, on 1 May, International Workers' Day, it was such warm, bright weather that it seemed as though Lenin Prospect, which I looked out on from behind my desk in the hotel room, wasn't in the centre of Moscow at all, but somewhere in Malaga, Jakarta or Rio de Janeiro. I opened the windows wide. The golden church domes in the distance were in a permanent conclave with the sun. Everywhere in the gentle breeze, light red flags fluttered. Lorries with loudspeakers on their roofs drove by to wish the people a happy holiday.

Julia had suggested going to Red Square to watch the parade. But because I still had to finish some work, we stayed home. A little while later, we switched on our black-and-white TV to see the live pictures of the events that were taking place about three kilometres away.

As was tradition, workers with banners were filing past our country's leaders, who were standing atop Lenin's tomb. Given the tense situation in Leningrad, the authorities in that city, worried about disturbances, had cancelled the entire event. But of course, the capital Moscow couldn't lose face. Gorbachev stood among his loyal comrades, as of old, looking slightly bored as he surveyed the workers' parade, as though it were his daily routine. Every now and then he raised a chubby hand with a smile, the May sun glittering on his bald, birth-marked skull. But, for the first time in more than seven decades, the Kremlin didn't seem to have total control. There was a fear in the corridors of Soviet power of the wrath of the vulgus, the crowd, who had paid the price for the reforms of these last few years; this fear was now perhaps as great as it had been among the czarist elite just before 1917.

Instead of the usual slogans, like OUR ATOMIC MISSILES WILL HIT EVERY TARGET IN EUROPE! or LONG LIVE THE LEGACY OF LENIN! and SOVIET POWER WILL CONQUER ALL!, banners bearing messages such as DOWN WITH PRIVATE PROPERTY! and NO MORE EXPERIMENTS! and WE DON'T WANT A MARKET ECONOMY! were held aloft by steelworkers, miners, and others whose lives over the last few years had become sheer hell. A direct slap in the face of the father of perestroika and glasnost. But Gorbachev remained stoical, calm, composed, as always. Even when something happened that no one could have thought possible: a group of demonstrators came marching up in formation from the direction of the Alexander Garden and the red-brick building of the Historical Museum to further interrupt the parade.

Julia looked on from her chair in silence, grumbling occasionally. I'd stopped my work.

Red Square was being stormed by a sort of vexillological resistance, which transformed it into a battlefield of flags, with people holding up the red, yellow, and green Lithuanian tricolour and the black, blue, and white national flag of Estonia to the apparatchiks who were wreathed in red Soviet banners. The parade in front of the Lenin mausoleum took on quite a macabre character when placards appeared that didn't just call for a change of direction by the current regime, but for its revolutionary end, stating COMMUNISTS, YOUR DAYS ARE NUMBERED! and DOWN WITH THE POLITBURO! As well as MARXISM-LENINISM IS ON THE DUNG-HEAP OF HISTORY!

'*Bozhe moi*, good God...' Julia sat half upright in her chair, watching the bizarre scenes with anxious eyes. 'Do you realise what's going on?'

That afternoon, Rena called, just as we were about to head out of the door to see if there was anything for us to do — maybe some stalls in Gorky Park with food or drink. She was in a public phone-booth close to Riga Station. She apologised for her abruptness two days earlier and insisted that we visit her at seven o'clock that evening.

'I despise everything communist, but after all it is a holiday,' she said.

I remember as though it were yesterday the second meeting with this kind-hearted Russian woman in her shabby, thirty-five-square-metre apartment. The wooden table in the cramped kitchen was chock-a-block with all sorts of snacks, which she'd clearly denied herself, and there was also a bottle of yellow liquid: home-made advocaat, deliciously sweet and mixed with vodka.

Once again, she was a waterfall of words. Her chattiness, I'd soon learn, was not only because she had a lonely life without a husband or children, and barely any interaction with family; it was also compensation for a life mostly lived in fearful silence. Despite their thirty-year age difference, Julia and Rena were soon talking as though they were sisters. Rena had last gone to the May Day parade when she was a child, and she didn't have a TV. She was entirely oblivious to the dramatic events that had unfolded on Red Square a couple of hours earlier. She had been hunting all day for a cut of beef, which she'd lightly seared, and now served in cold slices with horseradish and dill. When Rena laid home-preserved chanterelles on our plates, in clouds of vinegar and garlic, the women began a discourse on the joys of mushroom hunting, while I concentrated on the hip flask of Armenian cognac that our hostess had taken out of the cupboard especially for me. In the blackened courtyard, the birds in the chestnut trees were ranting like lunatics. After about four glasses, the cognac made me feel delightfully relaxed, and I almost dozed off; the life story of this red-faced Russian lady came through to me in snippets.

Rena's half-sister Sima was seven years older, and had left for the Netherlands permanently a year and a half previously. Their mother had been born in 1896 in a Ukrainian town on the Dnieper, the eldest daughter in a big, poor Jewish family. A worker in a tobacco factory, who rolled cigarettes for ten hours a day, she soon joined the Bolsheviks. When the civil war broke out after the revolution of 1917, she smuggled Lenin's brother, Dmitri Ulyanov, over the border from Kiev to safe territory. In the 1930s, Rena, her half-sister and their mother had lived for a while in the Uzbek capital of Tashkent, where her father — Sima's stepfather — had been offered a job as a commercial director in the recently opened big department store. In spite of the poor circumstances in which they lived there too, as a child she'd enjoyed the sight of the camels, the woven carpets, the warm weather and the fresh fruit, which you couldn't find anywhere in Moscow at that time. But from one day to the next it was over. The family had to return to Moscow, where Rena's father was arrested by the KGB and disappeared into prison and later to a penal camp. He would never return. During the war, the three women left Moscow for the industrial city of Sverdlovsk in the Urals, after which the two sisters undertook dangerous quests together in search of food, while their mother continued to work half illegally in a factory and look after the baby that Sima had borne to a soldier when she was nineteen, who had left for the front.

Julia sat there listening quietly, as she slowly and mechanically chewed on pieces of black bread. Suddenly, she said to me in Dutch that she desperately needed to go to the toilet.

'There, on the right in the passage,' Rena said almost without hesitation in Dutch, with a slight German accent.

My girlfriend and I looked at each other in astonishment.

'Yes, I can still speak a few words of Dutch …' Rena continued in Russian with a shy smile. 'After all, my dear father came from Amsterdam …'

As if by magic, I woke from my alcoholic slumbers. Idiot that I was! Why hadn't I realised this sooner? I'd been aware of the existence of the woman opposite me for years. I could remember as clear as day, almost word for word, a piece I'd read the newspaper about Dutch people who'd worked for the Russian secret service. The author remembered one day in 1936 when the Dutch communist Jef Swart was playing with two girls. 'Jef was on the street,' he relates, 'giving a demonstration of what girls call "yo-yo-ing" by one leg: he held each of them upside down by one of their legs and yo-yoed them. The girls loved it.'

And now, fifty-four years later, in a Moscow kitchen, one of those girls was sitting opposite me. Her half-sister Sima was the daughter of perhaps the greatest revolutionary the Netherlands has ever known: Henk Sneevliet, one of the instigators of the Jordaan revolt, the only rebellion against the authorities in the Netherlands, where the proletariat fought for two days on barricades decked with red flags against the army, as they once had done in the city of Petrograd, leaving seven dead and two hundred wounded. When I asked Rena if she was indeed the daughter of Jef Swart, the man who'd run a shabby stationer's shop on Warmoesstraat in Amsterdam before the war, as a cover for his activities as a secret agent for Russia, who then disappeared almost without trace a few years later in Stalin's meat-grinder, Rena looked at us in astonishment. Of course, but we knew that, didn't we? Hadn't her sister told anyone in the Netherlands?

If anyone had told me at that moment that this woman, whose mother had once smuggled Lenin's brother across the border to safety, would later stand beside both of my parents' coffins in turn with tears in her eyes, I would have thought they were mad.

Although the law of chance may be predominant as a rule, the law of preposterousness trumps all, of course.

# CHAPTER NINE

The summer of 1990 was one of the happiest of my life. I spent it mostly in and around Moscow, with a few trips to Leningrad by night-train, partly to get to know Julia's parents.

Despite the ongoing impoverishment and increasing political chaos in the country, I was acquiring more and more of a knack for business. One success after another followed. I was in love, my father was almost completely healthy again; if everything carried on the way it was, I'd have earned enough money by the end of the year to take Julia to Europe, to write my first book there in peace, and at the same time to think about the future.

But things would all turn out differently.

I hadn't seen the two academics from Novosibirsk for months, but from May onwards, they were almost permanently in Moscow because of their tomograph project. Both of them had their own suite in my hotel, on the upper floor. The million Deutschmarks from Germany were now within reach. All the formalities had been met. The application had been submitted, supported by concocted research reports, recommendations, prognoses, a stack of paper at least half a metre high, covered in signatures and stamps that the gentlemen, as masters at their university, had manufactured themselves. I'd taken it in portions to the German embassy, in big

brown envelopes, where I was always given a receipt, and likewise
a stamp.

Because I was able to live in my hotel room for a song thanks
to them, Khinshtein and Trofimov made endless demands on me.
One morning a report had to be hurriedly translated from Russian
to German; it was more concocted evidence, where the gentlemen
explained that the tomograph was needed very urgently in Siberia
to investigate special neurological and bone abnormalities that
appeared primarily in children, although the cause was unknown.

After Julia had translated the piece, slaving in a nine-hour
session, and Khinshtein had then more or less yanked it out of her
hands without the least thank you, let alone any payment, she had
a sort of mental breakdown for the first time. Who were these two
frauds? Why did I surround myself with these types? How long
were we going to stay in this hotel full of drunks and whores? What
sort of life was this? She'd studied for years; she was determined
to get her doctorate on the German baroque, but meanwhile she
was sitting here behind a desk for days on end, and now she had
to translate fairy-tales from wooden Russian, written by a pair of
charlatans. However poorly and miserably she may have lived in
Leningrad, she was increasingly homesick for her books, her piano,
and her bed.

'What else are you planning to do? That Pozorski phoned me
again yesterday afternoon. I didn't want to tell you, but he does
that quite often. One time, he even invited me to a restaurant.
When I told him I loved you, he said, "But he doesn't need to
know anything about it, does he?" Yesterday, he had to speak to
you come what may, but when I told him you were out of the city,
and there's no such thing in the world as a telephone to call people
remotely, he started raving at me. He called me a *cyka*, a bitch

... He sounded pretty tense ... Strange that he hasn't called back again today. I wouldn't trust that Pozorski for a kopek, him with his pretty face. How do you know him anyway? I bet he's an old friend of your partner Swindleman?'

I'd always kept this close to my chest out of embarrassment; only now I told her that Pozorski had been my contact a year and a half ago in Leningrad for my smuggled bibles.

'Smuggled bibles?'

I briefly explained my history with Siderius.

'Oh, and what else are you keeping from me?'

'Actually ...' I replied, talking over her, 'I only ended up here in the Soviet Union through the word of God. Otherwise, we'd never have met. We've been brought together by faith.'

Julia mumbled something, dissatisfied that I hadn't given her an acceptable answer. Then I came clean about my plans, how I'd slowly got tired of this life here too, that I would soon have earned enough money to get by for a couple of years, and to write somewhere in peace.

'Write? Are you a writer then?'


From the beginning of June, it was almost unbearably hot. As soon as the opportunity arose, we left the city by *elektrichka*, one of the hundreds of often still coal-powered slow trains — with wooden benches inside; the comfort of the turn of the century — that conveyed travellers away from the concrete misery, the exhaust fumes and the ever-present scarcities, to the blooming countryside that seemed to pay no heed to the human crisis, with its blue ribbons of clear, babbling brooks, sun-seared, birch-green canopies, and the singing of nightingales. The gardens produced an abundance of strawberries that were sold along the side of the road. The Russian strawberries were small, dark-red, black-speckled and honey-sweet. We rinsed them off in the brooks and devoured them by the kilo to banish winter from our bodies for good.

Julia was sorry that we couldn't cook in our room. Each year, she made strawberry jam — the pink froth that was produced when she was making it was the tastiest — and then spoon the jam into jars to preserve it.

Sometimes we'd stay somewhere overnight, amid the cacophony of the wakening woods, where woodpeckers were hacking at tree-trunks with their drilling beaks, and owls with their bass voices proved themselves to be the rulers of the forest, and one morning — in a hut that we'd come across deserted the day before — two young deer were ogling us, their big-eyed faces curious and astonished.

When we got back to our hotel room in Moscow, the new faxes were lying in waves of paper on the floor. Once, after I'd been unreachable for three days — because Julia and I had gone back to the cloister in Suzdal where we'd made love for the first time — Swindleman got so angry that he ended up hanging up on me. Ten minutes later, a fax arrived where he'd scribbled in his tiny, curt, and almost illegible handwriting that I wasn't in Moscow on holiday, that the whole point was for us to get cracking now, and that he was expecting new initiatives from me. He stated that he'd be back in Moscow from 1 October. We'd trade places. He'd move into Akademicheskaya Hotel 2, and I could take over the work on Javastraat.

We had a third business-sector trip at the start of August. The second one at the end of June had been something of a commercial disappointment – the thirty doctors that Baldwin Borger had assembled had quibbled over the price at the very last moment. Still, we made fifty thousand guilders gross profit from them.

This time, it was a bull's eye though, just like the first. The thirty *captains of industry* — from soap giants to dredgers, from rich ship-owners to wealthy chicken farmers — paid the four thousand guilders on top of the cost-price with no complaints. In return, they got an itinerary in which I'd even arranged a meeting with an advisor to the rising Boris Yeltsin ('If Borya comes to power, gentlemen, you'll be able to earn billions of dollars in this country! I'll give each of you my calling card in a moment!'), and once again Swindleman began bellyaching that the 50 per cent commission that Borger took for drawing up a simple list of participants was way too much.

When I told my partner on the phone a week later that the savings I'd lived on so far were almost gone, and I'd like my share of our joint earnings, Swindleman asked why I hadn't mentioned it earlier. But, of course, he'd arrange it right away! The next morning, a Russian friend of his was at my hotel door, handing me an envelope — with Swindleman's compliments — containing fifty thousand dollars. I exchanged five hundred of them for black market rubles, took the rest of the day off, and dragged Julia along to a couple of cooperative shops that had just opened, where they sold nice fashionable clothes. She kept on the dress and pumps that she eventually chose, after endless prevarication; then she stuffed her old clothes and shoes in a plastic bag. That evening we again ate in the pizza restaurant on Kutuzovsky Prospect. The windows were wide open to the almost subtropical evening air, and when we drove back home, with the warm breeze blowing into the taxi, I told Julia that I'd be going back to the Netherlands in October, that I still didn't know what I was going to do — man the office in The Hague, or write my first book — but that we'd have to set a few things in motion, the most important of which was obtaining a visa for her, of course.

'But how do you do that?' Julia was so nervous and agitated at what I'd said that she began to stutter.

'You just wait, I'll sort it out …'

The next morning, I went to the Dutch embassy in Moscow for the first time; it was a former minor city palace in yellow-ochre tints, a place where I would often come later, where I would live out a couple of the most beautiful moments of my life, but which now seemed like an impregnable fortress.

The guard at the door wouldn't let me in. When I told him why I'd come, he grunted that I was in the wrong place, that all visa requests had been transferred to the Bolshaya Ordynka, on the other side of the city centre, across the river.

'Is it a visa for a Jew?'

'What do you mean?' I asked.

'Go to the Bolshaya Ordynka,' the guard said swiftly, and he told me the house number. 'You'll be able to find it when you get there.'

I took a taxi, which drove over the Stone Bridge, with the Kremlin to my left, and then stopped a little later in front of a building with a Dutch flag hanging limply from the façade. The street out front was a hive of activity. They were selling books from stalls, like many places in the city now. As well as the increasingly obscure anti-Semitic publications, and opposition papers that probed those in power, the kiosks sold all sorts of hurriedly translated pulp fiction, soft-porn junk, and books with titles like *How I Became a Millionaire in Six Months, How Do You Find Work in the United States?* and *ABC for the Emigrant to Europe.* Here were *The Blessings of the Promised Land* and *Introduction to the Jewish Laws of Kashrut* and *Myths and Truth of the Palestinian Terror.* A year and a half before, when I'd been dragged out of my bed in my hotel room in Bukhara by three Uzbek cops in their green linen suits and made to undress right down to my genitals, I'd thought that the elder of the three was only spouting anti-Semitic nonsense when he accused me of being a spy. But it turned out to be true that the Dutch were helping Jews escape the Soviet Union; Israel didn't have its own embassy in Moscow, and for some reason, the Dutch consulate had taken on the responsibility.

After waiting in the queue forever, and then to my delight hearing a couple of old men with intense, white faces and ruddy beards speaking in sing-song Yiddish, it was finally my turn to be served; a Russian-speaking woman asked me cattily if I was here for a visa for a Jewish Soviet citizen.

'No,' I answered, still unaware that this wasn't entirely the truth. 'For an ordinary Russian woman.'

My accent betrayed me.

The woman disappeared into the back. A few seconds later, a bald Dutch man of around 30 approached me in a blue blazer. He looked at me with self-assurance, introduced himself, and began to tell me that in the year and a half he'd been here, he'd seen a number of men leave for the west with a Russian woman, and in many cases it had gone badly. Did I know what I was getting myself into after what had presumably been a very agreeable holiday here? The man even dared to give me a wink. Many Russian women were out to get their hooks into a foreigner. Once they were in Europe, the misery usually began. I was so shocked by his rude remarks, so completely stunned, that I didn't respond to what he was saying, but calmly repeated the question of what formalities I needed to satisfy to obtain a six-month visa for my girlfriend.

'Fine, I'll pass you back to my assistant,' the diplomat replied, clearly piqued, as his high-born jaw muscles tensed. 'She'll arrange things further. Good day.'

The Russian woman behind the counter had caught a whiff of her boss's displeasure. She immediately realised she had *carte blanche* to make things as difficult as possible for me, and her tone switched to the most cutting setting as she informed me that I'd first have to come back tomorrow with my partner and the necessary documentation — she gave me a photocopied list — and, as though I'd suddenly turned to air, she turned to the person behind me in the queue. When Julia and I were at the consulate again the next morning, the diplomat didn't put in an appearance, and after the assistant had cast a quick glance over the papers, she announced that she couldn't possibly accept Madam's application for a visa to the Kingdom of the Netherlands because she was still married to a Russian.

'My girlfriend is a widow,' I said.

'It says here she's married.'

While Julia was standing next to me as quiet as a mouse, barely even daring to breathe, almost genetically programmed to be terrified of everything to do with the authorities, I explained that her husband had been in an accident three years earlier, and that his body had never been found.

'Then I would like a death certificate ... Sir, come back as soon as you have one ... Next, please ...'

Julia was officially registered in Leningrad. That same day, we took the night train there and arrived utterly exhausted. We picked up her birth certificate from her pigeon-coop apartment on Vasilyevsky Island, along with her workbook and other necessary papers, after which something happened that I can't explain. Because there was no telephone book, as in all Soviet cities, Julia called a girlfriend to ask if she knew of a good notary — and of the thousands of notaries that the city was rich with, we found ourselves thirty minutes later in front of the gate to a notary's office on Tchaikovsky Street, sixty metres away from the house that we'd move into fifteen years later.

'A death certificate?' The notary, by the name of Wainstein, was a little guy with an Adam's apple covered in stiff orange bristles, which made it look like there was an unknown tropical fruit sprouting on his throat. He looked at us indignantly from his chair which was upholstered with worn green leather. 'Madam, you do know that we are here to apply the law, not to violate it?'

When we explained the case, the lawyer nodded. He bared his teeth, slowly pressed all ten of his opal fingertips together, and named a price. That very same day, we took the night train back to Moscow, in possession of the necessary document.

Julia's first husband was now dead on paper too. And she was officially a widow.

The million Deutschmarks for the Siberian academics came earlier than expected. At the end of July, Khinshtein and Trofimov left for six days in Bonn, Berlin, and the beautiful Bavarian capital of Munich, where they became acquainted for the first time with wheat beer and decided on the spot never to drink anything else for the rest of their lives.

They opened a bank account there, as the subsidy could only be paid by Giro deposit. The German authorities wanted to avoid any appearance of promoting their own economy, so the gentlemen could freely decide where they bought the tomograph. It could be in Germany — the Federal Republic had an excellent reputation in the field of medical equipment — but also in the United States, Japan, or any other country. The million Deutschmarks was a gift from the German authorities to the Russian people, to the Soviet country that was going through such a difficult time at that moment, and even though the word *Wiedergutmachung*, or reparation, was scrupulously avoided, Khinshtein knew, with his Jewish origins, that the benefactors were like beeswax in his hands. When he learned at the meeting with the committee in Bonn that the affair was almost entirely settled, but there were a few extra documents necessary to speedily arrange the definitive approval, the academic grew impatient and went for broke. He began to sob and hid his face behind his imposing Siberian fingers. While Trofimov looked on in silence, Khinshtein let it be known via the interpreter that his great-grandfather too — a doctor in a *shtetl* near Minsk — had had to look on helplessly as children died like insects in his hands because the czarist authorities had cut off their access to medicines. There'd been a glass partition between the Jews and the rest of the inhabitants of the Russian Empire. In the 1930s, just before the outbreak of the war, things were no different. Did people here realise how the fate of hundreds of children in Siberia, who were suffering from mysterious bone abnormalities and neurological complaints, was in their hands, because they needed immediate tomographic examination? Every month, every week, every day there was another. His own father — God save his soul — had lost a hand at the siege of Stalingrad by the Nazis, it was only because of ...

'*Agreed!*' the chairman of the subsidy commission sputtered. '*You will get our help immediately!*'

A week later, the money was in their Bavarian bank account.

While Trofimov told me the finer details of how his partner had conned the Germans, Khinshtein sniggered the whole time. In his youth, he hadn't been entirely without talent as a stage actor. Before he entered the faculty of natural sciences, he'd considered choosing the arts, but thank God he'd opted for science.

Since their triumph, the fortunate duo couldn't keep away from Moscow. They wore stylish foreign suits and their jawbones were smoother than ever. They invited their mistresses from Novosibirsk to come and stay at their suites. One morning, a black BMW with a chauffeur appeared at the door of our hotel and ferried the foursome through the city in an unending festive celebration. They'd picked up the flash car for a song. The family photo of the original chubby-cheeked German owner was still wiggling on a magnet on the dashboard, even after the car had been stolen and conveyed through the now porous east to Russia, and then illegally imported and traded on the black market. When I went to a restaurant with the two academics, Trofimov's blonde girlfriend tore off the magnet, opened the window and tossed it out with disgust.

One Sunday afternoon, Khinshtein had a monstrously big box of French chocolates delivered to Julia. That kind of thing cost a fortune in Moscow. My girlfriend would murder for chocolates but dropped them into the toilet one at a time with a splash, flushing a few times as she did so, grumbling how she didn't want to have anything to do with such frauds. In the meantime, it had become clear to us what kind of trick these two Siberians had pulled, now that they'd popped back to Novosibirsk for a few days. They'd managed to get hold of a cheap second-hand tomograph via a middleman, installed the equipment at their institute, and after the festive opening, they had sent photos to their subsidisers in Germany, and stuffed the rest of the tainted sum in their pockets.

Once again, they wanted me to arrange a visa for them to Spain. They were planning to spend three months on one of the Canary Islands with their ladies. And also, wasn't property ridiculously cheap there? Marta from the Spanish consulate had fled for good, but the visa application proceeded without a problem. The West was becoming ever more relaxed — people understood the possibilities of Russian tourism — although the icy lady at the Dutch consulate continued to make my life difficult. I had to produce a statement from the Netherlands that I had enough income for the definitive granting of a visa for Julia. When I was unable to produce that quickly enough, my parents had to act as guarantors for her; they lived off the tips that they'd hung onto after a life of drudgery, but the letter that they eventually sent was sufficient and the visa was to be issued. From mid-August on, Julia began counting down the days till we left Moscow. She hung a calendar on the wall, and early every morning, after ticking off each day, she sighed that time was passing so terribly slowly.

Swindleman kept peppering me with faxes, insisting that I come up with concrete proposals to get to grips with the tulip trade next year. Things weren't proceeding fast enough for him. He also wanted to move into artificial flowers: after a century of drabness in the Soviet Union, there was a demand for anything that yielded colour.

I was to be found regularly at the office of my old bible-smuggling contact, Pozorski, at the back of the KGB headquarters, where the workforce literally increased by the day. The underwear arm had moved and had now taken over an entire wing. A trial delivery of French *dessous* from Taiwan proved to be a huge success; it was a batch that Swindleman had picked up for a pittance at a closing-down sale in Rotterdam and half-illegally sent to Moscow concealed between the furniture in a removals lorry. They wanted more. Swindleman began faxing Taiwan, going directly to the source of the luxury lingerie.

Pozorski cautiously sounded me out as to whether my Dutch partner, given the reputation of Amsterdam, could browse around for adult toys. The people here were aching for such things, although he was always cautious about this: a guy in Rostov-on-Don was arrested recently with an overnight bag full of dildos, sentenced for violating the Soviet law of public morals, and then disappeared into the cells for three years. The capriciousness of the judges in the country was still immense, while the sudden wealth of the new elite made for bad blood with some Soviet officials who were caught in the straitjacket of ruble poverty and hadn't even had a sniff of the pleasures of the new age. However well-heeled and apparently untouchable someone seemed, the axe of jealousy, of revenge, could strike them just like that. Nobody was safe. The members of the brand-new club of ruble millionaires understood this. They were a group of people mostly in their twenties and thirties, some of whom were outright brilliant — even crazily so — and some of whom would hurt anyone that got in their way; the most successful were able to combine the best of both qualities. They hid their prosperous lifestyle as much as possible. Nevertheless, one of them had been picked up a couple of months earlier after he'd offended a militia commander in public in a restaurant (in his drunkenness, he had called him a poor Soviet fossil). The next evening, there was a police van in front of his house and he was taken away to a cell, where there was a sodomy case pinned on him — there were photos of his crime — while he was also charged with the offence of spreading STDs — the witness statement was ready and waiting — and the ruble millionaire disappeared off to Siberia for three years, where despite perestroika and glasnost, there were still more than a million people dying in the cramped barracks that were riven with TB and other diseases.

'We have to be careful in this country, comrade,' Pozorski added brightly from behind the orange sheen of his glasses. 'But if you don't take the risk, you don't drink the champagne.'

However head-over-heels in love I was, cohabiting in the two hotel rooms with my girlfriend sometimes felt claustrophobic. Now and then I needed solitude — to be able to think, to be able to function well. I often wandered alone through the city — which was as hot as an oven, where gritty dust scurried over the asphalt like volcanic sand, as though it were somewhere deep in southern Europe — abandoned to my meditations. I hadn't yet figured out what I was going to do with my life. Although I wasn't yet thirty, the lives of most of my friends in the Netherlands had already crystallised into something. Our youth had flitted by at an astonishing rate.

As I was wandering around Moscow, I was gripped by a sudden sadness that almost caused me physical pain. I'd grown attached to life in the Soviet Union, if not to say addicted. By now, I knew Leningrad and Moscow better than Amsterdam. The idea that my girlfriend and I would be leaving in a couple of weeks gave me an eerie sense of foreboding that I would perhaps never come back to this country. The shifting of the tectonic plates of history carried on inexorably. I'd witnessed it. Just like in an opera, the saga threatened to reach a dénouement. And now, of all times, I'd have to leave it all behind me and exchange it for an entirely uncertain future in the Netherlands.

Seven days before our departure, something happened that would bring my intense gloom to an end for quite a long time. At eleven o'clock in the morning, Pozorski called me to ask if he could meet me in an hour in the lobby of the Mezh.

'The *Mezh*?'

'The Mezhdunarodnaya, of course!' Pozorski was speaking in an anxious, almost tormented tone that I'd never heard from him before.

I said I already had an appointment at the Dutch consulate to pick up my girlfriend's visa, which had finally been issued.

'Damn your visa to hell! In the lobby of the Mezh in half an hour … I'll be sitting somewhere under the cuckoo clock.'

Hotel International, better known under the literal Russian translation Mezhdunarodnaya, had risen a few years earlier on the bank of the Moskva River, opposite the stone dripping-candle of the Hotel Ukraina from the 1950s. The immense lobby had the form of an inner courtyard and the gleaming glass lifts went up and down continuously like in an American film. The time travel that you experienced in Moscow that year was greater in this place than anywhere else. Men in tailored Italian suits walked by with diplomatic briefcases, held meetings, were already having an early lunch in one of the many restaurants, or having a nose around the little boutiques, where items were on sale that elsewhere in the country could now only be viewed in museums by a salivating public because of their exotic scarcity — these scarcities were becoming greater not by the day, but by the hour.

I'd taken Julia there once. We bought boots, then we ate *Eisbein* with *Sauerkraut* at the *Bierstube* on the second floor. '*Sauerkraut!*', she said in her almost perfect German, as though she hadn't been born in Leningrad but somewhere in Hamburg. 'Do you know that was the first word in German I learned? *Sauerkraut!* The second one was *Scheisse*, the third *Liebe* ...'

The seats directly below the cuckoo clock — which filled half a wall and was the hotel's showpiece — were all empty. Less than a minute after I'd sat down, a terribly refined gentleman of sixty with a green diplomatic briefcase came calmly walking towards me. His nut-coloured skull was evenly bald, he had a grey goatee and dark eyes, which had a warm, glowing expression.

'Mr Pozorski?' Before I could answer he'd already sat down next to me sedately. A gold watch rattled around his wrist, and he gave off a lemony scent with the odd whiff of nicotine.

I told the man that I wasn't Pozorski, but a friend of his, and that I was actually waiting for him.

'Ah, I understand,' the man said in English with an accent. 'Where's the merchandise?'

'The merchandise?'

At that moment, the gigantic cuckoo clock above our heads began to chime. The mechanical birdsong reverberated through the hall eleven times. Some people stopped still for a moment, including a slim woman and a girl toddler — obviously expats — who looked up at the spectacle, licking their ice-creams in delight.

It still hadn't ended when I heard my name paged over the intercom — like in an international airport.

'Telephone for Mr Waterdrinker. Please proceed to reception.'

I got up, gave a friendly nod to my exotic neighbour by way of goodbye and walked to the reception desk, where a girl was already holding up a telephone for me impatiently. It was Pozorski. He still sounded nervous, but a little less agitated than an hour ago. He asked if I was already there — fine, fine … — and told me that I had to ask at reception for a Tanya Panteleyeva. She was a friend of his. She'd give me a key for a locker. The lockers were at the back of the hall, right next to the cloakroom. I was to take out a briefcase, hand it over to the man who'd sat down next to me in the hall, in exchange for his briefcase, and that was it.

'Why?' I asked Pozorski. 'And tell me, how do you know that a man has just sat down next to me in the lobby anyway? What's all this about?'

I could hear a sigh on the phone. Unfortunately, Pozorski was stuck on business in the vicinity of Oryol. He would have loved to have come to the hotel himself, but he simply couldn't make it and his customer was flying back home in a couple of hours. In the meantime, he'd been informed of everything. An emergency. As an old comrade and friend, I could damned well accept a briefcase from him, couldn't I?

'I'll come and pick it up this evening … Thanks for doing this, man! We'll go and have a good time again in the Aragvi soon!'

Once back in my hotel room, I laid the briefcase under the bed, put the kettle on for an instant coffee and began drawing up a new application for thirty second-hand Volvos. An hour and a half later, Julia arrived back with a delighted smile on her face. She'd been to the zoo, where two white Siberian tiger cubs had been born. They'd been displayed to the public for the first time that day. She'd stayed there for an hour, shot an entire roll of film and was eager to develop it somewhere. When I told her about my meeting in the Mezhdunarodnaya and the briefcase, she turned completely pale. Briefcase? What kind of dope was I? Why had I just taken it? Maybe it was a bomb or something.

'A bomb?' I laughed. Why would anyone want to give me a briefcase with a bomb in it? You've seen too many Hollywood films.'

Julia was pretty piqued and shot back that she'd never even seen a single Hollywood film in her entire life, but that apparently, I didn't know what was going on in this country. Only recently, a mafia boss and three of his bodyguards had been blown up by a car bomb in the Urals. And similar things had happened in Leningrad and other cities too. She knew it, she'd sensed it: I never should have let myself be taken in by that Pozorski.

'Sweetheart, sweetheart …' I said to calm her down. 'I know exactly who and what Pozorski is, but he's never screwed me over. Come on, I'll get out that briefcase, and then we'll know what's inside …'

I hadn't even finished saying it before my girlfriend had flounced outside to the passage. She shouted through the door that it was up to me, that she'd warned me.

While the muggy heat of the late August day hung in the room like a kitchen rag, I bent down, took the case from under the bed and lay it on the bedcovers. It opened easily with two curt clicks. When I saw the contents I had to snigger, and that soon turned into liberating roars of laughter. I'd briefly felt a bit of tension that maybe there was something explosive inside. I'd grown used to dealing with hard cash, but the immaculate wads of greyish-green dollars grinning up at me impressed me mightily.

From the passage, there were grumbles about why I was laughing.

I cheerily called something back.

Julia crept back into the bedroom like a cat. She stared at the money for a moment, then asked in a whisper how much might be inside.

I picked up a wad, took off the paper binding and quickly counted the smooth new notes. A hundred. Ten thousand dollars. There were a hundred wads. A million. So that's what a million dollars looks like.

It looked like nothing.

Nevertheless, it was a life full of freedom.

I still hadn't heard a thing from Pozorski by the next afternoon. However often I called, he didn't answer. And there was no sign of life from my Russian partner the day after either. After I called his office for the umpteenth time, a secretary finally picked up. She informed me in an apologetic tone that the telephone had been out of service for two days, and that Mr Pozorski was out of the city, but was expected back towards evening.

I'd hidden the briefcase among the clothes in the closet, but all this time we hadn't been able to leave the hotel. Who'd leave a million dollars behind in cash, unattended? After we'd ordered the *boeuf stroganoff* from room service again at around eight that evening, and I'd hung up the phone, the Bakelite telephone on my desk began to ring.

Reception. There was a Mr Pozorski downstairs in the lobby. 'Can we send him up?'

'With the greatest pleasure!' I said with elation.

While I got the briefcase out of the closet, Julia grouchily mumbled that she was staying in the bedroom. She didn't want to see the Russian. I hadn't even made it into the passage with the briefcase before Pozorski lurched out of the lift with an alcoholic grin on his face. He greeted me full of pathos as though on stage, and gave me two warm kisses.

'My apologies, my great friend! The militia in Oryol kept me locked up for two days. What do you think about that? People who help this country to get ahead, who've fixed their sights on the future, are locked up. While the slaves of the state, the arch-idlers, walk around freely. Ah, that's fine, very fine …' he continued, after I'd pressed the briefcase into his hands. 'Well, what do you think?'

'Of what?' I asked, not understanding.

'Don't tell me you didn't take a peek inside. That would be completely normal! A million dollars. You're one of the few in this city who I trust. A million for me today; tomorrow, or the day after, for you. Where's your sweet girlfriend, actually? What, in Leningrad? Anyway, we'll see each other soon in Aragvi. Buddy, this man's dog-tired and is going to have a lovely long kip. Farewell!'

Back in our double hotel room, Julia was lying stretched out on the bed reading. Another Dutch textbook. This time she read out a poem by Martinus Nijhoff slowly and assuredly; the rhythm reminded her of Joseph Brodsky.

The next morning at eight o'clock, after I'd barely got properly dressed, the telephone on my desk rang again. It was reception. Asking if I could come downstairs.

There were two militia officers in the vestibule. They made me go straight back upstairs to fetch my papers, and a little while later they carefully scrutinised my passport and visa, after which they showed me a grainy photo of Pozorski and asked if I knew him. I told them I'd seen him the night before in the hotel.

'At eight o'clock in the evening?'

I nodded, knowing that they were checking the information they'd been given by reception, who were legally obliged to note down the name and passport number of every visitor. They asked me kindly to accompany them to the station. There, I heard that Pozorski had been found at twenty past eight the evening before, barely a quarter of an hour after I'd said goodbye to him, with bullet holes in both temples, by the side of the road close to Gorky Park.

'So, you're here in this country doing tomographic research?' one of the interrogators asked. He was a controlled Russian in a grey uniform.

'Among other things,' I said.

'And what do you know about a briefcase?'


Pozorski was the first person I'd known who'd been shot to death. Once again, I resolved to leave this damned country for good. Not knowing that the Russian who I'd met through my bible smuggling would be the first in a long line of people in my life to be murdered.

In truth, everything was yet to begin.

# CHAPTER TEN

One day, I went to the old city villa of the ballerina and former lover of czar Nicholas II, Mathilde Kschessinska, for research for my book on the Russian Revolution.

It was pleasant, mild May Saint Petersburg weather. The blue minarets of the nineteenth-century mosque nearby glittered majestically in the sunlight. In the little park behind me, the birds capered and chirped in the fresh green. For a long while, I stood in front of the balcony of the house that had been built in 1906 in the modern style, from which the famous ballerina had fled right before the February Revolution (warned that her life was in danger), after which she'd ended up in Paris where she died in 1971, shortly after her hundredth birthday. Just like the provisional premier Alexander Kerensky, she too would have heard the Beatles and the Stones at the end of her life, and presumably, as a sprightly elderly lady, would have seen the TV pictures of the foul napalm war in Vietnam, having previously shared satin sheets with the czar for three years as a teenager. She was subsequently taken good care of in a variety of ways by his family (and after her affair with the czar, she had two more affairs with Romanov grand dukes).

Lenin moved into the sumptuous villa in April, immediately after he had arrived on the train from Switzerland. The place had been stormed and occupied shortly before this by his Bolshevik comrades with their red flags, and afterwards the vengeful ruination of the building began. The antique furniture was shoved aside roughly and the sub-tropical palms allowed to wither in their pots. The dancer's legendary Roman bathroom degenerated into a rubbish tip for cigarette butts, paper, rags, and other junk while the vestibule was turned into a transit house for stinking soldiers who smoked the whole damned day and spat out sunflower seeds — as well as opportunists and other folk. The white grand piano from Berlin that adorned the private dance studio was scratched and stained with spilled tea, vodka, and other drinks, and the ballerina's Eastern-furnished bedroom became the nerve centre for *Pravda*, the Truth, the paper that spoke the truth as infrequently in those early days as seventy years later when I read it as a student, my fingers blackened by the printer's cheap ink.

Here on this balcony was where the victory march of evil began — the forces of darkness, of death. Lenin — with the strains of the *Marseillaise* and the *Internationale* still ringing in his ears after they'd welcomed him just before at the Finland Station — had extracted himself from the welcome dinner, gone out and began speaking in a shrill voice to a small crowd that was waiting expectantly on the street below. This was as a prelude to a speech that he would give indoors a few hours later, when — to the astonishment of most of those present — he rejected any collaboration with the Provisional Government, because it would amount to the betrayal of socialism. Continuing to screech, he made his first appeal for total destruction.

At that moment, the fate of Russia and many tens of millions was sealed. By one man.

———

I'd often visited this building. The former living quarters of the Russian ballet legend had been transformed into exhibition spaces, where the October Revolution and the other subsequent political upheavals were represented by artefacts such as firearms, propaganda posters, original documents, photos, and moving images. Naturally, this was with the seal of approval of the current authorities in the Kremlin. Virulent patriotism was the new ideology. I liked to look endlessly at the silent film clips of the last czar dressed as a simple Cossack, or Lenin orating to a crowd, but mostly Nevsky Prospect in February 1917, where people passed by in the snow on foot with an anxious, jerking gait.

Now I found myself back here briefly for my book. Non-fiction, my new métier, demanded the constant checking of reality.

I was about to go into the building when a cultivated man of around sixty, who had been photographing the architectural flourishes of the house with a professional-looking camera a little way off, addressed me in English with a thick French accent.

'*Mister, dzies is dze famous balcony?*'

Beside him stood a girl of about sixteen. She had pitch-black punky hair, glamorously styled, as though she'd just come back from an expensive hairdresser, and a piercing in her lower lip. Her rebellious eyes were black smudges, and the rest of her clothes were pitch-black, just like the army boots on her feet.

'*Ma fille!*' the man said with relief in his voice, after I'd answered him back in French that this was indeed the balcony where Lenin had first spoken to the people in the spring of 1917, after an exile of almost sixteen years.

The man was a retired photo-journalist, and a year ago he'd swapped his Paris apartment for the family home in the Ardèche. He was already sixty-one, and rarely got into the city: the young should be given their opportunity now. When he said this, the girl rolled her mascaraed eyes, as a sign that she was embarrassed by her father's words and was also bored out of her mind. For a Frenchman, this chap was uncommonly talkative. He hadn't expected this nice weather here. At Charles de Gaulle, it had been raining. He'd done a lot of work in Asian, African, and Latin American countries. But strangely enough, he'd never got around to a trip to the former Soviet Union, although he'd been a supporter of the revolution in his youth: Lenin had been a hero to him for a long time.

'I'm trying to protect my daughter from the same mistakes I made back then,' the man continued, while the girl stared morosely at her iPhone. 'Although, I think it may be too late.'

'What do you mean?' I asked.

At that moment, the child suddenly came to life. With a tone that suggested she hadn't said a word to her father since breakfast, she sighed the word '*putain*', cast me a challenging look, drew aside a black rag from her upper body and showed me her left collarbone and shoulder, on which the head of Lenin was tattooed in blue-and-black tints.

His daughter, the man continued in a scornful tone, had taken on the burden of those oppressed in the world. Her boyfriend, who was ten years older, was one of the leaders of the extreme-leftist organisation in Nantes. Together with other anti-Fascist organisations, he'd gone into action at a number of Le Pen's meetings. He'd smashed shop windows, but also carried out attacks on banks and law offices, in protest against capitalism.

'*Putain* …' his daughter muttered again.

I'd never heard a Frenchman speak with so much self-mockery. He'd invited his daughter and future-son-in-law to come to Russia with him, to the city where the Red Terror had begun. But his daughter's boyfriend didn't want to have anything to do with a cultural itinerary. He yawned at the idea of a visit to the Hermitage, and refused to go to that historical spot. Even before the second day had started, he was sitting in a cellar from early morning, drinking with a couple of Russian comrades who he'd fished up on the internet, who harboured the same extremist ideas as him.

The Frenchman's monologue was interrupted again with a contemptuous '*putain*', the stop-gap word used by the French youth these days, whether it was fitting or not. The pair began to bicker in such an unexpectedly aggressive way that the man quickly gave me a nod as a goodbye and dragged his daughter towards the park. At the same time, my telephone rang. It was Julia. Her brother had unexpectedly dropped by and wanted to speak to me.

'Kschessinska's house?' my wife sniffed when I told her where I was. 'Who's interested in that outside Russia? Come home quickly … We're already on the coffee … I've made a chocolate cake …'

When I got home fifteen minutes later, my brother-in-law was sitting at the round table with a smear of chocolate cake around his mouth, and the scrounger Peach was purring for attention on his lap.

Because of my stay in Moscow, I hadn't seen Alexei for a long time. He looked just as youthful, fresh, and optimistic as always. He and his sister had just decided to go to their father's grave the next day. It would soon be a year since his death, and they wanted to spruce up the headstone with a low fence around it.

'Why don't you come with us tomorrow?' my brother-in-law asked.

I mumbled that I was too busy. I try to avoid cemeteries as much as possible; I've been to them too often. While Julia lay a second slice of cake on my plate, I quickly changed the subject and observed that my brother-in-law was looking very sun-bronzed.

'The open sea,' Alexei said. 'A person doesn't turn brown as quickly anywhere else as on the water. Last week, my partner and I took the *Nautilus* out of its shed, what a racehorse! We cleaned everything with chamois leather, checked the rigging … Do you know that we already have forty people for the course next summer? And we still haven't started advertising. The sailing school is going to be a hit … And that's the reason …' Alexei cast a quick glance at his sister, took a sip of coffee and continued: 'And that's the reason I've popped by … I've started up the glycerine trade again, but it's hand-to-mouth, hand-to-mouth … Because of the crisis, everyone is reluctant to pay up … Sometimes I have to wait two, three months for my money … And now something's happened, something small, but I need to talk to you about it … It's about the future of my new business.'

Three days before, my brother-in-law and his partner had gone out onto the Gulf of Finland for a trial run. Everything on board was gleaming, the sails were taut in the wind, the hydrofoil boats full of tourists on their way to the spurting fountains of the Peterhof, the Russian Versailles, were thudding past on the waves. Far out at sea, they drew their sails to test out the motor. It didn't start. At first, they thought it was a leaky fuel pipe — when they thought about it, they both seemed to remember smelling something as they were leaving. But the pipe was intact, and the tank was full. Whatever they did — both were trained engineers — the bastard just wouldn't start. They hoisted the sails again, but once they'd moored up, there was no way to get the motor going.

They brought in a specialist, and after fiddling around, he told them in an ominous tone that the suction system was buggered, that replacing it would cost just about as much as buying a brand-new car. Because of the collapse of the ruble, the import of components had become insanely expensive. 'My partner can put up another two thousand of his own money,' my brother-in-law continued. 'That would mean me needing to borrow a little under three thousand euros extra from you. But given the enrolments we've already had, and the overwhelming interest, I think that I could already pay you back most of that money and all the rest in the autumn.'

Even without my wife's imploring look, I would have agreed, naturally. My brother-in-law leapt up from the table in joy. After he'd left with the cash, I immediately felt like a pauper.

'What are you so worried about?' my wife asked. 'I teach as many German lessons as I can. And you still earn enough, don't you?'

I didn't have any complaints for the time being, that was true. But the fear of unemployment had taken hold of me like poison.

'You're spooked, I think ...' My wife lifted Moesha onto her lap and began to stroke her furiously. 'How many times have you risked your life for that newspaper? To say nothing of all the nights that I lay awake at home eaten up by nerves after you'd left for another rotten war. These guys aren't ogres?' She smiled and went on, 'But thank you, bunny, for helping Alyosha. Since Papa died, he's had a much tougher time than he shows ... He's so brave ... I hope that everything goes well from now on ...'

———

That evening, I got two emails from the Netherlands. The first made me happy. The second sank me deep in doubt.

The week before, I'd emailed a few excerpts of my Russia book to a friend, whose judgement I'd always trusted, and who combined erudition and a literary sense with a successful life in the world of e-commerce. It had made him a millionaire. He'd read the pages I'd sent him. They contained some pretty decent passages, but he felt I was missing out on a great opportunity by emphasising the wrong things, and by treating some things too summarily. The differences I'd sketched between the rich and poor in Petrograd at the time weren't bad, but he wanted more of that: about the fortunate neighbourhoods of the well-off on one side of the Neva, with their neo-classical city palaces and billiard rooms, ballrooms and orangeries, where pineapples were harvested for desserts all through the year, and the theatres, cabaret restaurants, and the brothels; and on the other side of the river, the proletarian areas, the stinking factories and shipyards, the soup-kitchens and the slums where the workers lived, suffering from scurvy, lice and hunger. He'd never known that the exploited masses had literally crossed the ice *en masse* one day to mete out justice to the privileged. Didn't I see the parallels with the present day? With the newly arisen meridian of injustice?

This time, it wasn't a river but a sea. The Mediterranean, which legions of wretches had crossed over to Italy and Spain; thousands of them had drowned beneath the waves. This time, it wasn't the aristocracy, the bourgeoisie and the rich merchants in Petrograd that people were revolting against, but there was an almost global uprising against the fleshpots of hedonistic Europe.

*I've told you often: literature isn't something elevated
anymore. Everyone writes. And without engagement,*

*you won't get anywhere. In the arts too, it ultimately all comes down to what's slick. You have to connect your work to what's currently going on. To get on the talk-shows on TV. And if when you get there, you have to put on a bit of an elevated air every now and then, then so be it. Warmest regards, Felix.*

He'd written the note from his roof garden in Cap d'Antibes, where he has a *pied-à-terre* among the aromatic parasol pines, with a view over the azure sea, and where he spends most of his time now. Growing rich from e-commerce is something you can do from any place on earth these days.

After the first strike in the Putilov Ironworks munitions factory in 1917, the workers also downed tools in the northerly Vyborg and Petrograd quarters of the city. Then the hungry hordes — men, women, and children, led by left-wing demagogues — again crossed the ice in the direction of the city, after they'd been blocked by police cordons and Cossacks on the bridge. The rage and hate of the populace, which had been stored up for centuries, was first focused on the members of the feared czarist police, who were known as 'pharaohs' because of their headgear, which looked like shaving-brushes, and who to the very last mercilessly hacked at the rebellious human mass with their sabres from atop their black stallions. Manhunts were organised for them. They were driven at bayonet-point from the frozen roofs, where they'd dug in and fired on the demonstrators. Many crashed to their deaths in the snow to resounding cheers. Others drowned like rats in holes in the ice of the channel. The heads of slaughtered pharaohs were borne on poles through the streets as trophies, amid cries of triumph. The rebels passed the façades of elegant shops (*On parle français, Man spricht Deutsch*, English spoken here), desirable places full of luxury imported wares, where just shortly before the members of the foreign community and the aristocracy had made their purchases, greeted by doormen in dresscoats who obligingly held the doors open, inviting the clientele with a bow of their heads to walk up the royal blue carpets and come in; but these shops were now barricaded with planks and boards. The crowd filed past the houses of the well-to-do citizens, most of whom had no real idea of the collective social downfall that would all too soon be awaiting them as representatives of the *burzhuaziya*.

The red-brick fort of the Kresty Prison is on the bank of the Neva (if you go halfway down Tchaikovsky Street and turn right, you'll be walking straight towards it). There, the Bolsheviks freed the detainees, not only the political prisoners, but also the criminals — the thieves, rapists, and murderers. They almost immediately returned to marauding, plundering, murdering, and raping, sometimes disguising themselves as soldiers or revolutionaries, this time with the blessing of the socialist revolution that had been proclaimed in the name of humanity. In a flash, they'd sprung from the hell of prison into the heaven of total anarchy, in which the laws of the people no longer existed, nor those of God, and they could abandon themselves to the delightful pulsations of the blood, whipped up by alcohol, cocaine, and hormones, or all three at the same time. Those that belonged to the old imperial guard — the cadets who hadn't surrendered after the Bolsheviks had seized the Winter Palace, or been grabbed by the runaway human herd — desperately tried to rip the czarist epaulettes from their shoulders while in their hideouts. They were ready to give away all their possessions in exchange for the simple jacket, the leaky shoes and the torn work pants of a proletarian. But generally, their pleas went unheard and they fell prey to the Red Guards. At the Hotel Astoria, the British officers stationed there had destroyed the liquor store in the famous wine cellars, emptying out the barrels of cognac and whisky, before it was stormed, to avert the worst of the looters. But eight months later, it turned out that hundreds of private wine cellars in the city were still intact, including the Romanovs' in the Winter Palace. The Red Guards who were sent to destroy them, intending to prevent the total outflow of the Augean stables, didn't have much success. Many couldn't resist the temptation of the champagne and the wine that they'd never before drunk, having been born in the mud of their villages. With the popping of the first champagne corks, the large-scale plunder began. The catacombs of the Winter Palace were the scenes of tableaux worthy of Dante, in which men up to their ankles in wine shot at each other, the blood of the dead and the wounded mixing with the alcohol. Outside, on the street, sailors, soldiers, and random passers-by lay filthy drunk in the gutters, their craned heads licking and supping the wine that streamed from the bottles that had been lost and broken in the robbery.

Zinaida Gippius kept her diary a hundred metres from my house on Tchaikovsky Street; she was the chronicler of all human turpitude, but she barely complained about her own deprivations. On 26 October 1917, a day after the Bolsheviks had seized the Winter Palace, she predicted with prophetic vision: 'The way this government does things will be seen by those that make it through this alive. Not many people who can read and write will be left, I think. The Saint Petersburgers are now in the hands of a disorderly gang of some 200,000 men: the garrison, under the leadership of a handful of villains.'

In the following months, her diary becomes a testimony of despair: an inky-black, meticulous account of the downfall.

In June 1919, the civil war in the country was raging. Everything in the city had already been nationalised, 'Bolshevised'; the emporia, businesses, and factories expropriated. The bodies of those that were still alive were swollen with hunger, the activities of speculators and thieves flourished, floods of people were arrested, and even Gippius had her house searched twice because of communist snitches. She wrote, 'We've already been living so long with a stream of (official) words like "crush", "strangle", "eradicate", "devastate", "destroy", "choke in blood", "beat down into the grave", etc, etc; but the daily repetition in the press of these vulgarities, which actually shouldn't even be printed, no longer has any effect on us; they remind us only of the kind of stammering of the elderly (…) This has never before been seen in history. An enormous city committing suicide. And doing it under the eyes of a Europe that doesn't lift a finger.' Then she intones charismatically at us from behind the lectern of the past, 'I emphatically state that none of the things that the Bolsheviks have told Europe are true:

*There is no revolution.*
*There is no dictatorship of the proletariat.*
*There is no socialism.*
*There are no Soviets, not even those.*

The basis, the mainstay, the fundament on which the Bolshevik regime rests, and which is also its infallible weapon, is *the lie* … We are readying ourselves for the grave, in the icy cold, the complete darkness and the deathly silence … I've dreamt … About the Bolsheviks … That they are brought to a downfall … By who? By new, strange people … When? On the forty-seventh of February …'

From the very first minute of the tragedy, she'd figured it all out.

Ultimately, the forty-seventh of February became the 26 December 1991, when Mikhail Gorbachev stepped down as president of the Soviet Union, after the earlier August coup against him failed and he returned from his captivity in Crimea to Moscow. And so the USSR officially ceased to exist. The brand-new Russian president Boris Yeltsin announced that the possessions of the Communist Party, including the headquarters, the schools, and the hotels, would be nationalised.

The circle was complete.


For weeks, I'd wanted to visit Gippius's house to find out who was living there now. But how could I get in? One warm, rainy June afternoon, I went to the immense building with the little towers and pressed a bell at random. A guard with repulsive, bulbous eyes immediately dashed out, with a pistol on his hip. Before I could properly ask my question, he began to bark that there was no Gipsus or whoever living here, and never had been, that this was a private house and the occupants were very attached to their privacy. He asked for my papers. When I refused to show him, he began to lambast me again. *Blyat*, all whores, I shouldn't think as a foreigner that I had any special rights. On the contrary! He could report me to the police for hooliganism. There were video recordings of my attempt to get into this building illegally.

Back home, I settled behind my desk and resumed my writing. Two hours later, Julia came home from the college near Finland Station where she'd been teaching German for the last six months. She was worn out and collapsed into her bucket-seat, surrounded by our two remaining cats. As usual, she immersed herself in her pile of French cookery magazines. After a little while, she said, 'I had such a lovely dream last night. Just lovely ...' Although I was of course happy that there was still dreaming going on in Tchaikovsky Street, a century after the nightmare recorded by Gippius, I did suspect that my wife was making things up. She'd dreamt that my book about the revolution was a success, that we had enough money to go on holiday for a whole month; she looked at me mischievously, with a barely concealed smile that swiftly froze. 'Sometimes I'm so totally fed up of our life here. Someone at work was fired again today. Because she's supposed to have said something critical about the Kremlin to her students. A couple of months ago, her nephew took part in the demonstrations in Moscow. The poor boy's still locked up. Almost all my friends from my old German faculty want to leave ... They're sick to death of the corruption and arbitrariness of it all ... Say, bunny, shouldn't we, you know ... Hey, Peach, you scoundrel, what are you up to?!'

Our tomcat had scampered up the curtains. He was just hanging there, making sure that everyone was watching. After he let himself drop, he dashed off with one swift motion to the bedroom, leaving my wife and me behind with tears in our eyes.

From laughter of course.

# CHAPTER ELEVEN

Maybe it is better for a person not to write about revolutions in the past, but rather those in their own lifetime. However tedious, planned, and *apparently* well-balanced a life may seem, there's always at least one fault line that stands out in hindsight as having completely changed one's direction. For me, it was the autumn of 1990, when Julia and I swapped Moscow, which always felt like a trembling, thudding high-pressure cooker, for the low-lying country of the Netherlands, where I was born.

Pozorski's liquidation had little to do with it. We'd already decided that Swindleman would trade places with me. But at that moment, I was quite relieved to take my leave of the settings that I'd been roaming around in for the last two years. I couldn't wait to collect the rest of my money from my partner. I calculated that it was just under two hundred thousand dollars net. Enough to get by for years. I'd sometimes hinted to Julia about renting a little apartment somewhere in Amsterdam, or maybe in Rome, Barcelona, or Paris, with complete freedom to write, after which we could maybe think about ... but she always cut me off, out of superstition, and also because she couldn't believe that she'd been given a six-month Dutch residence visa — in the end, the consul on the Bolshaya Ordynka had been pretty accommodating — and that the light-blue KLM tickets from Sheremetyevo-2 to Schiphol for the end of October were ready and waiting in the drawer of the desk, where we'd consumed our first inedible *boeuf stroganoffs* earlier that year.

Meanwhile, Pozorski was stone dead. Before we left, I went to the militia station for interrogation three times, where they soon started asking about my business connection to the murdered Russian from Leningrad (which I couldn't deny, so didn't), and kept coming back to the briefcase. I didn't know which briefcase they were talking about: the one that I'd handed to the foreigner or the one that he'd given back to me, the sea-green one with the million dollars in cash. I flat-out denied everything, playing at wounded innocence, until the sergeant with the predatory grin in the greyish-blue uniform, who'd been putting me through the wringer this whole time, yawned last night's vodka out of his gob for the umpteenth time and yelled, 'All right, now piss off. The fact that a swindler like you could steal army secrets is completely down to those idiots in the Kremlin. But their days are numbered. It'd be better for you if you didn't show your face in this country again.'

Then he took my passport, which he'd taken off me at the start of every interrogation, and flung it on the desk in front of me, filled with loathing.

Standing outside Schiphol airport, we could both smell the sea right away.

'It seems as if the air's lighter here,' Julia said.

My parents didn't have a car, so I'd told them flat out not to come to the airport. We'd take a taxi and be home in half an hour. A few days earlier, my father had ordered the best steaks from his regular butcher. When we arrived, my two brothers were already sitting at the table laughing. It was strange to lie beside my Russian lover that night in my old room, pressed together in my boy-sized bed. My parents hadn't been able to arrange a bigger one in time. And they didn't know what my plans were.

The next day was the day of the great sniff. My mother took a sniff of Julia, my girlfriend took a sniff of my mother and father, and I took a sniff of both my parents who I hadn't seen for such a long time.

'And so, lad, what are you going to do now?' my father fished. His frame was terribly reduced because of all the surgical procedures. He didn't know anything about my successes. Every time we'd talked to each other on the phone in the preceding months and he'd asked me how things were going with business, I'd keep it light. I wanted to surprise him. As soon as I'd collected my share of the proceeds from Swindleman, I'd lay one of the envelopes bulging with thousands of guilders on my parents' table and thank them for everything they'd done for me, so that they could at least live with no cares for the next few years.

I'd called Swindleman from a phone booth just after we'd landed at Schiphol. I'd left all the papers, the contacts, and the ongoing business, in fact our entire correspondence, neatly arranged in Moscow, in the double hotel room that he would take over from me. There was a made-up bed ready and waiting for him, although I hadn't yet let him know about the death of Pozorski, which meant he'd have to look for another partner for his prospective flower business. I'd decided by now to quit the Intersoviet Consultancy, but would of course man the office in The Hague for the first few months and help with looking for a replacement, before withdrawing as a partner for good.

'This is the answering machine of Ragnar Swindleman. For important or urgent business, please leave a short message after the tone.'

I didn't just get his answering machine when I was at Schiphol, but the day after too, when I tried to reach him from my parents' living room. In the end, I tried an alternate number for the office on Javastraat. The girl on the line hung up the moment she heard the name Swindleman. When I called back and asked for Baldwin Borger, the same thing happened — the connection was promptly broken. When I rang Swindleman's home number shortly after, he finally answered. My partner greeted me very jovially. He asked me how my journey was, apologised for not having been available, and said we should meet the next day at around four in his new apartment in Amsterdam. He was still in Paris now. He'd re-routed his home telephone to the one in his hotel room. 'We have a lot to discuss … What did you say about old Borger? That's a story in itself … Tomorrow I'll tell you everything … I'm going to go off and enjoy myself now…Paris in the autumn, there's no more beautiful place in the world … I'm trying to recharge physically and pep up my morale too; months of grey Russian misery lie ahead of me …' He gave me the address of his new place, in a street close to Nederlandsche Bank.

That morning, Julia and I walked for hours over the beach and through the dunes. The sky in North Holland was a gleaming blue dome. The October sun was almost warm. Even though there was an absence of pine trees here on the coast, it reminded my lover of the former German seaside resorts on the Baltic Sea. One day, she said she'd take me to that fairy-tale blond, amber-riven coast where Thomas Mann had once had a country house built.

'Thomas Mann?' I asked, astonished.

I told her how the seaside resort where I'd grown up had

looked before the war. A pearl of the *belle époque*, with chic shopping arcades, an opulent Pavilion, a covered circus theatre and restaurants that even the former Austrian empress Sissi had twice visited. There was a photo of Anne Frank at the beach, taken a couple of years before she was murdered. Julia gave a quick feline flutter of her eyelashes as she peered up from the coastline with disbelief at the treeless boulevard, an ugly hotchpotch of flats and Jerry-built houses from the 1950s. Inconceivable, she sighed, that the same Germans that had besieged Leningrad for nine hundred days had also wreaked havoc here to build the Atlantic Wall. The fact that one people could be capable of such things!

Earlier that day, I'd taken Julia to the supermarket to get some fresh bread rolls. I hadn't really thought about it, but at a certain point she found it dizzying among the full shelves. The shock of the sudden abundance was too great. She flew into a brief but intense rage at the realisation that for all these years she hadn't only lived in the universe of the big Soviet lie, but most of all in one of scarcity, a scarcity that tens of millions of her countrymen still had to cope with, while this had been here all the time, and was completely normal. And then the rage passed.

After we'd had a coffee with some shortbread that my mother had made, I asked her if she was coming with me.

'Where?'

'To Amsterdam. I have an appointment with Swindleman.'

For the first time, Julia watched the Dutch landscape passing by from the train window. Once we were walking along the canals through Amsterdam, she sighed that she had the feeling that she'd come home now. She'd stood in front of the paintings of the Dutch masters in the Hermitage hundreds of times. The images were lodged in her mind like an encyclopaedia.

At three-thirty, I left her at the Rijksmuseum. I'd come to pick her up again at six, and then we'd eat in an Indonesian restaurant that I'd sometimes visited in my student days.

'A ticket, please,' Julia said to the lady behind the till, in Dutch with almost no accent.

I wandered along the canal to the neighbourhood where Swindleman lived. I stood for a moment on the corner of Van Woustraat, peering into the basement apartment that I'd lived in for almost three years during university. I'd never been unhappier than then. Lonelier too. I was a bad student, rarely went to class, had various part-time jobs through the week, could connect to almost no one and nothing. In the streets full of litter and graffiti, in the avant-garde temples to music, at the university — the winds of revolt had been blowing everywhere. The protesters cried, 'No home, no queen.' There were riot police. Some of my fellow students had broken off contact with their parents. Those bastards with all their cash, who'd had it so easy in their youth. But us? We were studying for unemployment; in their minds they had *no future*.

On Fridays at four o'clock, I'd take the train to the seaside to work with my brothers until Sunday evening in the restaurant, hotel, and banquet room cum eternal workhouse that my grandfather had started in the 1950s, which was now on its last legs. I stood behind the stove with my father. He could no longer pay for staff. Because of the problems, he'd begun to drink. Halves of lager. His always pristine white cook's apron hid a slack belly, which was only growing in girth. A combination of goodness and naivety towards their fellow man had broken the family. For twenty-five years, my father and my mother's three brothers, who'd built the business up together, had placed their trust in a

Mr Van Keulen, the bookkeeper. He came by to see us twice a year with his grey bird's head, always in a grey pinstripe suit, with a waistcoat pocket with a gold watch-chain dangling from it. Every year, when the summer season had come to a definite end in late September, and the period began for the winter club-life, parties, and festivities, and most of all the marriages, Van Keulen would park his big American car right in front of the door, step out and walk into our hotel, with the air of a diplomat entering an embassy. By the day before, everyone was already tense. Although he was paid for his services, my father and uncles placed the maths whizz on a sky-high pedestal; he'd been helping my grandfather with the accounts since just after the war; he'd studied in America for a year, and was fluent in French, the language that he'd spoken with his family in his youth in Maastricht. I'd often heard my mother sigh how on earth it could be possible that while we all worked so hard, we had so little left over. My father would go on about the taxes, the social security payments, the insanely high insurance premiums for healthcare that you had to pay as an independent small trader. The couple of employees that we had were essentially better off than we were. 'But I'll have to ask Van Keulen sometime,' my father would say to shut up my mother. For him too, with his two classes of lower education, Mr Van Keulen was a sort of saint. Meanwhile, the bookkeeper hadn't only given my family bad, expensive advice for years, but had craftily embezzled from them too. When one day he asked for a temporary legal proxy to arrange a few matters with haste, no one dared to refuse him. He explained that he was going to convert the general partnership into a limited company, which was better fiscally and indeed for everything else too. I was thirteen. When I was in bed that evening, listening to my father and mother talking in the living room downstairs about the shining future that was waiting for us, I hoped for one thing: that we could all finally go on holiday together, preferably abroad, where I'd never been. In the following week, Van Keulen carried out a number of transactions, with our hotel as security. He did the same with seven other businesses that he had in his portfolio. Then he vanished. The fraud made the papers. Seven years later, it was reported that he'd been tracked down. All that time, he'd been living with a woman thirty years his junior in Montevideo, where he was found dead one morning.

It was a story like in a film. But the catastrophe was complete. My family was left with a mortgage debt that was worth almost 80 per cent of the building, which had already half been paid off in the thirty years before with their tireless work, often sixteen hours a day. The interest was more than 10 per cent. The debt slowly consumed our business from the inside out, like a malignant tumour. When my parents were sixty, everything was sold to avoid bankruptcy. My father had worked since he was fourteen. He had to cling on for his state pension with the forty thousand guilders that he had left. His private pension had been spent by Mr Van Keulen in Montevideo.

As a good son, I would now put everything right.

Swindleman's apartment was on the third floor of a historic building. It was a shame that I'd had to leave Julia behind at the Rijksmuseum; I would rather have shown her how fine the interior of some Amsterdam houses can be.

'*Bonjour!*' Swindleman opened the door with an electric buzzer. 'Hey, could you bring up the paper for me?'

I slowly climbed the stairs with a fresh *NRC*.

In the months that I hadn't seen my partner, he'd grown slimmer. His body had an almost athletic quality, although his face was still as puffy as before. The yellow tint had disappeared; the dominant colour was again poppy.

'The whole world is still lyrical about that Nobel Peace Prize for Gorby …' Swindleman pulled a frown over the front page of the paper after I'd handed it to him. 'But I reckon it's all yet to start. In every peace lurk the seeds of the next war. The same is true of what we're living through …' My partner dropped the evening paper onto the floor, casually stepped over it, and then grinned and gave me a bear-hug. 'How's it going, old boy? Damn it, am I glad to see you. But where's that lovely girlfriend of yours? I thought you'd bring her along. What do you fancy? A beer? Wine? Vodka?'

When I walked into the living room, my mouth dropped open in astonishment. The room and suite, which were illuminated by the yellow, blue, and pelican-pink art nouveau stained-glass windows, must have been ninety square metres. Modern and tastefully furnished.

'Well?' He looked at me enquiringly in his white sports shoes, which squeaked every time the soles slid over the parquet.

'A cold beer, please,' I said, and then told him of my genuine admiration for his new home.

He'd been able to buy the flat quickly and cheaply, he said when he got back from the kitchen with the drinks. He gestured for me to sit down on the black leather couch. He flopped onto a white leather bucket-seat. Then he looked at me with a smile. He licked his tall glass with his wet tongue, as if it were an ice-cream. I told him that I'd left Julia at the Rijksmuseum but, of course, the three of us would have to meet up again before he left for Moscow.

'So how are things going with that flower project?' Swindleman said, getting straight down to business. 'I want to start exporting this spring, but I haven't had any feedback from you …'

When I told him that Pozorski had been shot dead in a liquidation the week before, he didn't betray any astonishment or dismay. He only grunted something, took a swig of his rum and coke, and rolled his tongue inside his right cheek.

'A dog deserves a dog's death,' Swindleman said. 'I've never told you, but I already knew Pozorski before I met you. When you told me about your Russian contact for those smuggled bibles, I knew straight away it was him. I did a few jobs with him in Leningrad too. He was a shit, but I didn't dislike him. When you first suggested him, I thought fine. Do you really think you're telling me anything new? I got a call from my friends in Moscow an hour after it had happened. He seems to have been tied up with nuclear material. The greedy fool ...! But anyway, there are thousands of other Russians who would like to get into the flower trade with me. It's going to be a goldmine! Every drama has a number of acts. The curtain definitively fell on Baldwin Borger two weeks ago too. It was stupid of me to pay him half of the profit from our first business trip. Fifty thousand guilders for drawing up a list of names, phew! When I told him he could kiss goodbye to his ridiculously high commission from now on in, he was livid. He threatened to kick me out of his building. One afternoon, I picked up my stuff and left. It's fine working here at home too. A telephone and a fax, you don't really need anything else. I'll show you my bedroom and study in a bit ...'

I was so taken aback by his words that I stayed silent. I hardly dared to tell him of my decision to withdraw as a partner. I hesitantly asked when I could expect my share of our profits. For the last few months in Moscow, I'd been living mostly on what was left of my savings. For now, I was staying with my parents, but I wanted to rent somewhere with Julia as soon as possible.

'What money?' Swindleman asked.

I assumed that he hadn't heard what I'd said, so I repeated my question, adding that I'd brought the number of my giro account with me. I thought it would be best to deposit it there.

'What money?!' my partner repeated, getting redder and redder. 'First, my friend, all of the money is in my account. That is to say, what's left after buying this flat. Second, you listen carefully to me. I'll make you an offer to come and work for me. You'll get a good salary, with back pay, of course. If need be, we can also talk about bonuses, but from now on you'll NEVER talk about that money again. Who was the major instigator of this project? How did you manage to live there in that hotel in Moscow almost for free this whole time, with your girlfriend? That's entirely down to my Siberian contacts! Without my daily direction, nothing would have come of it. In short, I'm offering you a good salary, with the promise that in six months you can go back to Moscow on behalf of my company as a senior consultant ... Meanwhile, I've registered the company in my name as an LTD. OK, yeah! You can stand up angrily if you want, but that doesn't worry me one bit. Keep your hands to yourself, mate! I've been at the gym every night for the last few months ... Sambo, the Russian martial art! You'll be sorry for not taking up my offer ... Sue me? Go ahead and sue me! You've got no proof — there is no proof ... I had our entire correspondence removed from the hotel room this morning ... Now it's safely stowed away somewhere in Moscow ... I'll ask you one more time, are you going to work for me? No? Fine, *adios*! But what's your plan? With no money? And say hi to that girlfriend of yours! See how long the love lasts now, and do teach me all about these Russian bitches!'

Half an hour later, I was standing outside the Rijksmuseum again. It had started to rain. I sheltered in the brick vaulted arcade beneath the museum that cyclists continually rode through. I was at the exit around six. A little later, Julia stepped out into the drizzle with a blissful expression on her dark face. She said, 'Oh, I'm so terribly happy. Of course, the collection of Rembrandts at the Hermitage in Russia is much better. To be honest, I found *The Night Watch* a bit of a disappointment. But I spent an hour and a half in that room with the small Dutch masters. And don't they have some wonderful historical pottery here! What are you looking so glum about? Well, where's this restaurant of yours? I'm starving. Don't put on such a sad face, eh! It's only a shower … I love rain, actually … Oh, isn't everything and everyone here so wonderful, nice and kind …'

# CHAPTER TWELVE

On my first day at the grammar school one hot August, I realised that conforming to and hiding within a group not only manifests itself in cowardly silence or an approving round of applause among adults, but among children too.

The summer season was still in full swing. Although my mother would have preferred me to take the bus for those first few weeks, I insisted that I wanted to try out my bike. Everything was new: the Batavus bike, my satchel that smelt of saddle-leather, the textbooks that an aunt had covered with smooth brown paper. For twelve years, I'd been going to Haarlem, to 'the city', in a grey NSH bus with my mother for a pair of shoes, or clothes, or for a visit to the optician, who'd discovered that I had an acute form of short-sightedness when I was eight. But from now on, I'd be going there for school. And all on my own.

The summer holiday had taken an eternity. For six long weeks, my elder brother and I had helped our parents as much as possible. Out in the courtyard, we sorted empty bottles into crates. And in the scullery, we scrubbed greasy pans with iron scouring pads. There were loads of other chores, like peeling hundreds of kilos of potatoes that we then put in the chip-press, my brother and I taking it in turns to crank the handle as the blue plastic bowl steadily filled with smooth pale ingots that my father would toss into the boiling oil a little later, for the first round of the frying process.

In the early mornings, we'd help our mother sort out the dirty bed linen in the rooms; sometimes we'd howl with laughter about the suspicious, almost colourless stains that we found on the sheets. We already knew all the ins and outs. Sometimes, Mama would laugh along with us on the sly, a failed look of disapproval in her eyes. By eleven, you could usually find us on the beach, where we sunbathed and swam. We turned as brown as toffees. Our parents gave us money to buy ice lollies, but we were haunted by guilt because they were still working at the hotel. Every now and then, Mama would join us for an hour or two at the beach after lunch. My father never put in an appearance.

We'd get back to the hotel at around six, where we lived upstairs in a couple of cramped rooms. My father would still be downstairs in the kitchen, as in the preceding hours, amid the hiss of gigantic purplish-blue roasting pans full of half chickens, and steaming pans of soup, vegetables, sauces, and other things on the three-metre-long stove; now though, he wasn't getting ready for lunch, but dinner. By this stage, my mother would have swapped the morning's blue work-apron for a white blouse and a black pencil-skirt with a little white pinny, just like my three aunts. While my father ran the kitchen, one of my uncles performed as the manager, while another rinsed out glasses, tapped beer and poured drinks behind the bar, and the third had acquired the status of a jack-of-all-trades over the years. Sometimes a beer barrel would need to be fetched quickly from the shed, or a lamp would suddenly blow out, or a fridge, or a kid's bed would need to be taken up to a room, or, because it was unexpectedly busy, we'd immediately need extra schnitzels, steaks, or cod (the butcher and the fishmonger were usually closed by now, but they'd given us the keys for the cold store: everything was done on the basis of trust); every now and then, when we were running short of glasses, cutlery, or crockery, he'd quickly don a hard, green waterproof apron and help out in the washing-up area, where a boy of nineteen with a bum-fluff beard (we referred to him as 'the student' in awe) operated the mighty steel machine, something that I and my brother often helped with too. My parents thought that we were too young to work the machine on our own; we would only be allowed to do that later.

Usually by nine-thirty, my brother and I were lying beside each other in bed under a single sheet, with rosy faces, listening to the sounds rising from the street and from downstairs. Eventually, we'd doze off, and every now and then I'd wake up at around twelve, when my parents came upstairs, and after a brief clatter of water, went straight to sleep because they had to be back up again at five-thirty for breakfast.

'Bye, boy, bye, dear boy! You watch how you go!' My father, who was dressed in an immaculate cook's uniform, and my mother, wearing her work apron, waved me off that morning at seven-thirty. My brother had stayed in bed with a hint of malicious delight. His school in the village started three days later.

The route to the town passed through the dunes, partly over tiled bicycle paths with majestic villas to the left and right, some with thatched roofs and lawns out front as big as half a football field, where people were sitting having breakfast at little tables underneath parasols. I'd been to the school once before, again on the bus and with my mother; my father had had to cook for a wedding and couldn't come.

The journey on the Batavus bike felt like a trip around the world to me.

Forty minutes later, when I arrived at the brown-brick fort, there was quite a commotion. Swarms of cyclists. Some of the pupils were already so old that both the girls and boys had adult voices. Lots of kids my age were brought in by car, and their papas and mamas kissed them and waved them goodbye at the gate that led to the impressive school playground with a flight of steps and an old-fashioned bell. Most parents looked remarkably young, sun-bronzed and relaxed. Many were wearing sandals; some were dressed in snow-white tennis clothes. People were busy greeting each other back and forth. The parents knew each other. I was leaning to the side as I walked because of the bag of books that I was lugging; on the way, it had slipped off twice because of the weight. I was scared to death; my heart was beating in my throat the whole time. Some of the kids in the class that I'd been put in turned out to know each other already. They called each other by their first names. They all came from Haarlem and the well-to-do villages dotted closely around the school. For them, the first form was just the extension of top class in primary school. Given their churchy youth, they were destined from the earliest age to end up at this chic Christian grammar school. What I didn't know, but would soon come to understand, was that I was an exception, because I had a father who despised the church to the depths of his being, and a quiet believing mother, but most of all I was one of the few who was an 'outsider'. From a village on the coast. With the social *odeur* of rotten fish.

Our very first lesson was taught by our form teacher, who also did geography. He was a small man with a thin, sunburnt face, steel-rimmed glasses and a fuzzy beard. He must have been around thirty, but he struck me at the time as ancient. In spite of how warm it was in the class, he wore a coat with all sorts of coloured stitching. It was an Afghan coat, he told us. He and his girlfriend had gone to Afghanistan on holiday this summer. Did anyone in the class know where that was? Afghanistan? Fingers shot up to the left and right. Scared to death that I was going to be found out and would immediately be carted off to a lower grade, so that the headmaster of my primary school would be proved right after all, I remained motionless in the back row, where I'd nestled myself.

'In Africa ...' I glanced to my right. The girl who had answered had freckles, a ponytail, and the curvature of breasts.

'That's wrong, Chantal ... But you're close ... How's your daddy doing by the way?'

'Fine,' she answered morosely.

'Will you pass on my warmest regards?' the teacher continued in a familiar tone. 'Fortunately, the theatre season is starting to pick up again. Yes, you there, what's your name?'

'Theodor,' said a boy with a head like a hedgehog.

'Do you perhaps know where Afghanistan is?'

'In Asia,' the hedgehog answered in a tone suggesting that it was entirely obvious. 'It's surrounded by other interesting countries, such as India and Pakistan. I know that because my grandfather worked in India for Philips. We've already been there three times to visit.'

The form teacher nodded in assent, and then uttered a word that was completely new to me: introduction: We had to *introduce* ourselves to each other. In a moment, we were supposed to take turns to say our names, tell everybody what our parents did, and where we went on holiday this summer. I stared at the linen map of the world with its cracked brown varnish on the wall to the right of me, and was happy that they'd started with the first row, so that I had time to see how the other kids did it.

The first pupil was called Caspar. His father was a dentist, his mother did the housekeeping; they only went to the south of France again this year. The father of number two, a girl called Nicole, was the director of a hospital, her mother worked as a dental hygienist; they'd hiked around Switzerland for three weeks. And so it went on: lawyers, notaries, there were even the children of two professors, although I didn't yet know that professor was another word for teacher. Most of them had spent their holiday in France, but Spain was in second place, and one had gone to Germany. I learned of professions and countries that I'd never heard of (the father of one girl was an 'actuary', and they'd camped near 'Andorra'), after which my neighbour, a boy with a blond, child-film-star face, told us that he and his parents — who both worked at the university — had toured in an RV through the United States for four weeks, which had been really cool because they'd even seen bears in the wild.

'Well, and you there, boy?'

All eyes turned on me. I began to register the world around me in slow-motion, like some depression sufferers do. I told them my name, and hesitantly told them that my family had a hotel-café-restaurant, but we didn't...

'Aha, an entrepreneur!' the teacher interrupted in a jolly tone. 'You see there, children: we have the son of a capitalist!'

I'd never heard the word capitalist before; I suspected that the majority of my new classmates hadn't either. But when the grin beneath the form teacher's beard spread into a false-toothed smile, which then turned into howls of laughter, just about the entire class began to laugh along and whoop horribly, as though on command.

'You see that, children! We finally have the child of an *entrepreneur* in class again, a capitalist's child!'

I could see my father standing on the street this morning, smiling and proud in his cook's uniform. I didn't want him to give me a kiss in public any more, but after my mother had kissed me, he gave me a little pinch on the neck, a sign meaning: make the most of it boy, I love you.

So, that man with his wrecked body was a capitalist. I assumed that was something awful.


It took three days before I was able to tell Julia about Swindleman's deception. What? Did he keep all the money himself? Did we slave for almost three-quarters of a year in that hotel room in Moscow for nothing? But that was inconceivable, surely? Then Julia cried, 'If that Swindleman won't give you your fair share of the money, I'll murder him!' And she raised her clenched fist, just like her Jewish great-grandmother had done in 1917 when she was one of the first revolutionaries and had enthusiastically taken part in destroying the orthodox crosses on the golden church domes.

She asked me for his address, to go and see him straight away.

'Leave it, sweetheart,' I said.

'What do you mean, leave it?'

'We have the rule of law in this country,' I said. 'Maybe you could take the law into your own hands in Russia, but here we have a judge. I don't have any proof — all of the papers are in Moscow. If I filed a lawsuit, the judge would dismiss it in five minutes.'

My coolness was an act. On the inside I was a volcano. I was trying to keep up a front for my girlfriend. It was depressing that Swindleman had robbed me of the opportunity to make my parents happy with a sizeable sum of money after they'd been living on scraps for years, even more so than the crushed prospect of a couple of years of financial peace for myself. I'd managed to hang on to twelve-hundred dollars from my stay in Russia. Grubby notes that had passed from hand to hand in Moscow, from whores to black market dealers. They stank. The decay of the USSR rose from the paper in fumes. One morning, I exchanged them at the bank. When I stepped outside with the notes in hundreds in my jacket's inside pocket, I was overwhelmed by despair. I could get by for a few months at best. But after that? Go and apply to be a lawyer in some office after all? I'd have preferred to go abroad right away. But now I had Julia to look after, who after only a week had optimistically enquired about the possibility of getting her doctorate at the university in Amsterdam. She dreamt of a PhD.

In those first few days, every joint meal with my parents was a festive occasion. We hugged each other all the time — we could barely get enough of each other's company. But soon enough, domestic life revealed its first cracks. Because we didn't have anything in particular to do, we were all on top of each other. My mother could accept the fact that Julia took a shower every day. But twice a day? In the morning *and* the evening? Wasn't that a little over the top? Money didn't grow on trees.

Once, when Julia offered to cook for us all, my mother dismissed it out of hand. Minor irritations started to creep in. A young couple in love should, of course, not live with parents. I'd been thinking about making a start on my book. I bought a couple of notepads, and got to work as soon as Julia walked out of the door, but couldn't concentrate. Short-term worries completely consumed me. Sometimes I woke up in the middle of the night bathed in sweat — the butcher's knife that I'd wanted to plant deep in Swindleman's chest floated before my eyes in blue specks like mist. I took the train to Amsterdam often, hoping to meet old friends in the pub. Julia didn't mind. She even encouraged it. Meanwhile, she'd lie on the bed, sumptuously buried beneath a mountain of books that she'd borrowed from the village library on my mother and father's library card.

Her Dutch was progressing insanely well.


This, dear reader, is how I ended up in journalism. It went like this: the day after I'd been to Amsterdam once again, where I'd had a drink in a café on Kloveniersburgwal, someone phoned me. It was a friend of a friend of a friend.

'I've been told that you know a lot about Russia,' the friend of the friend of the friend began, after introducing himself.

I mumbled that I'd been there on and off.

'I've heard you want to write,' he continued on the other end of the line. 'Well, maybe I have something for you.'

The next morning, I was on the train to Amsterdam-Sloterdijk, after a sleepless night of tossing and turning in despair, where I'd felt like a general on his camp-bed in his tent, beside a battlefield, who knew he was soon going to surrender.

I hadn't told my parents anything. I'd decided not to tell Julia anything either yet. I'd always thought journalism rather vulgar.

The journey to the station, past office buildings, where the wind raised welts on my face with gusts of cold rain, struck me as an ignominious retreat from my former life. Plumes of smoke were rising in the distance. The furthest outer suburb of Leningrad wasn't any more miserable. But as soon as I was inside, the comfort of a well-stoked central-heating system covered me like a coat, like something I could only describe as human warmth.

'Ah, good to see you so soon ...' After I'd reported to reception, a young guy with trendy glasses came down the stairs. He was the arts editor, and turned out to be the one who'd called me the day before. 'Our godfather's ready for you.'

A moment later, I entered the editorial office, a landscaped space beneath a polar sky of fluorescent light where there were men and women drinking coffee, smoking, relaxing and talking together, or casting sideways glances at one of the many TVs that were scattered around.

'Well, here he is …' said the young guy in the trendy glasses.

I was led to a glass cubicle where a handsome man of around fifty with a blue suit jacket and a pleasant bulldog's face was calmly sitting behind his desk leafing through a magazine, its cover adorned with a naked blond model.

He was the editor-in-chief of the country's biggest daily.

'*Dobroe utro!* Good morning!' The man got up and greeted me with his outstretched hand. There was a red gleam in his eyes, as though he'd just left the bar at the student society. 'Don't worry! It's the only Russian I know. My brother studied Russian, so there you have it … What was your name again?'

After I'd introduced myself, the godfather invited me to sit and we immediately got down to it. For the last couple of years, they'd had an excellent correspondent in Moscow, a really great guy. But since the fall of the Wall, things had progressed. The godfather didn't have much of an idea about all the ins and outs, as he freely admitted, but he sensed that everything in the Soviet Union was far from over. In short, he was looking for someone to work in the editorial office who could keep an eye on developments. A position had recently become available on the Foreign desk.

'What did you study, by the way?' the editor-in-chief asked.

'Law,' I answered.

'Great, me too. It'll be no use to you at all. I always call it "intellectual snake-oil". And what did you do after your degree?'

'Recreation leader,' I answered.

'Give me a second ...' Thought furrows appeared on the newspaper man's endearing dog's face. 'Recreation leader, that's ...?'

I told him I'd graduated *cum laude*, had received my diploma in the *Athenaeum Illustre* at the University of Amsterdam, and two months later I was in a Hawaiian skirt on stage in a hotel in Tenerife. I was supposed to entertain a room full of a couple of hundred sun-tourists every evening with a band. Quizzes, beauty pageants, open mics, that sort of thing. I spent a year and a half living on the Canary Islands and the Spanish mainland.

'Ha ha! Priceless!' the newspaperman grinned. 'And then?'

Then I moved on: 'I went to work in the Soviet Union for a travel company' — I kept it vague.

'And now you want to write?' he said.

I nodded as agreeably as I could.

'Fine, fine ...' A full-figured secretary came into the glass cubicle. She told her boss that his car was out front. 'I'll be right there, Estelle ... Where was that lunch again? At Braakhekke, right? Two minutes ...' The bulldog's cheeks turned towards me again full of well-meaning attention. 'And what sort of things have you written over the years?'

'Nothing,' I answered.

'Nothing?'

'But you can write?'

'I believe so,' I said.

'You're hired!' As he scribbled something on his paper, the editor-in-chief stood up wheezily. 'I have to go now, there are always these damned lunches ... Oh, yes, one more thing, what's your political orientation? What? Social Democrat? Ha, ha, sissies ... You amuse me, lad, you amuse me ...' He handed me the paper. 'Give this number a call, use one of the million phones in the editorial office. First press nine. Then you'll get a lady who'll arrange everything with you. Yeh, yeh, I'm coming, Estelle, I'm coming ...'

So the spectre of having a salaried office job, which I'd managed to avoid since I graduated, was now becoming a reality after all.

After I got home from Amsterdam-Sloterdijk and told them that from next week I had a regular job as an editor with a pretty decent starting salary, my procreators beamed with pride.

'And what are you going to be doing there exactly?' my mother asked.

'I don't know myself yet.'

Just three weeks later, my first month's pay was deposited in my bank account. Shortly after, Julia and I moved into a rather musty rented room in the centre of the village, but with its own entrance, shower, and cooking facilities. I'd imagined us living in Amsterdam, but my girlfriend had now grown used to living close to the beach and the sea.

On my very first day of work, a supervisor told me that the position on the Foreign desk hadn't gone to me, but to someone else, a guy who'd worked on the Home Affairs desk for seven years and had earned his spurs, spurs that I would still need to earn myself — his tone sounded pretty sceptical.

The editor-in-chief who had taken me on, and who I maybe could have complained to, had gone to Oman for a week.

So, I became a headline writer.

Apart from re-reading, correcting and tailoring copy submitted by journalists from all over the country, the work at the newspaper's office consisted primarily of thinking up headlines, the gripping headlines that the people's daily had been renowned for since its foundation in 1893. That first week, I was awful at it; the second, I was worse. While I went through the usual humiliations of the newcomer, constantly getting sent to the drinks machine to fetch coffee and tea, I thought up ways of pumping things out as quickly as possible. I sat brooding over a headline under a fluorescent light, with a beaker of weak java, wreathed in my colleagues' cigarette smoke. It was for a piece about a pregnant cat that had been saved from a chestnut tree. After I'd sent it to the copy-editor, I received the following reply: '"Pregnant cat saved from chestnut tree." What sort of sloppy work is this? It's pretty much the content of the entire article. And what's more, when that headline's typeset, it's three letters too long! The headline has to draw the reader into a story right from the start. Why did they ever take you on?'

But after a month, that was all over.

Once I'd got the knack, I had to stop myself working too fast. I soon acquired a certain reputation. But I couldn't believe that a person could earn his money thinking up a few words to stick above an article.

About six months later, I got a letter from the housing association where I'd been registered since I was eighteen, saying that 'my number' had been allocated a flat on the edge of the dunes. When Julia and I went to look, we couldn't believe our eyes: three whole rooms just for us, with a view over a riding school, where young ladies from the village with half a black coconut on their heads rode around a sand-pit in docile circles. After we moved, Julia began preparations for the Dutch entrance exam at the University of Amsterdam. We lived as frugally as possible. We used all the money we had left over to furnish our flat. We could both hardly believe it when a new three-piece suite was delivered. We stood there staring at this set of furniture for fifteen minutes in silence, then tried sitting on it, and beamed at each other the whole time. Meanwhile, I travelled by train to the newspaper where I alternated day, evening and soon night shifts. I corrected the journalists' copy, wrote the headlines, and was always happy when I could rejoin my beloved.

My history with Swindleman stuck in my throat for a long time. But slowly it subsided. It dropped into my stomach, into my rectum, and one day I shat it out with a vengeance. I seldom thought about it again. Likewise, I didn't think about writing, about a life as a novelist. When Julia and I passed a playground, she'd sometimes lift up a toddler and hold it above her head in delight, as she'd later do with our cats. One time, she got a mouthful off a mother. When Julia quickly apologised, and the woman could tell from her accent that she was a foreigner, she told her to damn well bugger off out of this country. Once, when I asked Julia what she thought a nice name for a girl might be, she cut me off right away, 'No, I'm not going to talk about it. Superstition.' By now, our life had settled into a calm equilibrium. I was happy. I think that happy people never think about writing, although I don't know that for sure.

Our Dutch years flew by. But the Soviet Union that would soon disintegrate into Russia and fourteen other countries still remained a central *leitmotif* in our life. This began with a tragic incident on one of the first cold winter days of 1991, when I nearly had to go back to Moscow immediately.

I was working late. An editor and I were meant to be holding the fort from ten in the evening until three in the morning, answering the phone for the news line, keeping a tab on the press agencies, just in case something happened after the first edition of the paper had gone down to the printers, such as a disaster or something else media-worthy — a murder, a major fire, the death of a national or international celebrity.

I was supposed to call the printers downstairs right away, to tell them to stop the presses. And then I had to call a journalist on standby, and if no one was available (which was often the case), I had to throw something together myself based on press releases. It was work under high pressure. That shift was considered forced labour and was given to the paupers in the editorial office. It struck me as quite bizarre that control of the biggest paper in the country passed at night to someone who'd never even been in an editorial office just a few months before. Usually, nothing happened. I spent my time drinking coffee, chatting to the editor and anyone else who'd hung around the office, and sometimes someone would go out and get croquettes.

This evening, the telephone rang at about eleven. I answered. The disaster I was informed of didn't involve an event that needed to reach the columns of the newspaper, but an internal affair. A panicked and confused Dutchman who didn't introduce himself told me that the correspondent in Moscow was gravely ill. He was in a really awful state. There was a Siberian chill in Moscow. The correspondent had taken the battery out of his car that evening to stop it freezing, and then gone to his flat upstairs where he'd become unwell. It was something to do with his heart. He needed help fast. I wrote down the person's number, hung up, and was briefly overcome by an ominous feeling. Somewhere in the city where I'd been living a few months before, a city closer to me than Amsterdam, there was someone of my age in a life-threatening state.

I phoned the editor-in-chief.

Barely fifteen minutes later, he rushed into the editorial office with a red face, in a blue blazer with a hockey scarf slung around his neck. The godfather had been in Haarlem, in a restaurant with some friends, and he'd immediately leapt into his chauffeur-driven official car. Less than five minutes later, the deputy editor-in-chief and two editorial desk heads were gathered around the telephone on the news desk, each in their personal alcoholic haze. As soon as I'd filled the gentlemen in and given them the contact number in Moscow, I was invisible to them.

They began making arrangements, calls were made.

Telephones started to ring on all sides.

Soon, it was plain that the correspondent needed special medicine post-haste, which couldn't be found anywhere in Moscow. The name of the medication was passed on. A little while later, they confirmed that the medicine needed could be delivered to Schiphol airport by taxi within half an hour, but the next flight wouldn't leave until ten-thirty the following morning. A private plane could be arranged within the hour, but that would cost forty thousand guilders.

'I don't care if it costs me forty million!' the editor-in-chief thundered, as he efficiently led the entire operation. 'The boy needs saving ... And you there, lad ...' the godfather suddenly addressed himself to me. 'You know that country well, don't you? You're getting on that plane ...'

But it was too late. A little while later, the phone rang again and the news came through from Moscow that the correspondent had died. It was snowing when his body was brought back to the Netherlands, and he was consigned to the earth a week later in North Holland; it was like an adaptation of *Doctor Zhivago*. About five days later, the godfather came up to me quietly in the editorial office. He beckoned me enigmatically, and asked me to come to his glass cubicle. 'You haven't written a single word for the paper yet. But I have a good eye for people, I don't doubt you can do it ...' and he asked me if I'd like to be the successor to the correspondent in Moscow, who'd passed away from a congenital heart defect.

I stared at the tips of my shoes for a second, and thought of how intensely happy Julia had been when she'd come home the day before. She could sit the Dutch entrance exam for the university in just a couple of months. Someone had asked if she'd be interested in working two days a week in a shoe shop on Kalverstraat. I thought about our new flat, pictured the centre of Moscow in my mind with its shabby façades, where souls deprived of nourishment shuffled along like Wayang puppets, and decided, without talking to Julia first, to turn the offer down.

That spring, Julia passed the Dutch entrance exam for the University of Amsterdam with distinction. The dean of the Faculty of German invited her for an audience, where he didn't only call into doubt the status of her degree in German Language and Literature from the University of Leningrad, he also turned out to be an unadulterated bigot. 'What did you say? You want to do a doctorate? Ha, ha! But madam, I've often been to the Eastern Bloc, and from my visits there I know one thing: people can't think independently. We in the Netherlands are accustomed to thinking *independently* and *critically* about all the issues of life from the earliest age. Here at the academy, there's no fear of the authorities. I think you should first internalise that trait, as well as a thorough knowledge of the contents of our curriculum, of course …'

The fact that Julia had already published a series of papers about the German Baroque in a number of Soviet journals did not impress the academic in the least. He generously offered her the chance to start in the second year of an undergraduate course, where for the first few months, the class would read Goethe's *Faust* chapter by chapter. Julia felt like a grammar-school pupil who'd been banished to a comprehensive school. She quit after two months and soon decided to do a doctorate in Slavic Studies, specialising in late-eighteenth century Russian literature. Through her, I soon got mixed up in the Amsterdam milieu of Russian émigrés. A world laced with knowledge and culture that Julia flung herself into like an excitable dog in a pool of cool water on a hot summer's day. She was bursting with energy. Alongside her studies, she'd also begun working for two days a week in the Manfield shoe shop on Kalverstraat. During December, there were all sorts of discussions going on about the future of Russia in the many clubs for Russian and Dutch intellectuals, now that the one thing had taken place that few people had thought possible: the Soviet Union had simply ceased to exist, dissolved by the presidents of Russia, Belarus, and Ukraine in a luxurious hunting lodge close to the Polish border, where the gentlemen first copiously wined and dined — according to accounts, they consumed a whole wild swine.

The failed coup of August 1991 had finally been redeemed.

Julia and I sat in our flat on the edge of the Dutch dunes, watching the TV images from Moscow with pounding hearts, as putschists held Gorbachev hostage in the Crimea and tried to turn back the clock in Moscow. Despite the high costs, Julia spent the whole time on the phone to her family in Leningrad. After Boris Yeltsin had appeared on top of the tank outside the White House with his fist raised before the eyes of the world and promised that he wouldn't give up, we knew that a new age had dawned. Seventy-four years after Lenin's coup in Petrograd, a new Russian revolution had succeeded. For the first time since my return to the Netherlands, I was wracked by a yearning for Moscow, for the Russian city where the newspaper now had a new correspondent — a glamorous, spring chicken of a lad, for whose equally glamorous and thorough front page articles they let me make up headlines.

Meanwhile, I was slowly starting to be absorbed back into my old village life. People greeted me on the street and I greeted them back. My mother often reminded me that I should pop by to see Sima, the Russian woman whose half-sister we'd visited in Moscow and who was married to Theo Veen, who'd been in service with my grandfather. 'In service' — my mother's choice of words was rather bizarre. In the late 1940s, my grandfather had relaunched the antiques business that he'd had to shut down in the first months of the war. He eventually managed to buy the building, completely financed by the bank of the War Administrators Institute. And in the early 1950s, he began setting up the hotel-café-restaurant, after my father had quit his work as a cook's mate in the merchant navy. Because Theo Veen didn't have any work at the time, my grandpa took him into his employment. During the war, they'd distributed clandestine newspapers together – my grandfather *Fidelity*, Theo Veen *Truth*. According to many, he'd been a communist all that time. But in service?

The two of them had lugged cupboards and couches around for years and finally handed out plates of food. They'd slaved away together. There was never any question of a master-servant relationship, it was more a question of a common fate and friendship.

'What are we going to speak, Russian or Dutch?' Julia asked me when finally, for the first time one afternoon, we rang the doorbell where Sima and her Dutch husband lived.

'I don't know, let's see.'

Theo Veen was an agile septuagenarian. He had something goblin-like about him: a gnome with a bushfire of whitish-grey hair on his head and black horn-rimmed spectacles, which covered almost half his face — the stereotypical Dutch communist. After he'd opened the door and welcomed us amid a wave of charm, he led us along to a small, cramped living room, where two frozen chops were defrosting on the radiator, wrapped in plastic with a yellow reduced sticker. I could smell the sickly scent of pork.

'*Privet, rebyata* … *Kak dela?* Hi guys, how are you doing?' Sima Sneevliet, a slight woman with bright eyes behind thin-lensed glasses, smiled and extended a hand but remained seated in her chair. 'Excuse me, children, I can't get up. I pained my ankle walking on the beach yesterday …'

'Sprained …' my grandfather's former helper instantly corrected. 'Not pained, sprained. We say pained when we …'

'Oh, you and your constant remarks!' the Russian interrupted, in a lovingly snarling tone. 'You hurry off and make a cup of tea.'

From that first meeting, the two ladies began chattering to each other eagerly; it was as though Theo and I didn't exist. We listened, subdued and in silence. As they took tea with homemade peach conserve, they mostly talked about practical things. How they could help their friends, family and acquaintances back home in some material way, now that the USSR had disintegrated and there was chaos everywhere in the country. Sima had left two children behind in Russia, a daughter and a son, as well as grandchildren.

She often felt guilty amid all this Dutch luxury.

'You're still so young,' Sima told Julia at one point, 'but you are old enough to know what it's like: to live in the biggest prison in the world, knowing that you'll never be released.'

When I once bumped into him in the bottle section at the supermarket, Theo Veen told me that they'd finally managed to get Sima's half-sister Rena a visa. So one day, this friendly woman, who'd once received Julia and me in Moscow with home-made advocaat, came to live with us in the seaside village too. She was well over sixty, spoke almost no Dutch, but with her clear, gleaming eyes, open face and friendly smile, she quickly captured the hearts of many in the village. To earn a little on the side, she began working as a babysitter. After about six months, she spoke good Dutch. The language that she'd spoken for the first four years of her life miraculously resurfaced. My parents had had little contact with Sima, who was a bit snobbish and tended to pride herself on her intellectual status, but they often stopped for a chat with Rena on the street.

In that same year, my father met Hafid in the waiting room of the hospital in Haarlem, where they were both visiting for their check-ups. The Moroccan turned out to have lived in our village for twenty years, in the New North area. He hadn't yet reached his insurance limit for taxis, so he invited my father to travel back with him. A friendship developed between Hafid, who'd worked in a slaughterhouse for thirty years, and my father. Somehow, they had a lot in common. When it was nice weather, you could often find them on the boulevard, where they sat together on a bench looking out over the sea. After a while, Rena often joined them too. Once, when I wanted to get some fresh air on the beach, I slowed my pace and watched from a distance as the three of them sat there busily gesturing. There they all were: my father, who in his youth had been shot in the legs by the Krauts while attempting to flee, and had sailed with the merchant navy as a cook's mate and then spent his whole life behind a stove, until he had almost gone bankrupt and became ill. Hafid, who'd drifted in one day from the desert, and had spent his best years among the carcasses and the stench, and who had also been stricken by cancer and was now whiling away his final years here because of his children and grandchildren. And Rena, who'd lived through the Jordaan revolt as a toddler in Amsterdam, lost her father in a Stalinist camp, and after a childless life had returned to the land of her birth in her old age. These three entirely different souls sitting on a bench together made a deep impression on me. Sometimes they remained quiet, each submerged in their own private lives and thoughts, staring out to sea.

One morning, the godfather tapped me on the shoulder in the editorial office; he looked at me mischievously, and said, 'So, are you still happy making up headlines? You've been here almost two years now. Isn't it about time you wrote something yourself?'

'Maybe,' I said.

Well, anyway, the godfather continued, he'd received a letter that morning from The Hague. The wives of the presidents of Russia and Belarus would soon be visiting Amsterdam. It was totally informal. They'd been invited to attend an auction of children's drawings made by victims of the nuclear disaster at Chernobyl. The money was going to a good cause. He'd really like to have a report on the visit for the paper, and an official that he was friendly with had also asked him whether he knew someone who could guide the ladies around during their trip. Someone who could speak Russian.

'Show us what you're worth for once, lad!'

Two weeks later, I was driving in a cortège from Schiphol to Amsterdam. Despite the fact that it wasn't an official visit, limousines had been flown in from the former USSR. The wife of the new ruler in the Kremlin, the giant who'd stood on the tank with a clenched fist and flushed Lenin's legacy down the toilet, had never been to the west before. It was lovely weather. Amsterdam was bathed in a sumptuous prosperity and was at its most beautiful. On the first day, the ladies and I walked down Albert Cuyp Market, quietly followed by three bodyguards. The Belarussian first lady held a swede in her hands and asked me what it was. I didn't know the Russian word for swede, I still don't as it happens, but I managed to get by with the generic kapoesta, or cabbage. The auction was a success. I was terribly anxious the whole time. When I'd applied for my job, I may have claimed I could write, but I was still only a headline writer.

On the second day, we and the bodyguards climbed into a tour boat near the Munt Tower for a trip around the canals. A middle-aged woman joined us; she was a little plump, manly, with horseradish-coloured, close-cropped hair. She regally settled herself between the two presidents' wives, with a colossal handbag on her lap, and immediately took over. She seemed vaguely familiar to me. But, of course! She was the Russian woman that I'd seen a couple of times years before in Moscow in Dom Kino, orating from behind a lectern in the presence of Andrei Sakharov and other dissidents. Her name was Galina Starovoytova. She was now the advisor on nationality issues to Boris Yeltsin, an important position because the ethnic violence in the Caucasus had flared up again with all its vehemence.

'What are those ladies doing over there?' Madam Yeltsina asked me, with her head turned around, after we'd sailed into the red-light district.

I told her.

'But they're such nice girls. Look, they're even waving!'

The rumour had evidently gone around the red-light district that a boat would be passing by with the wife of the Russian president on board. Among the waving girls, a blonde had stepped out of her cubicle and was shouting something to the president's wife in Russian.

Shortly after, a muffled ringing arose from Madam Starovoytova's handbag. The Russian woman undid the clasp and took out a telephone with a battery as big as a chocolate log. The reason for the absurd size of the ladies' accessory became clear: it served purely as the case for the telephone. She pressed a button, turned her head away, then covered her talking mouth with her pale hand, and began to jabber. I didn't understand a single syllable.

When she finished the phone call after about three minutes, she carefully stashed the apparatus away and addressed herself to the Russian president's wife, '*Eto bylo Borya.*'

That was Borya.

While we were sailing over the Amsterdam canals, this woman

had just spoken to the man in the Kremlin! This was the early nineties. I'd never seen a mobile phone before.

What I couldn't have imagined at that moment was that I would come across this charismatic Russian woman with the horseradish hair many more times later in my life, at political meetings, gatherings, and press conferences, until she was shot dead at the age of fifty-two on a filthy November day in the portico of her house on the Griboyedov Canal in the old czar's city that had been rechristened Saint Petersburg.

After the murder of Pozorski, this was the second person I'd known in my life who had died by shooting.

A week later, the godfather walked into the editorial office at around eight in the evening, dressed in his student-like garb, with a red face. His aura of alcohol was nothing unusual. After about seven o'clock, a large number of the editorial staff were always on the beer, the whisky and other strong liquor — a tradition that I believe has now been dispensed with, or even banned.

The editor-in-chief walked up to me, told my section head that I had the rest of the evening off, and five minutes later I was sitting beside him on the back seat of his chauffeur-driven official car, which was waiting in front of the building. I could feel my colleagues' looks of bewilderment and envy staring after me.

'So, what do you fancy? For food ...'

I didn't really know how to respond; I mumbled that I'd leave that up to him, of course, not knowing what the reason was for this sudden invitation. A little later, we were standing at the bar of a restaurant on a canal, a sea of mirrors and lamplight, where we first drank a couple of cold beers. After a while, a manager invited us to come to a little room right at the back of the tastefully dark, wood-panelled building, while the largely female staff affably greeted the godfather. It was abundantly clear that he came here often. Even before the soup had been served, we'd drunk nearly a bottle of Sancerre. Then, because another *entremets* of Norwegian wild salmon was brought in, the godfather ordered half a bottle of Chablis, a so-called *entremets* wine. We polished off two bottles of Bordeaux with the main course and the cheese platter. When I popped to the toilet, I saw that my tongue had turned black because of the tannin, and I was happy that the house had brought in a refreshing *spumante* before the coffee came. When he realised that I didn't like sport, my editor-in-chief changed the subject to current affairs. We talked about all sorts of things, with him asking every now and then if it was true what they said: that Russia was drowning in beautiful women.

'Well? Spit it out … You can tell me anything.'

For the first time, I told someone about my years abroad before I came to the newspaper. The godfather listened with amusement, now and then grinning like a schoolboy. He paid the bill with a credit card and a red twenty-five guilder note beneath it. In this world, he explained, we should always think of the serving staff. When we were standing out on the canal and the official car drove up as though on command, the godfather told me that he'd drop me off at home. He lived near my neighbourhood, in the villa-village at the start of the road through the dunes that led straight to my flat. When we were near Halfweg, he mumbled that he still had a raging thirst. He invited me to his home, where he was greeted by a lonely cat that he quickly fed, murmuring a stream of sweet words to the animal in a paternal tone. Then, he came into the living room of this Bloemendaal house with a fresh bottle of white wine. At least I'd learned to drink well in Russia, he said with satisfaction. After he'd taken a swig of wine, a sort of gulping swig that someone very thirsty would take from a glass of water, he seemed to recover an inner equilibrium.

He began to tell me about his marriage, about the complicated relationship with his wife, about his children — a boy and a girl whom he loved to bits. After I'd been listening to him quietly from the couch for a while, drinking slowly and mechanically, I finally asked him why he'd yanked me out of my chair in the editorial office that evening and invited me out. Me, the headline writer, who was twenty years younger than him, and on the lowest rung of the ladder at the newspaper. He glanced at me in amazement with his watery eyes, and suddenly said, dog-tired, 'But don't you get it? At least you know a little about life … That has nothing to do with age … And you're not a boot-licker … most of them at the paper are boot-lickers and they've never experienced anything! And by the way, your piece about the visit of the Russian president's wife was outstanding. So there. And now I'm going to hit the sack … My chauffeur's still outside, he'll take you home … Tell him he can have the rest of the day off tomorrow … Wait, I'll open the door for you myself, otherwise the cat will get out again …'

Three months later, I was promoted to the foreign desk.

During the first two years in the Netherlands, we spent all our money on furniture, on doing up our flat, on tuition fees, and on books for Julia's studies. She was zipping through her exams like a slicer through a vat of butter. But because we were continually short of cash, we still hadn't been on holiday together. Then, one day in October, we were finally ready. We were going to the south of France. After two days in Paris, I steered boldly towards Nohant, to fulfil an old wish of ours: a visit to the manor house that had belonged to George Sand, the writer, who'd received just about all of the greats of her time. In the dining room, there was still an oval table, tastefully laid with linen, porcelain, silver cutlery, and ivory-coloured cards bearing the names of guests such as Flaubert, Turgenev and Chopin, who'd composed a couple of his most beautiful works on a grand piano in the rooms above. My own literary ambitions had died amid the rhythm of morning, evening, and night shifts. Rather than stories and novels, I'd just written a few pieces for the paper. We'd rented a spacious room for ten days with a separate kitchen in the hills of Nice. On the way, we stayed at a chateau, the property of a deaf-and-dumb aristocratic couple who served us delicious pork cheeks. In nearby Menton, we visited the Russian cemetery, in search of a Belarussian family member on Julia's father's side, who'd belonged to the lesser landed aristocracy, and who'd been able to flee to France after the revolution and was supposed to be buried there with his life companion, a lady from Saint Petersburg. Later, this knowledge would be of great value to our children, Julia said, as she dragged me past the Russian Orthodox crosses overgrown with thistles. A person has to have roots. You're lost without roots in this life.

We couldn't find the grave.

Every evening, my girlfriend stood cooking in the kitchen for hours, going back and forth with the ingredients that she'd bought at the market, while I finished off my first bottle of wine and read the pile of books that I'd brought with me.

One afternoon, after searching endlessly, we found Ivan Bunin's villa in Grasse, ringed by a charming garden. Below it in the distance glittered the azure of the Mediterranean. The man who'd picked up girls as a youngster in old Moscow, and written fabulously about it, had come to live here with his wife after winning the Nobel Prize for literature in 1933. There could barely have been a greater hater of Lenin. Just like Zinaida Gippius, Bunin had initially welcomed the revolution. As the scion of an impoverished aristocratic family from central Russia, he'd written against poverty, injustice, and exploitation under the Romanovs, as he rose from assistant-editor to journalist. He soon switched from reporting to literature. After he'd witness the first massacres of Jews by the Bolsheviks in Odessa, he quickly lost faith in the intrinsic goodness of ordinary people. He was one of the first to describe the greed, the desire for vengeance, and the hypocrisy of the Red Leaders. 'They are sea dogs with big pistols on their belts,' Bunin described these usurpers with disgust, 'pickpockets, criminal scoundrels, and clean-cut dandies, dressed in military jackets, skin-tight britches and dandy shoes with the inevitable spurs. They all have gold teeth and big, dark eyes, I suspect from cocaine.' When Julia and I were standing in the profusely overgrown garden, among the fields that produced the flower petals for the perfume industry that flourished some way away, I pondered how the 50-year-old Bunin had finally climbed on board a ship with his wife in 1920, and headed into exile, until his death in 1953. 'This is the last time I'll see the Russian coast. I'll burst into sobs.'

That evening, Julia started chattering at me from the kitchen while she was cooking. Our visit to Bunin's house had made a deep impression on her. Pretty soon, she was only talking about Russia. She hadn't seen the city of her birth for a couple of years now. She knew that things were awful there. Her brother and parents could barely get by. They'd be doomed without the money that we regularly sent to Saint Petersburg by banker's draft. The corruption and crime that we'd seen the first signs of in Moscow had now taken hold of Russian society like an aggressive form of scabies. The masses looked on silently and powerlessly at the formation of a new dynasty. She was aware of all this, but she was still feeling homesick. She'd begun to idealise a few things. An evening of ballet at the Mariinsky Theatre, for example. A plate of *pelmeni* with a little cooking water, salt, and sour cream in a canteen. A snowstorm, while you're sitting safely inside. Naturally, she longed to see France and Italy, Germany, and the rest of Europe too. But she did miss Russia. Shouldn't we head back there again sometime?

'Well? Hey, why don't you say something? Are you sleeping or something?'

On a whim, I'd bought a couple of notepads and a fountain pen earlier that day in a tourist shop on the boulevard. My love was standing cooking, I was drinking wine, I was staying in Nice, but in my mind, I was back in my youth, in the little hotel on the Dutch coast where I'd spent the first years of my life. I wasn't sleeping, I was writing. In big strokes. Feverishly and lightning fast.

I'd begun my first novel.

# CHAPTER THIRTEEN

After four and a half years in the Netherlands, Julia and I finally returned to Moscow in 1996. We moved into a flat in an outlying suburb, where the young guy that we'd taken over from had lived together with his flamboyant girlfriend. Before us, they had taken over from the widow of the correspondent whose heart had stopped one day and whose corpse had been laid out in our bedroom. Sometimes I woke up in the middle of the night, with a constricted feeling around my chest, certain that my time had come too. I felt neurotic. Until I heard that my predecessor, who was a well-balanced person in everything, had had exactly the same experience a couple of times.

In the years that we'd lived in the Netherlands, we'd popped by to see the couple in Moscow once or twice. They'd transformed the flat into a hospitable den of drink, food, and wild eroticism, with a Bohemian allure. You entered it as though it were a Russian novel. My predecessor would grow into a journalist and editor-in-chief of some allure, and his wife became one of the best post-war columnists in our country.

On the day of the transfer of the post, which came with a secretary, a house-keeper who was secretly in the service of the KGB, and a chauffeur with a round head covered in fleshy pimples, my predecessor gave me the book *To Moscow with Two Jars of Peanut Butter* by Karel van het Reve, bearing the inscription:

> *And five jars of patience*
> *And ten jars of humour*
> *And a hundred jars of money*
> *And after five years, they'll come and fetch you, and you*
> *can head back home again. I wish you much success!*
> *Ph & S*

It would turn out to be a bit more than that.

But let's return to the revolution of 1917.

Lenin's coup was only the start, and was followed by a civil war, a struggle for domination that would last until October 1922 — five long years of destruction, plunder and murder, with ten million dead as a result. Former generals and officers of the czarist army, joined by a mishmash of Cossacks, blue blood, ordinary citizens, and intellectuals of various political plumage, competed with each other for glory, fighting against the Red Army, which was led by the merciless organiser Trotsky, while armoured trains of often rival armies moved in confusion through the gigantic country like a travelling circus. The Whites eagerly exterminated another hundred thousand Jews to the celebratory crack of the Cossacks' short whips, and hanged Bolshevik priests from trees, as they screamed from beneath their beards for God's help, with sharpened sticks shoved up their anuses, skewering them to their throats. Sometimes, captured officers and soldiers of the White Army had cages bound around their naked bodies that contained a rat that would bite through the living flesh of the victim.

Those aristocrats who hadn't already been finished off in the first weeks and months of the revolution, or who had gone underground in anonymity, now fled the cities *en masse*, first to other parts of Russia, like Kislovodsk — that delightful spa city where people still drank the iron-rich mineral water, or took restorative mud baths, or listened to classical string quartets in the open air of botanical gardens like a sort of Baden-Baden in the Caucasus — which soon became an unsafe destination too, after the White Army's resistance had almost completely collapsed in Siberia and elsewhere in the country. Then, the former elite began to gather in the Crimea, the peninsula that would soon become a geological funnel out of the country for those that could afford it. The Crimea, which was as blessed climatologically and scenically as the Caucasus, where the Greeks had once built their amphorae, and where later descendants of the empire of the Golden Horde had forged a fairy-tale Islamic empire with glazed mosques and colourful wooden palaces (the beautiful remains can still be seen). In the middle of the second decade of this wonderful new century, I would bear witness to its annexation by little green men from the first hour, with my pencil and notepad in hand. They seemed to have dropped from the moon, soldiers without any insignia, spreading out over the peninsula and taking up positions at barracks, air-fields and strategic roads — men with black and green balaclavas, armed to the teeth with modern weapons, who later turned out to be soldiers from Moscow. This was geopolitical retribution for yet another revolution in contemporary European history, namely the Maidan in Kiev, which I would also witness from the start. I would see the hastily erected barricades of snow and junk, the soot from smoking cars' tyres, fighters at each other's throats with knives and sticks, and people sheltering in little tents with wood fires outside, like a medieval army camp — a surreal contrast to the drinking and flirting in bars, restaurants, and brothels all around — until the cockroach-violence of the security forces, who were entirely clad in black with their gleaming full-face helmets and shields, proved insufficient, and then the snipers came. Bullets were fired from rooftops by rifles with silencers; men, women, and teenagers fell soundlessly in front of the doors of McDonald's and the hotel where I was staying, gnawing my lips and not believing what I was seeing, which marked the beginning of the end of the Ukrainian president, who ultimately fled like a thief in the night, while the next day his palace was stormed by the masses in triumph, like the Winter Palace in Petrograd had been in 1917.

This was followed by a filthy guerrilla struggle in Eastern Ukraine, which was characterised as a 'hybrid war' by the experts who had suddenly emerged from all corners of this world; and there was me, with my 50-year-old-plus body, uninsured because I was a freelancer, among the falling trees and roadblocks, braving drunken nutcases with machine guns, biting back my disgust and fear, and driving around in a hired Lada in the archipelago of towns like Donetsk, Kramatorsk and Sloviansk. Then one night, I was arrested, taken from my bed, and dragged to a rickety ambulance beneath a dulled lamppost on the street, where it stank of formalin, ether, and spilt blood, while the sons of bitches kept the diesel engine running, and it droned as I was told by these jokers that they were going to put a bullet in each of my kneecaps. I didn't even know if they were from the Ukrainian army or the pro-Russian rebels, men and boys whose fathers and grandfathers had once marched together behind the socialist red banners, but had suddenly become enemies because of the degenerate revolution of

1991. By some miracle, I managed to escape. And afterwards, I carried on writing features and reports; the odd time I had Julia on the line from Tchaikovsky Street, I made light of everything — 'Dangerous? You should never believe what they write in the papers about a war like this.'

I'd started hearing voices; not only the thousands of men, women, and children who had died on the ground, whose dismembered bodies I can still see before me, but also the 298 innocents who were shot out of the sky, including 198 Dutch. The bodies of those who had moments before been thinking of sun and palm trees now drifted down in a human rain, onto sunflower fields and among the ripened summer grass in the district where I'd been on the battlefield shortly before. I wrote a second novel that was an homage to the victims and loved ones of this tragedy, a book that became a mirror of its time as I wrote it, that showed some people to be terribly ugly, and not least the author. I tried to sketch a panoramic view of old Europe that was once again adrift; but both the five hundred pages of the novel and I myself were immediately drawn into the caverns of a deathly-sick consensual discourse that swung between good and evil. What I had written didn't fit into the current *narrative*, though, and when I realised how nothing would ever change, my repugnance for the literary business grew so intense that I decided to call it quits. I would die anonymous in occupied Crimea, on a terrace shaded by grape vines, opposite the old Khan's palace in Bakhchysarai; a patch of earth blessed with overweening nature, where in the autumn of 1920, fifty thousand people were hanged and executed on the order of the commander of the Red Army on the ground, Mikhail Frunze. The majority were members of the former privileged class, and only the most prudent had brought their jewels and money with them; most had left their valuables behind in the vaults of Petrograd and Moscow, sure that their wealth would be safe in the banks. But unknown to them, the vaults and safes of both the private and state banks had already been plundered three years earlier, unlocked by clerks and officials, with pistol barrels at their heads held by cursing fighters of the revolution.

One day, one robber stuffed five million rubles in a velvet bag, jumped in a car and a little later dropped the booty in triumph on Lenin's desk, in his office in the Smolny Institute, which had been commandeered as the headquarters of the Petrograd Soviet. It was an unparalleled, elegant Palladian building, topped by five monastery domes, where once aristocratic girls had learned to dance beneath the chandeliers that I still see burning on sombre Saint Petersburg days during my often sombre walks (it's ten minutes from Tchaikovsky Street at a moderate pace). These girls were the most desired trophies of the communist murderers in their black leather coats; at least, those who weren't lucky enough to have escaped to the Crimea, or across the Black Sea on one of the last boats fleeing to Constantinople, where in the morning mist over the Sea of Marmara the gleaming minarets of the Hagia Sophia and the Blue Mosque suddenly became brothers of the Statue of Liberty in New York. Many of those who remained went underground, became prostitutes, sold their bodies often for less than a hunk of black bread, to the peasants and the proletarians who had the power now, or to Philistines who could still live out their sexual urges with death hot on their heels.

Among the refugees on the Crimea route then were Vladimir Nabokov and his family; the writer, who together with Chekhov and Turgenev, had led me to the Slavic seminars in the Spuistraat in Amsterdam, and whose widow I would meet as a student one day in the Grand Palace Hotel in Montreux, on that similarly magical lake where she still lived. Many years later, I would bump into their son Dmitri by chance, beneath the Stalinesque chandeliers at the Leningradsky Station in Moscow. We were both on our way to Saint Petersburg by night-train. That brilliant and mercurial Nabokov, whose intellectual coldness and lack of social concern would aggravate me more and more over the years, however much I liked to bask in the halo of his artistic sun. The youthful Nabokov had wandered as a frail dandy with a walking stick among the proles and common herd of the revolution, with the same arrogance that his mother used to treat the servants in their house in Petrograd and their estate outside the city — they were less than invisible to her. In the family's adventures on their way to the Crimea, he amused himself more or less delightfully, as though nothing could overcome him, which indeed proved the case. While millions of people his age died, he became a student at Cambridge, that privileged universe of white trousers, punting, and the English aristocracy.

Zinaida Gippius, her husband, and two others managed to flee Petrograd in the winter of 1919. Helped by a high-placed official in the Smolny Institute who'd given them safe conduct, they were supposedly touring the country giving readings for the Red Army. They left their house on Tchaikovsky Street on a winter's day with mountainous drifts of snow everywhere and biting frost, never to return again. Within four days, they were able to escape the Bolsheviks for good in a wagon that was full to bursting with soldiers, hoarders, and every possible kind of riff-raff. They first stayed in the Belarussian town of Zhlobin, before escaping to Poland as refugees, after which they finally ended up in Paris, about which Zinaida would later write: 'I prefer not to think any more of those days ... We were always negotiating. One moment with a suspect smuggler, then with another after the first one had deceived us. We continually lurched from hope to despair, only to recover again ...'

They then fell into the hands of people smugglers.

But in contrast to the wretches all over the world now who are searching for a safe haven, back then it was about those who were robbed of their wealth.

After our return to Russia in the spring of 1996, I hardly thought about Ragnar Swindleman's treachery again. I found myself on a rollercoaster of energy: travelling, writing articles for the paper, an immensely busy and whirling social life, sometimes speaking five languages in a day. Despite some controversy with my first novel, I'd carried on mucking about a bit with literature. But the greatest literature for me was often life itself. Oh, yes, those days were just like pages!

The fact that I'd once guided the wife of the Russian leader through Albert Cuyp Market, and explained to her the finesses of love for hire behind neon-lit glass, hadn't done me any harm at all. She'd left a phone number for me, which gave me some degree of access to the Kremlin. One day, the president walked out of a crowd towards me, at a meeting in Siberia that I'd followed him to attend for the paper, and thanked me for chaperoning his wife in Holland.

The openness of Russia in those years was quite phenomenal, despite the permanent chaos: currency depreciation, collapsing banks, murders in mafia circles, a constant parade of new ministers and cabinets, and the continual rumbling of the war in the

Caucasus. Suddenly, everything was being shown on TV. No taboo was undiscussed. Sex, lotteries, and fortune-telling swept across the country. Careers were made and broken. The shops and kiosks had turned into overflowing horns of plenty. The market was a sponge that sucked up everything. I sometimes involuntarily thought about Pozorski, who would have been among the richest Russians on earth now, if he hadn't been murdered on that foul autumn day just after our last meeting. At the headquarters of the KGB, you could walk right through security, simply by putting on an arrogant look, or self-confidently holding up a library card. Anyone who wished to could grub and ferret through the archives. Many people saw foreigners as sent by the Lord, even more so than before; you could arrange anything with a snap of your fingers. Until, on the last day of the old millennium, an ex-spy and KGB member, who grew up among the cockroaches and rats of a Leningrad *kommunalka*, got his hands on the power of the old sick 'czar'. I heard about it in the queue at the supermarket, where I'd just filled my cart with drink, potatoes, tins of peas, gherkins, cold beef, and mayonnaise for the traditional Olivier salad on New Year's Eve.

The rules of the game changed all too quickly now; the restoration had begun. Resentment at the collapse of the Soviet Empire, and the accompanying conspiracy theories, swept across the nation. TV broadcasters, newspapers, and other media were again restricted or destroyed. Some journalists were hunted down, others fled the country. The KGB building became once again a fortified bastion; I watched the employee car park transform within a year from Volgas to expensive foreign sports cars. The apparently inexhaustible streams of money from oil and gas flowed like underground rivers of gold. The army rubbed its hands, cursing those that had handed over the fatherland in the preceding years to the evil western democracies. There was brooding over revenge all around. The atmosphere of fear had returned, of *proizvól*, of the time of Czar Alexander III, who didn't only have his secret police, the Okhrana, pick up terrorists, dissident politicians, students, and writers, but anyone who was suspected of subversive activities, even those in the highest echelons of power. Uncertainty and fear, especially in the circles of the new president, were the best guarantee of enduring domination. Meanwhile, everything remained possible. Friends of mine who were already rich now grew immensely rich.

Shortly after the new lord took up residence in the Kremlin, the rent on our flat in a distant suburb of Moscow was raised insanely, so we were just as well off looking for something in the centre.

Julia had begun dreaming of our own home in Saint Petersburg, but there wasn't much to be bought with the thirty thousand dollars we'd saved.

We did find a magnificent rented apartment in the centre of Moscow though, near Clean Ponds, in a pre-revolutionary building with a grand entrance and a large bay window in our living room, which had a phenomenal view out over the boulevard, and which was reminiscent of Paris. We received friends in our home; the wine flowed like mineral water from a biblical mountain cleft. Those that dropped by from the Netherlands were all talented, successful, famous, or soon would be. One day, Julia came home with something woolly in her hands. It was Moesha, six weeks old. For the first few days, the cat kept out of sight under the couch that we'd bought on sale in Haarlem, that had adorned our flat on the coast for years. But she soon made herself mistress of our new home with her downy, furry presence. We were intensely happy as we followed her exploratory expeditions, like the first footsteps of a child.

I went on a bear hunt in the winter woods in the Urals, to find out what the fascination with killing was among middle-aged men. On holiday, Julia and her father took me to the former East Prussian coast for the first time, to the scented pine forest with darting game and roaming elk, where they showed me her grandparents' old German house, where she'd partly grown up. The apple tree in the garden, too, had survived the bombardments of the city and the fury of the Red Army storming towards Berlin. It yielded big, red, tasty apples. My father-in-law took me to his old primary school, where he'd been in the same class as a future astronaut. Then, this intensely good man, who is now feeding the worms in the Russian soil, gave me a gift that I cherish as one of the most precious things in my life: a little milk jug about the size of one and a half thimbles, bearing the black letters *Nordbahnhof, Königsberg*. It keeps me occupied endlessly. What people may have held this jug in their hands in Hitler's Germany?

I would sit drinking tea and wine for long evenings with a painter who had a studio in the attic of our apartment block, a sea of space between the wooden beams, which creaked frightfully when there was a storm, and likewise a sea of light that shone directly through a milk-glass roof panel. The artist was around forty. With his straggly beard and greyish-blue eyes and stringy eyelashes, he looked like he'd just escaped from one of Tolstoy's stories. He mostly painted religious themes: mother and child, medieval churches and monasteries with onion-shaped domes of various sorts. But occasionally, a creamy, snowy landscape too, in which a sleigh glided past, with the silvery tinkle of bells almost spattering off the canvas, the passenger a Russian beauty draped in blindingly white fur, with red lips and eyes like grey crystals, viewed from the side of the road by a couple in rags. After taking off his cap, the man pressed it with one hand to his crotch, while he made the sign of the cross with the fingertips of the other.

This Russian's deeply concealed homosexuality was clear to me from the start. Sometimes, he started fishing for information about life in Amsterdam. At Easter, he took me with him to church, where services amid brocade habits, singing, and incense lasted the whole night, until at a certain moment the priests would announce: '*Khristos voskrese!* Christ has risen!' After which the faithful would cry in unison: '*Voistinu voskrese!* Truly, he has truly risen!' This artist, who had a continuous inner struggle with his sexual orientation, also liked hunting. One day, he was standing beaming with pride on the staircase, holding up the cadaver of a lynx, which he had shot shortly before in the woods around Arkhangelsk. That very same day, he would paint it in the attic, a *nature morte*, a so-called still-life, which he showed me a couple of weeks later.

The artistic Russian's pockets always jangled with golden ducats; he had rubles and dollars in abundance. Only later would I learn that he'd become the court painter to the new satrap, and regularly visited the new authorities in the Kremlin. His kitschy paintings, which were created with a religious, patriotic, and brilliantly masterly hand, were often given as state gifts when the president was travelling abroad. Not that long ago, I learned that this tragic man, whose sing-song voice I can still clearly hear, and who in other circumstances would without any doubt have become a classical master, chose the path of suicide.

But I didn't follow up on this; I'd rather not know.

———

In the preceding years, the doctors had rarely left my father in peace. After the intestinal operation and then the procedure on his throat, he'd undergone double-bypass surgery, and shortly after, his intestines began to play up again so badly that he had an immediate colostomy. He never complained or cursed his luck. The same was true of my mother who, one summer day, learned that she had breast cancer. She soon had to have a breast removed. I cursed myself when I was finally sitting opposite her in the living room a good two weeks later, having travelled from the industrial city of Norilsk above the Arctic Circle. I felt like the worst son in the world because I hadn't been there when she'd needed me.

'But my boy, we do know you love us?'

In the summer of 2001, something happened that no one had dared to hope: my parents felt strong enough to visit us in Moscow, along with my eldest brother and sister-in-law. Julia and I were at the high point of our lives. I was writing a book every two years, alongside my work for the newspaper, and she'd begun a one-person catering company, and had also had features in cooking magazines here and there. She did a lot of volunteer work, we no longer had any money problems, and our guests carried on visiting us unabated. In the summer months, we rented a dacha seventy kilometres outside the city, together with friends; it was a run down Pippi Longstocking house, with a lake nearby surrounded by tall spruce trees, which we hung hammocks between, and sporadically swatted the big Russian mosquitos with rolled-up newspapers, just waiting for the hour of salvation when we could take the first bottle of white wine out of the stream where we'd laid it to cool. The men would begin chopping wood — in Russia, there was still 'men's work' — and soon the aroma of roasting meat would spread through the undergrowth and the woods, while the mosquitoes flew to their crackling death in the big orange fire that we kept alight with freshly chopped wood beside the *shashlik* grill. At around eleven, someone would often slip off to find extra drink in the dusty villages in the vicinity around us; we'd sit around the fire till about three in the morning, then slip into our sleeping bags and be woken by the warm rays of the sun, take a refreshing dip in the lake, and start all over again.

My mother could barely grasp it, standing in our living room near Clean Ponds. Just this morning, she'd climbed out of her own bed and now she was in the middle of Moscow. She'd flown for the second time in her life. While my father was fussing over her, Moesha emerged from under the German sideboard that Julia had inherited from her grandparents and crept closer, and for the remainder of the next twelve days, she hardly stirred from my father's lap.

Everything trembled in the heat that July: Red Square, the broad shopping streets, and the palace gardens around Saint Petersburg where we went for two days by train. My father drank it all in with his swarthy Portuguese face; it couldn't be hot enough for him — indeed, if it was his choice, he'd have spent his life somewhere in South America, and not behind a stove on the Dutch coast. Now and then, he reached for the blue pouch on his hip, in which he had his colostomy bags; he was scared to death that he might lose them here. My brother and sister-in-law disappeared for whole afternoons into the Russian countryside, and lay lazily beneath the leaves of the trees alongside the burbling water, unaware of the two great sons that they'd have one day.

My mother, for her part, had a tough time with the heat

because of the radiation treatment she'd been having. She huffed and puffed the whole time, and had a red face; nevertheless, she sighed what a nice time she was having, and how much she was enjoying everything with my father. In her imagination, Russia was a country that was covered in snow and ice even in the summer; she was amazed that people were just walking around the city, and that there were trams and buses, shops, supermarkets with packets of butter and milk in the fridges, just like at home; that in certain respects, Russia was a country like all others. When I said that I'd told her this often enough on the phone, and even written about it too, she said, 'Yes, my boy, that may be so … But a person would rather believe what's on TV …'

My father thought the metro was the most impressive thing; he enjoyed himself like a child, taking the majestic escalators down into the depths, into the belly of Moscow, with its underground palaces for the people, paved with marble from the churches destroyed by Lenin's industrious ants, as well as from the monasteries and cathedrals, and the tombstones of the rich. When I told him that the tunnel system had been built partly by someone in Henk Sneevliet's circle, Sima's father, he raised his eyebrows in astonishment. 'You mean Theo Veen's Sima?'

After I'd put my family on the plane back to the Netherlands, I was sure that I'd never see my parents in Russia again. But things were to turn out differently — at least as far as my mother was concerned. My father, though, died shortly after their visit. My mother bore her grief in silence. Despite her own illness, she continued to be a great source of energy, amiability, and helpfulness to everyone, on the outside.

———

I only briefly knew my first ambassador in Moscow; he was a baron who looked like he could have been a distant cousin of the last czar, with his fragile but bolt upright, lightly bearded appearance. It was rumoured that he'd once been earmarked as the spouse for our sovereign. His equally fragile and extremely aristocratic wife was seldom in Moscow. She generally remained among the horses at their estate in Overijssel, leaving her husband, who'd been endowed with the same twinkle in his eye as Prince Bernhard, behind, alone in the nineteenth-century city palace where the residency was based.

Occasionally, we were invited for drinks or to lunch. Once, the ambassador received a delegation of MPs from the Dutch Lower House at the official residency. They were visiting Moscow to examine whether expanding NATO to the east was a good idea now that the Warsaw Pact had been wound up five years earlier. During a lengthy farewell in the vestibule with lots of consultation, the ambassador said to the parliamentarians, 'Gentlemen, don't do it! One day, you'll be sorry!' I can still remember it as clear as day, the more so because I thought exactly the same at the time, and I still do as it happens. Nonetheless, the MPs ignored the ambassador's advice, with Russia's annexation of Crimea and the war in eastern Ukraine as delayed aftershocks.

But it was not the first time that the building with its ballroom, charming dining rooms, and Venetian chandeliers had been the scene of historic decisions. Previously, it had belonged to the German embassy in Moscow, and here the negotiations were conducted for the Molotov-Ribbentrop Pact, down to the final comma.

The next ambassador, with his tall, pigeon-grey appearance, didn't look any less aristocratic than his predecessor, and this was equally true of his wife, a waterfall of unaffected elegance. Previously, he'd held the highest posts in the Middle East, the United States, at the ministry in The Hague, and elsewhere. The baron's successor was one of those rare, almost entirely extinct liberal diplomats who saw it as his task to fathom as best he could the country he'd been posted to, to fully participate in its social life, to attend the theatres and restaurants, between the congresses and the official visits. His home was a permanent buzzing hive of meetings with artists, intellectuals, members of diverse social organisations, and politicians of all kinds, and he systematically involved the rudimentary Dutch press in his activities. He took us with him on his missions to Siberia, to trading cities on the Volga, even to the deserts of Turkmenistan.

He was always present in a calm way, and was a later Moscow counterpart to the legendary British ambassador George Buchanan, who had been the leading representative of the *corps diplomatique* in Petrograd during the revolutionary days of 1917.

Buchanan had witnessed the demise of the czarist empire from close at hand, together with the American ambassador and self-made millionaire David Francis, and the French ambassador Maurice Paléologue, who would gossip with grand dukes in the salons and had great literary gifts. All of them had their residencies within a few minutes' walk of the apartment that I'd later occupy on Tchaikovsky Street.

On a frosty January day in 1917, these three and others were at Czar Nicholas II's final New Year's reception at the Catherine Palace in Tsarskoye Selo. While World War I was still raging some distance away, and forces were gathering all around to rapidly finish off the rich, they were taken to the czar's residence outside the city in a luxurious train — dressed in ceremonial knickerbockers, with feathered caps and buckled shoes, or in dress suits with wing collars — where they were met by a fleet of fur-lined sleighs that ferried them to the palace through an enchanted, nocturnal, fairy-tale landscape, amid the airy ringing of bells, lit up by thousands of lamps. They were then led through the marble vestibule with blood-red drapes, past two Nubian sentries with turbans and halberds, to the golden reception hall, where the czar welcomed the diplomats in his simple grey Cossack's tunic, and began making small talk and observations about the weather, as though there was nothing going on at all, although fear could be seen in the faces of those present, including in Nicholas II's own face, whose 'pale, drawn expression', according to Paléologue's memoirs, betrayed his secret thoughts.

One day, something happened that I'd never previously thought possible: the Russian translation of one of my novels was launched at Fontanka Palace in Saint Petersburg, a couple of months after we'd bought our apartment in the city, with a loan from a friend in the Netherlands.

When I asked my mother and youngest brother to come to Moscow for a few days at our expense, from where we'd take the train to Saint Petersburg, they agreed, after prevaricating for quite a while. As soon as the new ambassador and his wife heard about it, they immediately invited the four of us to dine at the residency.

Despite a life of washing sheets, serving, and scrubbing, my mother had the diction of a queen. She spoke astonishingly refined Dutch, as well as having a natural style which enabled her to mix effortlessly in all circles. I can still see her, with my diffident youngest brother in her wake, walking into the ballroom and taking a glass of orange juice from the silver platter that was offered to her by one of the servants, after which we went into the dining room that was adorned with works by seventeenth-century masters. The ambassadorial couple had asked their cook to prepare a traditional Dutch meal. Not because they knew about my mother's difficult taste in food, but presumably out of empathy and intuition.

While I could read in my mother's eyes that her thoughts were on her husband the whole time — my father who'd only been dead a year and could no longer experience all this — she nevertheless took a lively part in the conversation, smiled, and sipped her white wine. Meanwhile, the steam rose from the hotchpotch and Guelders smoked sausage in the national porcelain dinner-service, curling towards the Venetian chandelier, under which Molotov and Ribbentrop had once schemed over their devil's pact.

'No more divorces' is what Czarina Alexandra Feodorovna, originally 'Princess Alix of Hesse and by Rhine', wrote in Czar Nicholas II's diary shortly after their marriage in 1894; the diary always lay open for her. 'Together at last, settled for life. And when this life is over, we'll meet again in another world, reunited for eternity. I am yours, yours.'

Their marriage — which resulted in four splendidly healthy daughters and their haemophiliac son — was one of a deep and great love, mutual dedication, and complete harmony, in spite of the fatalistic doom that had hung over the reign of Nicholas II from the very first, beginning with his coronation in May 1896. The Saint Andrew's cross, one of the highest decorations in the empire, had come loose on his chest and eventually clattered to the floor; a couple of days later, this was followed by a disaster of almost biblical proportions. During the handing out of free beer, sausages, and commemorative souvenirs on a field outside Moscow, thousands of people were stampeded by the crowds, and in a few minutes, almost fifteen hundred had died and many more been wounded, a catastrophe that the young czar only learned about when he arrived at a ball given by the French ambassador to the city, the Marquis of Montebello.

Nicky, Alix, and the children liked to spend their time together in the rural Alexander Palace in Tsarskoye Selo, strolling in the grounds, singing, playing music, reading to each other from English novels, pasting photos and stamps of their travels in albums, far away from the big city that Nicholas II had always hated. Away from all the intrigues, the banal politics that tried to eat away at his God-given imperial omnipotence, Alexandra commanded her husband not to give an inch to any of it, and the fact that the people were dying like rats in the belly of a sinking ship simply didn't affect her. The family were far away from the Russian gossip press that had grown increasingly hostile at Rasputin's powerful influence over the court, and which painted the czarina as a German spy, a member of the fifth column of a people that holy Russia had been at war with for three years and which had already cost millions of Russian men their lives.

After the February Revolution of 1917, the abdication of Nicholas II in his train carriage near Pskov in March and his return to Tsarskoye Selo, Alexander Kerensky had probably extended the life of the czar's family by a year when the attempt by the Bolsheviks to take the city in July failed and he took power as premier as the successor to Prince Lvov. This was on account of his decision to evacuate the family to the city of Tobolsk, on the border of the Urals and Siberia. Along with some officers, the Romanovs were allowed to take a few trusted servants with them on the train, such as the private tutor Pierre Gilliard, the court physician Dr Botkin, the English teacher Mr Gibbes, and the chambermaid Anna Demidova. In mid-August, the train departed from Petrograd to the east under a Japanese flag. Each time it passed a station, the drapes were briefly lowered, but it stopped every day for half an hour somewhere at random in the wilderness, so that Nicholas could take his habitual stroll.

Four days later, the czar's family and their retinue boarded the river steamer Russ in Tyumen, where the tracks ended, which ferried them to the city of Tobolsk. On their way, they passed Pokrovskoye, the village where Grigori Rasputin was born, and whose prosperous house on the shore rose up over the others. As well as his polygamy, the Siberian charlatan had kept a family — a wife, two daughters, and a son. The fanatical monk had once predicted that his previous patrons would visit this place, a few years before he succumbed to bullets and arsenic in the Yusupov Palace. In Tobolsk, the Romanovs were housed in the home of the former governor; relatively, they had quite a lot of freedom, and could even visit the nearby church. In her letters and diaries, the czarina expressed the hope that they would one day be saved, that the monarchy would perhaps even be reinstated. But when Lenin came to power in Petrograd two months later, the mood grew very dark. In February 1918, every member of the family was put on the same rations as an ordinary soldier. They were taken to Yekaterinburg in the spring and placed under the direct control of the local Soviet. The previous idea that they could flee to England with the help of loyal monarchists, or if need be could be granted a quiet retirement at their beloved Livadia Palace among the eucalyptus trees in the Crimea, had now become an absurd abstraction. They were living the life of prisoners. When the soup and other simple fare was brought into the house, which was surrounded by a high wooden fence, a revolutionary would first press himself between the czar and czarina with his malodorous armpits, and holding a spoon, ostentatiously test the food, demonstrating his proletarian power and contempt for them. Their last commander was the Siberian Yakov Yurovsky, who Nicholas II managed to record in his notebook, 'This specimen is the one we like the least ...'; he would ultimately fire the first bullets at the czar and his young son.

On 14 July 1918, the cleric Father Storozhev was given permission to conduct a service in the House of Special Purpose; it struck him that in contrast to previous visits, everyone had now abandoned hope, except for the salvation of God. The devout sang songs in his presence. The Romanovs delivered their own requiem, sinking to one knee together — Nicholas, Alexandra, their daughters Olga, Tatiana, Maria, Anastasia, and their only son Alexei, who in spite of all the magnificent décor had, in essence, lived a simple life, sleeping on hard camp-beds, with cold baths, and had barely become familiar with the anger in this life.

When Yurovsky asked for extra Mausers and revolvers on the morning of 16 July 1918 because he was going to execute the family later that evening, some of the guards hit on the idea of first raping the czar's daughters: a golden opportunity that they whispered about with flushed cheeks as they swallowed their spit, but nevertheless had to let pass. Towards evening, the family was told that they were to be taken elsewhere later. They were forbidden to undress and go to sleep. Far beyond midnight, they were ordered to go to the cellar, which was closed off on the street side, with only a small dim window on the garden side. Nicholas II carried his

13-year-old son in his arms, followed by his daughters. Because everything was running a little late, chairs were brought in for the Tsesarevich and his parents. Their chambermaid Anna Demidova also brought soft cushions with her. When Yurovsky and his gang of murderers, consisting of ten militia members, finally filed in, he quickly rattled off the death sentence that had been passed on them by the Yekaterinburg Soviet. The astonished Nicholas II didn't even have time to utter his first protest before Yurovsky emptied his revolver on him and his son, with the latter showing an abnormal persistence for life, only cut down after a few more bullets. The empress, her daughters, and also their faithful physician Dr Botkin, Nicholas's valet Trupp, and the maid Demidova, who had all accompanied them, must have flung themselves to the ground in terror in the few seconds before it was their turn. The shots fired at them mostly made bullet-holes low on the cellar wall, with many of the rounds ricocheting off the jewels sewn into the czar's daughters' clothes, so that they needed to be finished off with bayonets.

The children's spaniel was killed too, in the cellar full of gun smoke, bangs, screams, and blood.

The spaniel was called Jimmy.


Eighty years later, on a sun-drenched day in July 1998, the skeletal remains of the czar's family were solemnly buried in Saint Petersburg in the Peter and Paul Fortress, having been found on a country track near Yekaterinburg seven years earlier. The confusion surrounding the Romanovs was still as great as ever. The matter in question was whether the bones that were to be laid in the cathedral that afternoon, where Peter the Great was also buried, were authentic. What should have been the closure of a bloody chapter in Soviet history turned into a controversy that fiercely divided the nation.

In those days, there was a glut of writing about the fate of the czar's family, with each report contradicting the last. According to some rumours, the heads of the czar and czarina were delivered on silver platters to Lenin's cabinet in the Smolny Institute in Petrograd shortly after their murder, just like the five million rubles in a velvet bag had been — one of the many concocted stories, myths, false legends, that swiftly arose in a world in which nothing is normal any longer. In reality, the bodies of the Romanovs and their servants were loaded onto trucks after their execution, and dumped outside the city in a mineshaft, after having been stripped of their clothes, which were burned. Because the pit wasn't sufficiently full of water, the naked dead bodies stuck out. So the next day, Yurovsky was given a roasting by the local Soviet leaders who'd come to check on the results of the crime. They issued their own imperial declaration to bury the mortal remains at a spot where they would never be found.

That night, Yurovsky and his accomplices hauled the bodies out of the mineshaft, tried to burn those of the czar and czarina, which they weren't able to, then put what was left of the remains on a truck and headed to another mineshaft nearby; but they got stuck in the mud on a country track. The gang of murderers (who would later be murdered themselves) hastily buried the bodies in this scrap of ground, known locally as Pigs' Pasture, until a geologist and a filmmaker dug three skulls from the ground in 1979, which had been mutilated by sulphuric acid and bullets. The men, whose expedition had begun with a thorough study of witness statements in the archives, brought the skulls to Moscow, where they requested a Russian Orthodox priest to solemnly bury their find, because they were sure these were the remains of the last

Romanovs. But after the priest reacted in panic, fearing the wrath of Leonid Brezhnev and his communist junta in the Kremlin, for whom the czarist past was still a taboo, the skulls were taken back to Pigs' Pasture to await better times.

Those arrived in July 1991, when, as the freshly elected president of Russia, Boris Yeltsin appointed a special commission to determine the authenticity of the now nine excavated skeletons.

Now that Yeltsin was sporting the colours of capitalist democracy, he anxiously tried to obscure the fact that as the regional red 'czar' of the Urals, he'd demolished the Ipatiev House in 1977 to prevent it becoming a place of pilgrimage for monarchists at home and abroad.

But it had already long been turned into a place of pilgrimage. When I visited the site of the murders in Yekaterinburg a year before the re-burial, the muddy field was swarming with people where the merchant's house had once stood, and where a wooden shrine had now risen, erected by the men and women who kissed icons, made the sign of the cross and muttered prayers, punctuated by their cursing of the Jews.

'Why the Jews?' I asked.

Didn't I know that the murder of the Romanovs was a Jewish conspiracy? Their executioner Yurovsky was a 'Yid', just like the overfed merchant Ipatiev, while eight out of ten Bolsheviks who were in power in the city at the time were 'Yids' too, which was equally true of the gang in Petrograd who'd sent the telegram with the order to murder the czar. 'And what do we see now?' A priest in a tobacco-brown habit leading a battalion of singing women in headscarves looked at me. 'Jewry is once more in power in Moscow. Look at the ministers, the bankers, the oligarchs. Jews, Jews, and more Jews! When will we finally be rid of this plague?'

———

I travelled from Moscow to Saint Petersburg for the Romanovs' funeral with a colleague and good friend, who has since become a great writer, and who I shared the Pippi Longstocking dacha with at the time.

The granite quaysides in the city were black with people, as the last heads of government, ambassadors, other dignitaries, and descendants of the Romanovs from the diaspora were arriving at the airport. We waited with a group of journalists inside the walls of the Peter and Paul Fortress; there, the ringing bells, the display of flags, and the sun playing tag with the golden spire, under which all but two of the czars were buried including Peter the Great, gave the spectacle a festive feel.

The bones of the Tsesarevich Alexei and his sister Maria still hadn't been found at that point. Extensive DNA examination of royal families from all over Europe had proven that the skeletal remains in the coffins flown from Moscow to the former czarist capital were 99.9% certain to have belonged to the five murdered Romanovs. But this was openly questioned by the Russian Orthodox church, to the delight of many of the faithful who continued to believe that it had been a ritual murder by the Jews, and they announced on banners along the road side that the beak-noses in the Kremlin were lying to the people once again.

The patriarch refused to attend the ceremony, and in his place he sent a Saint Petersburg priest, though he did choose sides in the split between the descendants of the Romanovs about the succession. Although the majority of the forty blood relatives of the last czar who had travelled to the city considered the 77-year-old Swiss resident Nicholas Romanov to be the only pretender to the crown, the grand duchess Leonida Georgievna of Paris advanced her grandson George, who lived in Madrid, a claim that Mother Church seemed to tentatively support.

At twelve o'clock, a thunder of cannons shattered the golden chiming of the bells. Thousands of pigeons took flight. The authorities had set aside less than a million dollars for the ceremony, one of the reasons for the demonstrative absence of the grand duchess.

After a little while, my writer friend and a colleague from the TV really needed to go to the toilet. While they went in search of a bathroom, I looked after a camera on a tripod and other equipment. The sun-drenched cobbled square where terrible executions had once taken place now lay all around me.

Suddenly Nicholas Romanov emerged from a neo-classical building with corn-yellow stuccowork, and came walking towards me with his natural stateliness, in a full-fashioned grey suit that subtly accentuated his elegant and aristocratic appearance. I only knew his distinguished face from the papers. The heir to the throne nodded at me amiably and asked in his whinnying Oxford English if I was the man from the British TV station for the interview with him.

'You mean the BBC?'

'My secretary told me that those chaps would be standing here.'

I shrugged my shoulders, introduced myself quickly, and asked him what he thought about the schism that had developed in the family around the succession. On this day of all historical days, the story had slowly turned into a scandal and spread all over the world.

'Schism?' The Romanov offspring looked at me in amusement with crow's feet at the corners of his eyes. 'Do you know what? Grand duchess Leonida Georgievna is entirely on her own in her claims. So how can there be any talk of a schism? Her grandson is more a Hohenzollern than a Romanov. I could compliment the chap on that. The family line of the Hohenzollerns is even older than the Romanovs. My deepest apologies, but unfortunately I have to carry on looking ...'

A little while later, when my friends got back and I told them that I'd just been speaking to the heir to the throne of the last czar, four eyes stared at me full of envious disbelief.

'We nip off for a piss and Waterdrinker talks to a Romanov,' my fellow-artist said, full of irony and disbelief.

Nevertheless, he immediately began fishing for information because while I only had to file seven hundred words, he had to write two thousand for his paper by the next day.

# CHAPTER FOURTEEN

The pounding of the jackhammers and sledgehammers over my head and underneath my feet just refused to stop. I was having a tough time of it, together with our cats who couldn't find any place to rest; they had fled to the linen closet in the bedroom.

We had recently acquired a third cat: a second tomcat, a scoundrel a couple of months old, with boundless energy and a black blotch on his white face, whose name is Kljaksitsj. Julia made the name up; it's derived from the Russian word for 'ink-spot', but because my tongue trips over it, I just call him Tooter. The young gentleman Tooter, who keeps the young gentleman Peach and the old lady Moesha company, here on Tchaikovsky Street.

The plaster that seeped into our house from the demolition was as fine as flour. My wife and I lay awake all night coughing, our throats like cardboard. Vacuuming and wiping it all off with a damp cloth hardly helped: you'd turn around and it was back again. I couldn't understand where it was coming from, until my eyes fell on the antique brass air grilles interlaced into the parquet floor and the walls. A fine vapour was clouding out of them, as though someone was smoking behind them. I asked Julia to buy tape at the DIY shop on the Kirochnaya Ulitsa on her way back from the night school where she teaches German, to paste over the grilles.

'What sort of tape exactly?' she texted back.

'The wide stuff,' I replied. 'The tape they always use to gag people in films.'

The refurbishment of the *kommunalka* above and below us came as a complete surprise. All of the occupants had left for an unknown destination. Nobody had any idea where, and I understood from the caretaker that I'd be better off not asking again. The move took place in the two and a half days that Julia and I were visiting friends in Pskov. When we got home, the worn stairs of our staircase were strewn with paper, wood splinters and other rubbish — a slipper, a flesh-coloured bra, half a cupboard door, books, notebooks, coat-hangers, torn-up gas bills, a bottle of Baltika beer with a broken neck, a dark-yellow puddle that had begun to stink, crumpled empty cigarette packs, tights, a card game that appeared to be making a run for it over the seven metres from the stairs to the front door — the skid marks of a hasty evacuation that were tidied up the next afternoon by a boy in overalls.

He'd been detached from the demolition crew to perform this chore; they were all boys and young men from Tajikistan, this country's Muslim slaves, who worked for peanuts sweeping the courtyards, including mine in Moscow. Clearing snow in the winter, climbing scaffoldings, and often boarding together twenty at a time in a dingy one-room flat, far away from civilisation, on the mouldering outskirts of the city, where the view is only of apartment buildings, factory chimneys, and exit roads, they saved as much money as possible to send to their families at home, who groaned under an autocrat who bathes his well-fed arse every day in a golden bathtub with golden taps. These are the *gastarbeiter*. They are the representatives of a phenomenon that was one of the first things to return to Russia after the implosion of the USSR: poor sods hacking away without face masks, carrying rubble by hand to lorries parked on the pavement in front of our house, earning much less than the Russians.

The demolition began at quarter past eight in the morning and would still be going on at quarter to nine in the evening. There was no point in complaining: the invisible hand of power was behind it. In the hall downstairs hung a stamped paper written on a typewriter that said permission had been granted for this rush job. They could also work on Saturdays and Sundays. My neighbour from Dagestan didn't answer, the diva from the top floor was on holiday with her family in the Caucasus, but I learned from a Russian who was standing in the stairwell with a pencil behind his ear taking it all in — who I thought worked for the contractor — that the *kommunalka* had been bought up by a bigwig on the city council. He was busily buying up portions of buildings — sometimes whole buildings — and even complete streets to turn into rented apartments for a song because the market was at rock bottom.

'How long is the demolition going to take?' I asked the man.

'Count on a month of noise.'

'And the renovation?'

'Oh, at least a year. You'll have to get used to it. But you'll have a nice hallway in return. We want to renovate the stairwell; you won't get any rent for a dump like this otherwise.'


It was late June and the White Nights were still with us. I had two months left to finish my book about the Russian Revolution. Over the last few weeks, I'd hardly written a thing. I wasn't in the right frame of mind. There was a clamp on me, a vice.

The greenery in the parks and the perfumed scent of the lilacs was overpowering; the *lunaria annua* of the moon hung in the pale blue sky all day long. Saint Petersburg would easily rival Florence with its *grande armée* of mint-green, pale-pink, bilberry-red and yellow-daubed stucco façades if it were located on a different latitude, in a different landscape, with the sun coming in at a different angle, without the endless grey months of rain, mist, and bleakness; if it wasn't standing on this miserable marshy ground that bears the bones of countless wretches who gave their lives constructing this city, but rather on a rock, in the midst of fine rolling hills, with the ink-black silhouettes of olive trees and cypresses. Everyone was at the street-side cafés! On Rubinstein Street, on the bank of the Neva, near the Mariinsky Theatre, but also in the dark streets behind, where a commemorative plaque could be bricked into every building because of the terror of the past, but where there is now clear vitality again — small businesses, offices, exhibition spaces, cafés full of young people, sipping at their cappuccinos, engrossed in their laptops. The sight is simply glorious.

After six, the soldiers from the barracks behind our flat would commandeer all the benches in the Tauride Garden, chewing sunflower seeds, spitting out the husks like machine guns. Some lay in battledress, stretched out in the grass, their caps over their faces to keep out the sun, just as Gippius had described in the hot summer of 1918, the first summer after the revolution. I still hadn't managed to find out who lived in her old apartment. I had no desire to be sent packing for a second time by the doorman, but my wine dealer from the Furshtatskaya told me that he might be able to help. A handsome Russian of around fifty, calm in all his movements, with lank boy's hair and a smile that contains a whole universe, he used to work on Soviet cruise ships and stopped notching up his conquests when he reached fifteen hundred. We always have a chat; I'd already told him how I'd really like to visit Gippius's apartment, with an eye to a book.

Oh, the Saint Petersburg White Nights! The devil tugs at your sheets all night and you can't fall asleep. At one o'clock in the morning, a mother-of-pearl dusk hangs over the city; it's only really dark for three-quarters of an hour at most, while the sounds of the day carry on till morning: cars driving off, drunken voices and music, the heated shrieks of girls and boys, a ship's klaxon on the Neva in the distance.

'What are you thinking about?' Julia asked one night, when she too was twisting and turning and couldn't get to sleep.

'Nothing,' I yawned.

'The renovation maybe?'

I grumbled something, giving the impression that I was indeed thinking about the renovation, about the months of noise that were ahead of us, about the fact that from now on our building wouldn't be the same and that I would presumably never see the old occupants again, who I'd grown used to, and who I'd portrayed here and there in my books.

In reality, I was protecting my wife; I was twisting and turning restlessly, brooding over that book, over my dead friends and their families. 'I'm drowning in coffins!' Flaubert had once complained in a letter, when he wasn't much older than I am now — while the maelstrom in my head was punctuated by banal thoughts about the future. How was I supposed to earn my bread if the newspaper really went ahead with my dismissal as they'd announced? Trade in vegetarian meat? Become a businessman after all? A shit-shoveller in a monkey cage?

I took Julia to Vitebsky Station. She was off for a week to do some volunteer work in a camp for orphaned children in the countryside, but mostly to be away from the pounding in our flat, away from the dust and summer heat in the city. When I was walking back to the exit beneath the iron station roof, in the midst of the melee of traders, passengers, and a group of young sailors who sounded like they'd been on an excursion to the palace in Pavlovsk, someone rang me on my mobile. It was Yuri, my wine dealer. He told me that the present occupants of Zinaida Gippius's apartment were at home at the moment. They'd just been to his shop and bought a case of wine, and when he told them about me, they said I could pop by that evening.

'I'll send you Sergei's number in a second. His wife's name is Tanya. A peach, but as you know, I've had my time on the cruise ships.'

After I received the message with the phone number, I scrolled with my fingertip and called the man.

'*Da* ...' he immediately answered, wearily.

I introduced myself, said that I ...

'Yeh, yeh, fine, fine ... We landed last night from Novosibirsk and were just about to have a lie-down. Yuri's friends are our friends. He always orders special red wine for me from Montalcino. I'm crazy about red wine from Montalcino. What do you drink?'

'Everything,' I said.

'Fine, how about eight-ish?' the voice continued in a friendly tone. 'Ring number 13, and the doorman will come.'

It was after four. That morning, I'd sent a couple of pieces to the newspaper; there'd be no more real writing that day. Anyway, I didn't feel much like working on that damned book, so I decided to kill the time with a walk. I strolled towards Nevsky Prospect with the calm gait of a middle-aged man, past Dostoevsky's former home, with a little market by the church where wrinkled old ladies were selling fruit, vegetables, lard, and fish from crates, as though the Soviet times were still ongoing.

The city, meanwhile, was a picture of prosperity that officially didn't exist, but was there anyway; the street-cafés were jam-packed again. Gorgeous girls in historical clothing were in the parks selling paper cones of caramelised almonds. In the canals, boats packed with tourists droned onwards over the motorways of foam, with the loudspeaker voices of the guides reverberating in an incomprehensible cacophony as they drifted beneath the low bridges. Millions of people could barely manage to get by, living in their pustular homes around the outskirts of the city, and also behind façades in the centre. Just as in Moscow, the streetscape was dictated by those with money — relatively few but, in absolute terms, disturbingly many. The smartphones and the fashionable clothes on their bodies were perhaps the only things they had, but the young populated the silver escalators of the air-conditioned, luxury department stores with the air of owning everything around them, or at least they would one day. Their natural hedonism was the continuation of the material desires of their parents and grandparents, who'd mostly grown up in Soviet scarcity. Most of them weren't interested in politics, just like the members of their generation in the West, as long as the continuation of the present and their daydreams about future pleasures were guaranteed. By way of an advance on the riches they were counting on, they went to the lobbies of the mega-cinemas, which were jam-packed in the daytime too, and bought mega-portions of popcorn and Coca-Cola at six hundred rubles a pop — more than ten euros — and in anticipation of the first gong they sat staring at their screens, sniggering together, in the trendy seats in front of the windows, beneath the illuminated posters of *Pirates of the Caribbean 5*, with a view of a stretch of street where the bodies had once lain piled high in the first arctic days of the February revolution of 1917, and later during the starvation siege by the Nazis. But could you hold that against these children? Wasn't mourning history something for the old, the outer layer of the battalion, ready to be the first thing to be peeled away?

Because I suddenly had sore feet, was tired, thirsty and seized with an uncontrollable urge to eat something, I ended up buying a cinema ticket myself, a half a litre of Coca-Cola and a mega-portion of hot, sweet popcorn, and flopped down in a delightfully soft seat, with curved arm-rests and springy foot supports, ready to glide through the world of illusion. I was delightfully entertained, but nevertheless nodded off now and then, and when I walked back out onto the buzzing street almost two hours later, the bright evening sun struck me like a fist. I put my sunglasses on and resumed my wandering through the city, away from Nevsky Prospect and the clammy throng, through the streets to my neighbourhood, where the revolution had once begun — about which factory-sheds full of learned works had been published, though the diary entries of the tragic Zinaida Gippius's were closest to me. I passed the city hospital a while later, a barrack-like building that was now almost completely hidden in a sea of bottle-green shade, where people were cared for at the time of the czars, and where the doctors had murdered my mother-in-law through criminal negligence. I was reminded of a passage of Gippius's, about the first months of the revolution. 'Do you know what Chinese meat is?' she'd written. 'I'll tell you exactly: The Cheka feeds the bodies of executed persons to the animals at the zoo, as we know. Both here and in Moscow. The executions are carried out by Chinese people. They don't hand over all the bodies: they hang onto those of younger people and sell them on as veal. Here and in Moscow too.'

I walked slowly, the impressions from fantastical Hollywood ebbed slowly away, and the time passed equally slowly, like viscous honey. Driven on by some vague feeling, I turned left onto Ulitsa Vosstaniya, the street of the Uprising that eventually runs into Tchaikovsky Street. A moment later I stopped in front of a nondescript Saint Petersburg building with a dark tunnel full of graffiti behind a wrought-iron fence that led to a stinking courtyard, where the tenement stood in which the current satrap had grown up in decently endured poverty. There's one thing that I'd quickly decided on in my writerly life: never, and I mean never, to sully my novels with current politics. But it was a fact, as naked as it was historical, that a century after the revolution of 1917, a proletarian son had assumed the power of the last czar of the House of the Romanovs, which had rivalled the Sun King's. What would come after him, nobody knew. Things could go badly. Things could go well. Things could also carry on just the way they were. I'd shaken the hand of the satrap twice in his palace; it felt limp — not powerful, not pleasant, but not unpleasant either. The majority of my Russian friends pay little attention to him anymore. His terror is that of the narrow-minded man who wallows in power and money, in appearance, with a preoccupation for the physical that is nothing more than a fear of dying, not that of the born psychopath who is bent on destruction and killing.

———

Not far from where the satrap used to live, there was a seedy cellar space with greasy windows that faced out onto the pavement and afforded a good view inside as you were passing by. There, on judo mats, boys in white jerseys and blue sports shorts were busy lifting weights, hitting punch bags, or messing around with each other, in contortions of gleaming sweaty muscle mass. It was a sports school of the lowest order, with shabby, rusty equipment, clearly discarded by other institutions, just like in a poor neighbourhood in New York: Harlem or The Bronx. Boys with proto-Slavic faces, and also those of Caucasian and central-Asian origin, were busy working on their bodies and their futures, which at first glance seemed only to promise the jobs of street-fighter, doorman, or extortionist — the same kind of street-fighter who had finally made it to university and become their president. Their underprivileged origins — childhoods of poor nutrition, continual worries, and having to stick up for yourself — were etched into these boys' faces. I stood there looking for a while, and felt some sympathy for these young guys, for their youth, their strength, their endurance. I harboured as much sympathy for them as for the teenagers who I'd seen the week before storming onto the street with liberated cheers, with sashes around their bodies, in dresses and jackets that were much too baggy for their spindly arms. These were the graduates of the grammar school that Julia had attended. They were getting ready for a lovely long summer holiday, followed by lovely years at a polytechnic or university, in the midst of the Empire of Evil.

I quickly walked on to Kirochnaya Ulitsa, past the building at number 12 where Rasputin had once lived. There were two good-looking girls standing by the entrance to his portico. Their pale-blue tattoos made their bare limbs look like Cologne pottery. They hugged each other, stuck out their tongues, kissed each other intimately.

When I got home, I took a bound Russian edition of Gippius's diaries out of the bookcase, which I was planning to give to my hosts as a present. Back on the mildly warm street, everything was illuminated by a dim violet glow. A cool breeze was blowing from the Neva. The bread factory was working summer shifts and was already pumping out its sweet, precious scent. I flopped onto one of the tasteful benches in the Furshtatskaya, which runs parallel to Tchaikovsky Street, and is one of the most beautiful streets in the city with its linden-lined central avenue. To the left of me hung the American flag, almost motionless on the façade of the building where the consulate is now housed and where the embassy was during the revolution. Back then, the ambassador David Francis brought from the United States his faithful assistant cum chauffeur cum valet — Philip Jordan, an African-American who was born in Missouri and grew up among the street gangs. He would develop in his letters home into one of the most incisive and moving chroniclers of the first days of the revolution in Petrograd. 'In Russia, the streets are littered with cut-throats and street thugs,' he would write one day, less than a hundred metres from where I'm sitting now. 'You can hear the machine guns and artillery thundering day and night, thousands of people are being murdered. In a house not far from the embassy, they murdered a little girl, twelve bayonets stuck into her body. We're like rats in a trap.' Not far from the embassy? Could the murder of the child perhaps have taken place in our street? What does a person really know about the past, goddamn it?

I had half an hour to kill and began leafing through the diary, reading a passage here and there. Gippius had really figured out the world! This woman, who during her poetic religious quest had lived an almost virginal life, but according to some had always maintained covert connections with the Khlysts sect (the flagellants), which Rasputin had also belonged to, whose rituals were accompanied by sexual orgies. She quickly and mercilessly exposed the hypocrisy, the stupidity, the ignorance, especially in the West. She pierced a whole generation of later fellow-travellers with her scorn; they were still singing the praises of the communist Utopia when I was a student. 'Europe sends "commissions" here and individuals too, in almost complete lunacy, to keep abreast of what's going on,' she wrote, shortly after Lenin had seized power. 'But they walk straight into the arms of the Bolsheviks. They build pretty décors, put them up at the Astoria, and have them guarded day and night without concealing it, so that it's impossible for them to get into contact with the outside world. If a country can exist in Europe in the twentieth century where there's such phenomenal and previously unwitnessed *slavery*, and Europe doesn't understand that or else accepts it, then Europe must meet its downfall. And that would be its just desserts!'

After fleeing Petrograd with her husband, the writer and cultural philosopher Dmitry Merezhkovsky, she stubbornly continued to warn the world about the Bolsheviks from Paris. In 1936, after all the horrors endured in Russia, Gippius could see that another war was taking shape; she wrote to a friend, 'I don't think even the devil knows what's going to happen in France or when. You have to understand that we don't have a cache of gold in England. Bunin does, and can go anywhere he wants, but we can't. For some reason, I just can't believe there's going to be another war, even though you can expect anything from that bastard Hitler.' But three years later, 'Those two devilish brothers: the Bolsheviks the eldest, and the Nazis the youngest, have turned the world on its head and nothing surprises us anymore. No person doubts that Hitler, that possessed one, will be beaten; that victory is all too obvious. But if the most important Satan, Bolshevism, is left to triumph unmolested, can Europe harbour any hope of a stable peace?'

Shortly after the invasion of Poland, she predicted the later occupation of Eastern Europe, the Cold War, until peace finally arrived with the fall of the Berlin Wall and the collapse of the Soviet Empire.

According to some, history was complete.

But history doesn't repeat.

It rhymes.

And only the future is complete.


'Who have you come for?' a voice asked on the loudspeaker beside the door, after I'd pressed the 13 on a metal panel.

I told the voice who I'd come for. The door was opened a few seconds later by the doorman with the abnormally bulbous eyes, who'd sent me packing a few weeks earlier and threatened me with the police. He'd evidently been informed of my arrival and behaved subserviently; he just about refrained from adopting the position.

'Take care, Mister! The third step's pretty slippery. There's usually a stair carpet, but it's been at the cleaners for the last three days!'

I climbed the impressive stairs to the second floor, having passed the cubicle in the hall where the doorman spent his days behind the desk with a bank of screens that showed all corners of the street and surroundings in black-and-white. In the passage, I was about to ring again, but a splendid leather-padded door opened on its own.

'My wife is still in the bathroom — that damned flight back from Novosibirsk has totally worn us out, we had a four-hour delay!' The man standing in front of me was my age; he spoke in a tone that suggested we'd known each other for years, he was wearing modern glasses and had wild ash-coloured hair. 'Do come in, no, keep your shoes on. We've been to Europe often enough to know the customs!'

I entered an apartment of bizarre dimensions; passages with high plastered walls fanned out in all directions like a labyrinth. The hall, in contrast, was pretty cramped and more or less merged into a modern kitchen that completely clashed with the painted ceiling, the glimpses of Greek friezes, and a grainy marble fireplace and antique furniture in another room. The windows partially looked out onto the gateway to Tauride Garden. After I'd introduced myself, and my host had briefly inspected my book, as though it had just dropped into his hands like a moonstone from the heavens, he turned the conversation to our common wine dealer in the Furshtatskaya. He insisted that I call him Sergei and addressed me informally.

'Wine is a weakness of mine … Yes, let's sit here, until Tatiana comes in …' The Russian sat down at the kitchen table, gave me a glass of wine and topped himself up from the bottle with a glugging splash. 'I only used to drink vodka, what else is there in Siberia? In the late eighties, you'd murder for a good bottle of Kristall vodka. A mate of mine in the car trade was sentenced to seven years in a camp after he knifed his old drinking buddy from the army with a penknife one night. They were friends, but they were dead drunk and they began to fight over one bottle of Kristall! He got seven years' maximum security for the killing, but after three he was already dead from appendicitis. There were doctors in the barracks, but at that moment they were all out hunting in the woods in the area, and they were dead drunk too! Foreigners can't even imagine …!' He grinned for a second, the grin of someone who has been busy for a while polishing off a bottle on his own and is pleased because he finally has company. 'What do you think? This one comes from Sicily, from an excellent grape … I always start with the white, then the red, mostly Italian. Yuri knows my taste. And he has those wines from Montalcino imported specially for me. But anyway, after the vodka came the beer. One beer brewer after another sprang up, then one brand of beer after another appeared on the market. Russia had suddenly become a beer paradise! I'm talking about the nineties now — before that there was only a sort of weak owl's piss that was sold from tankers on the side of the road. You even had to take your own empty jam jar with you – there was a shortage of glass, of everything at the time. Can you imagine? Practically everything. Some people had a few litres tanked into a plastic shopping bag. Ah, but how can you explain all this to a foreigner? Anyway, we were patriots and we drank the Siberian Crown brand! Siberian Crown! I was dealing cars — I bought up cars for price A and sold them on for price B — the money streamed in, but secretly we were all under the influence of Siberian Crown! Delicious, foamy, full-bodied beer. My mates and I drank an ocean of it in the *banya*, with *liverwurst* from Tomsk on the side and warm prawns. But guess what? I slowly started to get a belly like a rainwater butt. I already had kids, I was married. Then that sushi rage started up. My wife and I had already moved here from Novosibirsk a while before, and we decided to have a healthier life. That's partly the influence of youth: I've got a daughter in Moscow now in her twenties who does yoga. She wants Tanya and me to go to yoga class as well. For our mental and physical health. It's supposed to be good for the sex life too. We drink wine almost exclusively now. On the odd occasion, a glass of whisky, as a nightcap! But tell me … Gippius … Of course we know who she was … A poet, a writer … My wife and I are dealers, people of money, but we aren't Philistines. We even visited her grave in Paris. Houses where celebrities once lived are worth more. In trade, whatever trade it may be, you always need to know as much as you can! But to be honest, Tanya and I don't enjoy reading all that much, we prefer films … They live, move … Books are dead … Why would someone still read those dead books?'

I calmly drank my wine and let my host keep on talking, so that I had the opportunity to take a surreptitious look around. Apart from the kitchen, everything still seemed pretty intact. The interior of a grand pre-revolutionary apartment, once occupied by the Saint Petersburg upper bourgeoisie. The copper-green dome of Tauride Palace was gleaming through the trees in the garden of the same name, to the left of the spot where Julia and I had buried our middle cat Ljòlja one winter's night. As I'd passed the entrance to the courtyard, it had flashed through my mind how in June 1919, on a White Night just like this, Zinaida Gippius had been put on watch by the Bolsheviks at exactly this spot. 'All occupants of the house, with no exception, have to do regular three-hour shifts. Why it might be necessary to hang around in a dead quiet street that's always well-lit is anybody's guess. The sun is shining brightly. There's a lady sitting on some stone steps in mourning dress. She looks as though she doesn't have any strength left, as if she's given up all hope. Suddenly, she sticks out her hand, silently and in pain. She doesn't ask for bread — oh, no! Who can still give away bread these days? She asks for dried Roach.'

'They can complain about the Kremlin as much as they like,' Sergei continued, 'but there's still gold to be made in the auto business.' He sourced the second-hand cars at the top end of the city, or sometimes just over the border in Finland, and loaded the merchandise onto the train for transportation to his contacts in Siberia. His wife was in textiles, mostly ladies' lingerie that she acquired in China. She flew back and forth from Saint Petersburg to Shanghai at least three times a year. 'But would you like some more wine, or are we slowly going to make the switch to red?'

'I think this white is delicious,' I said.

'It's a special Sicilian grape,' my host replied, as he hoisted himself halfway up from his seat, and topped us up as if it were water. 'A golden tip from Yuri ... Damn, what is that grape called again?'

'*Catarratto*, my sunlight ...' said a clear woman's voice, which originated from a brunette with Botoxed lips of about forty years old. She entered the kitchen wreathed in a mist of bathroom freshness, clad in a canary-yellow kimono that showed off her full figure to good effect. 'Is there any wine left for me? I haven't totally woken up yet. I fell asleep again in the bath. Ah, you must be the gentleman that came for Gippius? I can tell you that she's supposed to have been an awful person, a bitch, haughty, elitist, the sort of shrew who thought she was better than everyone and everything. She was married to her husband for fifty years, but no children — that sort of thing sets the alarm bells ringing with me ... Tanya,' she introduced herself, offering me a hand, while her husband took a green-stemmed glass out of the cupboard and poured her a white wine too. 'Your name is the nickname of our city, by coincidence … Are you staying here long in Saint Petersburg?'

When I told her that I'd been in Russia for almost a quarter of a century, and that I was living with my wife in an apartment a little way away from here on Tchaikovsky Street — we were practically neighbours — I think I discerned some disagreeable confusion on the handsome face of the Russian woman, after which her husband asked me what I'd been doing here all this time.

'Communication,' I answered, knowing that my profession aroused suspicion in many in Russia.

'And now you're writing a book about Gippius?' the wife of my host asked, as though she was suddenly intensely interested.

I kept it superficial, answered that I'd been going around with the vague idea of writing a book about the Russian Revolution of 1917, and that I'd come across Gippius's diaries by chance — I nodded towards the bound work that I'd given her husband as a present, which was now living a lonely existence beside a damp sponge on the worktop — and how I was extremely grateful to both of them because it was important for me to see her former house with my own eyes to pick up something of the ambience.

'Then you should also write down that Rasputin was a frequent visitor here …' The brunette tasted her wine as though it were a ripe, juicy piece of fruit. 'Aahhh, it's delicious again, Sergei, that Yuri is such a dear treasure! We'll have to get a couple of crates of this right away …'

'Is that true?' I immediately got the conversation back onto topic.

'My husband doesn't want me to talk about it. He's superstitious. A bear of a guy, has done deals for a million cars, goes hunting every winter for wild boar in the Urals, but in the dark he's as frightened as a child. Do you see that cross around his neck? I gave him that a couple of years ago. Blessed by the patriarch. So that he doesn't have to be frightened when I'm in China for my lingerie and he's at home alone. At least, I hope he is!' She gave her husband a loving, challenging look, with eyes like stars, and he drained his glass in one gulp, playing at wounded innocence. And she continued: 'When we bought this house, there was an ancient woman living in the front room. She was way past ninety and was the daughter of the former caretaker. Everyone left, but she just carried on living here after 1917. We had to hand over another fifty thousand dollars just to get rid of her. Two nephews made a claim on the room, and they were awkward to the very end. She's the one who told us. About Rasputin. That he was often here in the lobby. But he wasn't necessarily here to visit Gippius in particular — a lot of prominent people lived in this building at the time, just like now ...'

'Well, I'm switching to red ...' Sergei got up, and conjured a bottle of red wine with a screw cap from the fridge, then flopped back down in his chair. 'We mostly drink red wine cooled too ... For the freshness ... Tanya, stop going on about Rasputin,' he said to his wife, who helped herself to the dregs of white that were still in the other bottle. 'Let's talk about ... There's a Gazprom director who lives in our building, as well as a former world judo champion who's now chief of military police in the city, and two lawyers who represent our state at the very highest judicial levels. I'm not naming any names, but the twenty-four-hour security in the lobby downstairs isn't for nothing ... This is one of the most prominent addresses in the city ... But just to get back to that revolution of yours ...' My host took off his glasses, quickly wiped the lenses with the corner of his shirt, put the glasses back on and then stared at me with a watchful eye, as his voice dropped an octave. 'What sort of communications are you in, actually? I might be in the auto trade, but I come from a family of intellectuals. A person doesn't have to read books to be an intellectual. Watching films, keeping your eyes peeled, coupled with common sense — that's enough! No offence, my good man, but Tanya and I are often in Europe. We're even thinking of buying a house in Spain, near Marbella. But every time we're in Paris, London, or Berlin, we have to explain ourselves … Imagine …' The Russian sniffed the bouquet of the red wine before he poured one for me and himself, and then followed it with a resolute swig of approval, and continued: 'There's a lot wrong in this country, but our leader is supported by the masses. We'd rather be ruled by a thief who gives you bread than a thief who keeps you poor. And makes sure that chaos doesn't break out again. You're in communications, I hope you're not one of those secret propagandists for "good intentions". Half of the world is on fire because of the good intentions of the West. It's not about good intentions, it's about whether they turn out well. I trust you *dorogoy*, my old mucker, but tell me, why are we always portrayed as collaborators in these European capitals? What does this have to do with the West?'

'My dear sunlight …' his wife interjected, pouting, and clearly bored. 'Maybe our guest would like to see the rest of the apartment, that's why he came after all?'

The brunette knotted the sash on her kimono, hauled her husband from his chair, and the couple guided me intrepidly through their flat.

The tiled stove in the corner of the parlour, with its ochre enamel tiles and painted moss-green arabesques, was still the original. The whole flat was like a showroom of a nineteenth-century furniture shop; the gigantic parlour was filled with two sofas covered with blue silk, a chaise longue with a tiger motif, and a variety of antique side-tables all thrown together, albeit littered with DVD covers, magazines, modern smokers' paraphernalia, iPads, and cardboard boxes containing little white boxes of ladies' lingerie. The dining room was modest — it was clearly rarely used — and there was a high-priced exercise machine in the corner with a display panel like an office computer. The plastered ceiling, painted with angel motifs, and the Karelian birchwood panels, were still intact, but chalk-white Greek pillars had been set against the wall and clashed totally with the original style. They were obviously supposed to lend a chic appearance, but they looked as though they were from a DIY store, which was presumably the case. These same pillars, though even bigger, had been set up in the bedroom around a platform that bore a four-poster bed made of honey-coloured, luminous wood, with a red curtain, of a size that a baby elephant could fit into.

'We're the only people in Russia with a bed like this,' Tanya said proudly, as she stepped onto the platform in her kimono, her hips swaying as though on a catwalk. 'We had all the furniture imported from Italy. It was made by an ancient carpenter who also furnishes palazzos for the aristocracy around Montalcino. That's where we drank the wine for the first time too, right, Sergei?'

I estimated that the apartment must have been about three hundred square metres. My host had clearly had enough of the excursion through the flat, but he led me to the bathroom, where the colourful mosaics, gold swirls, and dark speckled marble seemed vaguely familiar. 'Do you know the Arabian bathroom in Yusupov Palace?' Sergei asked, as he kicked something away with his foot, an intimate scrap that shouldn't be lying there. 'It was completely restored a few years ago. Rasputin was murdered there. I tracked down the craftsmen and had them do this bathroom. So, that's the lot.'

We turned back to the kitchen, through the splendid rooms that Gippius and her husband had only partly occupied, and which would have been as crammed with books as they were now utterly devoid of them. The kitchen was the heart of the house and the place where the occupants most liked to be. With one telephone call, the hostess had some warm meaty snacks delivered from a restaurant up the street. When the order arrived we were onto our third bottle. The couple drank the red wine at a rate that suggested the white had been cheap plonk. When the hostess asked me how many children I had, I answered without any hesitation two, to immediately get that subject out of the way, after which we started toasting the new generation, our parents, the wisdom of those who had to help the world on its way, and soon enough the satrap in the Kremlin too, after Sergei had once again turned the conversation back to politics. He reckoned that the world was at an international watershed. The Americans had finally come out of the closet, and now you could see what human garbage they had hidden there all these years! And wasn't the same true of Europe? Wringing his hands, he could only look on at how the top brass in Brussels launched their arrogant moralising every day, like a swarm of clay pigeons. It wasn't only the Russians, the Americans, and let's not forget the British, but the whole devilish gang throughout the world that was crazy! Crazy and hypocritical! Then his wife changed the subject to China. She'd been back there the week before to buy the autumn and winter collection of ladies' *dessous*. But doing business with the Chinese was always challenging —

if they could rip you off, they just couldn't help themselves. We were slowly being inundated by the Chinese, she declared. The airports throughout the world had become ant hills for them. And there were swarms of them in the city now too. The guides in the Hermitage and in other museums complained about their rude behaviour, how they touched everything, how they spat on the floor; it wouldn't be long before the first Chinese stuck their selfie-stick through a Rembrandt or a Renoir!

After the fourth bottle of red wine — this time a Brunello, as warm and broad as the sun, and lovingly opened with a corkscrew — the lady of the house suddenly disappeared. She came back a little later, slurring that she wanted us to tell her what we thought of the new collection of lingerie that she'd bought in Shanghai. Then she disappeared again. The heavy wine had taken hold of me. In a haze, I was catapulted back in time. I was once more in the office of my former business partner Pozorski, behind the Lubyanka in Moscow, at the agency of OLGA & OLGA SEXUAL LADIES LINGERIE, which Swindleman and I had once supplied with three shipments of *dessous* from Taiwan; we must have made seventy thousand dollars off them, even though I'd never seen one cent of it.

'This one's called The Spider Wasp …' The hostess had come back in again; she opened her kimono and displayed her full-figured, sunbed-brown body, clad in a fiery red slip with black ruches and matching brassiere. 'Well?'

'Classy undies, Tanya!' said her husband. 'Very classy!'

The show continued. The designs were all strikingly chaste; there was evidently something going on in the world of lingerie too. Sergei clapped his hands like a child, taking greedy swigs of his ruby red wine, looking at his wife with childlike adoration, clearly smitten. I disentangled myself from them, and made out that I was going to the toilet, but my bladder was wondrously light and empty, so I grabbed the opportunity for a last wander through the apartment, through the splendid rooms, with the shadows of the antique sofas and furniture, bathed only in moonlight, as though these were the exhibition rooms in a museum.

When I got back and told them that it was already one o'clock, and that I had to be up bright and early the next morning, they gave me a hospitable and understanding growl, and I felt a wet kiss on my neck, and a warm hand in mine. The padded door opened and when I was once again on the marble stairs in the hall, another doorman hurried up to me, a little guy with a mouse's face.

'Take care on the stairs, *gospodin*, they're slippery! Our carpet's at the cleaners for a few days ... That's very good. Goodnight, sir!'

The full moon was pale above Tauride Garden. I hadn't taken three steps before I felt the phone in my trouser pocket vibrating. It was a message from Julia at the orphans' summer camp. She'd been given a group of teenagers. Nice girls and boys. They'd just finished a walk in the woods, and then eaten the fish they'd caught themselves in the river earlier that day, and they were now sitting around a campfire singing together. It was Saturday, so the leaders were letting the kids stay up as long as they liked. And how was I doing? I stopped walking to answer, texted that everything was going okay, but that I was totally stuck with that shitty book, that I was too dumb to write a historical work, that I'd never finish it on time, and I'd prefer to be dead. Just then, the silver door of the spa salon to the right of me opened; I'd often seen men going inside. Now this guy came out, a bald Russian escorted by two girls who could be his granddaughters. The man looked like me. Of all the monstrosities in life, unexpectedly coming across your doppelganger, a person physically practically identical to yourself, is the most monstrous. You see yourself as others see you. Filled with disgust, I stood there as though I'd been nailed to the ground. The Russian was wearing an expensive suit, his wrist was gleaming with gold, and his belly quivered like mozzarella; he walked onto the steps with the two giggling girls. As if on command, a Jaguar came around the corner of the Furshtatskaya. I kept still, the bloke and the two girls got in, and the car slowly disappeared in the direction of Tauride Palace, from where I could hear the gruff barking of dogs …

When I again became conscious of myself, I realised that I was still standing with the phone in my hands. I hadn't sent the text to my wife. As my heart pounded, I deleted my drunken words, so that the screen was again empty. Then I typed in: 'Dear Julia, I'm going to sleep now. Everything's fine. Sleep tight. I love you.'

And I quickly walked home.

# CHAPTER FIFTEEN

As soon as Julia got back from summer camp, I left for Moscow. I'd made some good progress on my revolution project. A day has twenty-four hours — eight to work, eight to drink, eight to sleep — a pragmatic rhythm in which I've written ten books.

In Moscow, I was busy working for the paper. I made two short trips by train to the provinces, cooked, and slept, but one evening, I couldn't stand it any longer. I'd had enough of the talk in the papers and on TV, and of the press conferences as well. I called my Frisian beer-buddy Gerbrand, and an hour later we were sitting in café-bistro Zhan-Zhak as of old.

The girls were back again, spying from the corners of their eyes into the sparkling mirrored walls — or rather, they'd never been away. Gerbrand was more energetic than ever. He downed big jugs of beer. He looked at me mischievously the whole time, but what he was saying was actually pretty sad. For three and a half years, he'd tried to get a job in a Russian circus for his act with three black panthers, but he'd never managed to. The Russian who'd lured him to Moscow with tall tales of a golden future had fled, after wheedling ten thousand euros for arranging the air transport and quarantine and obtaining the necessary certificates. All his savings were gone. He'd briefly considered going back to Holland with his panthers, but the ban on predatory animals would soon apply from Trondheim to Gibraltar. As an animal tamer, he was a European refugee.

When I asked what he was going to do now, his eyes lit up like the diamonds on the collars of his panthers, who he'd always had enter the ring in darkness. At a party, he'd met a 40-year-old blonde, half-Russian, half-Uzbek woman, a former ballet dancer, who'd divorced her husband a year earlier, a filthy-rich Russian. Gerbrand had seduced her with his light blond Frisian head of hair, muscles like cables, and the photos of his panther act, and they'd ended up in bed together that first night. Within a week, she was completely addicted <u>to</u> him. She had the yoga studio in her villa in the Barvikha woods converted into a mini circus ring, with original props. And there he had to tame her, naked, with his whip.

'She's completely nuts …'

After a couple of beers, Gerbrand and I took a walk to another establishment close to Red Square. 'She always wants to show me off at some party, an opening or a premiere. Hardly a day passes without some event. That story about taming her in her yoga studio is doing the rounds like a bush fire among her friends. But anyway, she's given me a credit card with no limit. I have total *carte blanche*! She's got eighty million dollars. The kid has no idea of money. I take $5,000 out of the bank every day. No more, no less. She doesn't even notice. If I keep that up for a year, hopefully two, I'll be made.'


Back in Tchaikovsky Street the pounding, drilling, and hammering went on without end. The dust seemed to be getting finer, by some strange mutation. Julia roamed through the flat all day with a damp cloth, worried about the cats. I even found her one morning wearing a mask, one of those white face masks that the Chinese use; she was trying to fit a similar piece of junk over Moesha's snout. It was utter madness and I was stuck in the middle of it. How much can a person demolish?

The entire décor in this historical building above and below me was shot to hell. A young worker who I bumped into in the passage told me that the new sounds were actually from the renovation. All of the waterpipes, electrical and other cables were to be replaced, a process that would take at least eleven weeks.

At around five, Julia went to school — the evening school in Sadovaya where she doesn't even earn the equivalent per hour of a cappuccino on Nevsky Prospect, but which she's happy with and I encourage. Just after she left, her brother rang the doorbell.

'Brother-in-law, are you home?' he called up through the intercom.

'Yes, brother-in-law, I'm home,' I replied cheerfully into the telephone receiver, and pressed the button to open the outside door to the street downstairs.

I quickly checked whether there was beer cooling in the fridge. Julia had taken everything out to make room for the jars of preserves that she'd made from plums, blueberries, and strawberries for the winter. I put three bottles of Baltika in the freezer section, but once Alexei was sitting at the table opposite me as usual, with his shoulders sagging and his eyes glazed, he told me that he didn't want any beer, or tea, or coffee — nothing.

'There's been a disaster,' he said, stuttering with emotion. 'I'll tell you straight out, a downright disaster.'

The evening before, my brother-in-law and his friend and partner were having a drink on the Nautilus. Business was going well; the number of people wanting to do the sailing course was increasing, and sometimes they rented out the boat with a captain (mostly himself) to couples who wanted to have a romantic few hours sailing on the Gulf of Finland. In September, they could start repaying the debts to the bank and me. And now they'd finally had an evening off. A warm August breeze was blowing over the water; on the quayside at the little harbour, there was the sound of singing and an accordion that was coming from a group barbecuing meat in the open air. To celebrate their business success so far, they were drinking on the deck of their own boat like millionaires. Fool that he'd been! They hadn't even had much to drink — at most five glasses of apple liqueur — but despite not having much alcohol in their veins, they got entangled in a heated discussion about the future of their joint venture, and finally about politics, at which point my brother-in-law's partner called him a traitor.

In stark contrast to my brother-in-law, who'd travelled, spoke English, and followed the world news on the internet every day, his partner had only been abroad once: to Helsinki, in a rented van, to buy a new kitchen for his flat because everything there was half the price, even after paying the import costs. But as the offspring of a former Soviet military man, he was a patriot. He'd rather go on holiday in his own country, and he was proud that his son would soon be serving in the Russian army. As a good citizen of your fatherland, you have to be prepared to make sacrifices — if necessary, your own flesh and blood. After the NATO troops first began stirring things up in Ukraine, according to his partner, they were now right on the border with Russia, in the Baltic states. Poles, Americans, even Canadians, under the direction of Berlin!

Although my brother-in-law was the grandson of a sea captain in the Soviet navy, he was appalled by both the system and Russia's military posturing, and had done everything he could to keep his own son out of the army. One day, he'd paid a fortune to a medical officer to obtain a fake exemption certificate; you'll do anything to save the health and life of your child.

'Traitor,' his partner suddenly said to my brother-in-law on the boat.

'What do you mean?'

There was a brief silence, after which my brother-in-law's partner said the terrible word again. He was amiability itself without a drink, never looked for an argument, nor would he hurt a fly.

'Anyone that keeps their son out of the army is a traitor.'

In an attempt to keep the peace, my brother-in-law topped up their apple liqueurs, murmuring by way of appeasement that luckily, as friends, they could have different opinions, and then he carried on with his line of reasoning. The country was in the grip of people who didn't actually know anything about life. That went for the clique in Moscow, the governors from Kaliningrad to Kamchatka! Yes, they really had no clue! Maybe that was their greatest crime. They lived in villas and palaces, had private planes, sent their children to elite schools in the West, where they also had their country houses and their billions, but at the same time they followed the instructions of the satrap who said that they should detest the West, vilify it, hate it. How long could the country continue doing the splits? In the Kremlin, they only had the most modern smartphones, but the messages in their mailboxes came straight from the Soviet Union and from the Middle Ages! The country was going backwards, not forwards. And my brother-in-law, who in his stubbornness took after his father — my father-in-law — was paying for his propriety, after a life of hard work, with the pension of a glorified bum in a one-room flat, and now he told his partner that he <u>was</u> sorry he'd never really been to Europe. Not so much the museums in the fine city centres, or the coasts with their dunes and palm trees, but the interiors of countries such as Belgium, Germany, Denmark, and France, with their well-cared-for, ploughed fields, the cowsheds, factories, and small businesses that produced things that everyone wanted to have — otherwise they'd go bankrupt — and most of all the villages, the small towns and cities with their bakers, butchers, florists, carpenters, roofers, house painters, restaurant owners, publicans, and shopkeepers, who like the farmers didn't only have an understanding of their trade, but shared a *love* of their work, in contrast to Russia, where almost all craftsmanship had been destroyed by the communists, and a quarter of a century after the fall of the USSR, it still hadn't recovered, in fact it was suppressed.

In truth, those in power looked down on people like them: the enterprising lower-middle classes. How long had they had to beg for the permits for their sailing school? How much time did it take to get the right stamps? How many kickbacks did they have to pay to various people? How in God's name could his partner like these characters who essentially deeply despised him? The satrap had once lived abroad as a spy, distrusted everyone, was always on his guard. Later, as president, he visited most of the foreign capitals, but what did he know about *real* life there? Had he ever driven on a French country road with cattle grazing to the left and right, and fertile fields, not in a limousine with a motorcade stuffed with bodyguards, but as any free European citizen in a small car? He had no idea what a pleasure it was to stroll through a French market, where local farmers sold their fresh produce, doctors shopped for groceries with their families — doctors who helped people first and foremost because they *were* doctors, and not because of bribes.

Or what it was like to wander around towns where you could trust police officers and officials, where judges really administered justice and didn't just carry out their orders from above, where a person — in brief — could live as a person should.

'Russian tomatoes are the best in the world,' his partner remarked, not having understood my brother-in-law, or been willing to. 'And if things are going so well there, why is half of Europe in revolt? And what are you talking about those farmers for? Our grain harvests are breaking all records. We're the granary of the world again!'

My brother-in-law eventually sloped off. It was only this morning that he found out what had happened afterwards. His partner had stayed on the *Nautilus*. He'd opened a second bottle of apple liqueur. After a while, two figures had left the *shashlik*-barbecuing, music-making group further down the quay: two young women. They'd wheedled their way on board the yacht, where a broad-shouldered man was drinking to excess, alone by the light of a storm lamp. They began drinking with him, and soon persuaded him to take a boat trip with them over the water. My brother-in-law still didn't know quite what happened. In any case, his partner went sailing with his boozy head and, miracle of miracles, he made it back from the Gulf of Finland intact. But coming back, he must have run into something in his alcoholic haze — a mooring-post, a buoy, maybe the quay itself. In any case, the boat was so badly damaged that it was almost on the point of sinking. The *Nautilus* was totally smashed up and had to be repaired as quickly as possible — the damage would run to thousands and thousands.

'What a fool I've been!' My brother-in-law raised both hands to his head in despair. 'First to start drinking, and then to start a quarrel about damned politics. Usually, my partner's a nice lad, I swear it, it's always the cursed drink … What am I to do now?' Alexei looked at me with the sad, damp-eyed expression of a seal pup that's been abandoned by its mother. 'Go on, I'll have a beer then … How could I have been so stupid? I'm ruined, I don't know what to do, I'm totally wracked with nerves …'

When I came back from the kitchen with two ice-frosted bottles of beer, my brother-in-law took one straight out of my hands, mumbling that he didn't need a glass, and lifted the neck to his mouth. Then he began to say how his sailing school should under no circumstances suffer from the incident, naturally. He'd built up a reputation after all! What's more, the roster was full of people for the course till the end of September. While the *Nautilus* was being repaired, he'd have to hire a boat; he'd already been nosing around on the internet, there was enough on offer and his partner had promised to sell his car. That was enough for 70 per cent of the initial costs, but they were still stuck with that damned 30 per cent.

'How much?' I put the cold bottle of Baltika to my lips; a sharp pain jabbed into my front teeth.

'For me, it would be a question of three grand,' my brother-in-law answered. 'Tell me, what's that awful pounding upstairs the whole time?'

In the bedroom, Julia had covered all the furniture with sheets; it gave it a spooky feel, like a house where the occupants have gone away for a long time, but in the evenings we could at least crawl into a dust-free bed. I tugged a sheet off a dresser, bent down, opened the little door and took out a grey metal money-box. The money-box had always stood in my father's office, among the packs of macaroni, super-size tins of tomatoes, crates of wine, and other stock; there, he did the bookkeeping at a table that had previously been in the café, often while he was still wearing his chef's tunic. The money-box was one of the few things that I'd inherited from him. At the time, I'd left most things to my brothers, on account of their offspring.

I still had eight thousand saved — a hundred and sixty fifty-euro notes. I always kept the key to the mini-safe with me. Julia didn't know about the money. Every man has his secrets. I'd wanted to use it to pay off part of my home loan, but in the end I'd decided to set it aside for what the Russians call 'a black day'. I quickly counted out sixty fifty-euro notes. I put the box back, shut the dresser door, and pulled the sheet over it again; Tooter came to pay me a visit with his tail up, until the whine of an electric drill picked up again from above, and he quickly sped off to join Moesha and Peach in the linen closet.

Back in the living room, my brother-in-law was sitting there with a pencil and paper working out some figures, the tip of his tongue sticking out of his mouth. He glanced up at me and said calmly, 'If I don't have any more setbacks, I can start paying you back in the summer of next year. Don't worry, brother-in-law, I know exactly how much I owe you. One day, you'll have it all back. This damned country is finally condemned to success, and so are we!' His snigger turned into a guffaw, and although I didn't know if he was being serious or was really making a joke, I naturally laughed along with my brother-in-law.

Back in Moscow on my way to an appointment for work, I passed by October Square, where I hadn't been for quite some time. The majestic Lenin was still on his pillar; Julia and I had looked out on him from our double hotel room in the winter of 1990.

Lenin surveyed our city like a general would a battlefield, with his right hand in his trouser pocket, flapping coattails, and bronze revolutionaries at his feet. Back then, this neighbourhood had been the epicentre of the newly emerging market economy.

Meanwhile, in the present, capitalism had become as common as a Big Mac, but October Square and the start of Lenin Prospect was still one of the busiest traffic arteries in the city.

After the two Siberian scientists from Novosibirsk had received the million Deutschmarks for their tomography project, I never saw them again, at least not in person. Khinshtein had been appearing on TV for years, as a nuclear expert, and spokesperson for one of the parties that supported the satrap like an applause machine. He'd grown older, but in a way that didn't involve decline, rather a gradual conservation process. His helmet of blue-black hair had turned whitish-grey, but his sharp bird's face was as sharp as ever. He was the type of man who would grow to be very old. Soon after the duo had defrauded the German funders, his fellow member of the Academy of Sciences, Trofimov, had died. He disappeared into the waves in the sea near Mallorca; his body was never found. I only learned about it by chance when Khinshtein was doing an interview online about education in the Soviet Union, and he recounted the sad fate of his former good friend and fellow scientist.

The hotel of the Academy of Sciences where Julia and I had once taken a champagne bath had transformed over the years into a shabby transit house. There were massage parlours, and human traffickers stowed their living cargo here from the East, heading West. Bazaar-like shops had sprung up on the ground floor around the lifts in what had once been a fairly chic lounge, to which Pozorski had descended shortly before he was murdered.

This Soviet building, together with thousands of other Soviet buildings in the city, had been recommended for demolition, just like the apartment that I'd rented in the nineties. The places in Moscow where I'd spent the best years of my life were rapidly being lost. Maybe it was time to head off for good. But where to?

I'd been out and about that day researching a piece, which I wrote up in my flat on Bolshaya Tatarskaya. Then, in my inbox, I found a message from my friend Felix from Cap d'Antibes. Ten days earlier, I'd sent him the latest version of my book about the Russian Revolution of 1917, which still wasn't finished. I'd ignored the emails from my publisher in Amsterdam, asking where the manuscript was, and suggesting that, although I hadn't actually overrun the delivery date, she was getting to the stage where she wanted to know what sort of book it was going to be. What was getting in my way was fear: the eternal fear of failure. I was happy that everything would soon be over for good.

My friend's opinion hadn't changed very much, even after a couple of hundred more pages. I was a fool not to have developed the theme of the Neva more, and also connected it to the current state of affairs. In what was then Petrograd, the Neva had been the dividing line between rich and poor, wealth and want, exploitation and rule. The Mediterranean was the new Neva. The outcasts in the world were coming to claim justice, not across the ice this time, but over the waves in boats. The exodus from Africa to Europe continued unabated. Wretches who only dreamt of a humane existence drowned every day like rats in the cold waves, and right-wing bastards all over the world seemed to think this was okay, and did nothing, or even encouraged turning the sea into a floating fortress, supported by the plebs who'd crawled out of their lairs; the old continent had once again become a zoo full of political adventurers and agitators.

Oh, yes, my friend in the south of France was right: you only had to change the word 'SIRE', which the poor slobs had helplessly directed at the czar in their petition in the winter of 1905, to 'EUROPE', 'PETROGRAD' to 'AFRICA', and 'QUARTERS' to 'COUNTRIES', and the poem of history rhymed again:

> *EUROPE,*
> *"We, inhabitants of Africa, who come from various countries, our wives, children, and helpless elderly parents, have come here to YOU, EUROPE, to seek justice and protection. We are poor and oppressed, we toil endlessly, and we are degraded. (...)*
> *We are being suffocated by despotism and our lack of rights, we are gasping for breath. Oh, EUROPE, we have no strength left. We have reached the limit of our endurance. We have come to that terrible moment when it seems better to die than to continue in our unbearable sufferings..."*

During the first days of the revolution, the cold and bloody days of February 1917, it soon became clear that the czarist world was finished for good. Servants were ordered to drape the façades of the elite's neoclassical city palaces with red flags and banners, and rig private coaches and sleighs with red reins, as proof of their masters' warm support for the revolution. There may have been aristocracy living here, but they were *good* aristocracy, with their hearts in the right place. Of course they welcomed the Bolshevik revolution! Hadn't they pleaded all their lives for a more just society? More rights and opportunities for the poor? A fairer apportioning of the earthly pleasures and riches? Hadn't they secretly flirted with the ideas of the revolution in their younger years, as members of the privileged, intellectual, ruling class? Always read the right books, papers and periodicals? Oh yes, they'd kept it a secret — a person doesn't want to flaunt their goodness — but they had supported the *Narodnaya Volya*, the People's Will movement, which aimed to overthrow the czar, both morally and financially, even if no receipts actually existed. The red reins that they now had harnessed to their coaches were the proof!

The red reins would have to save their lives.

The revolt of 1905 had broken out after Czar Nicholas II had ignored the people's petition and had his troops fire on his subjects; the streets were suddenly strewn with the bodies of the rich, and the horizons of the countryside glowed orange and red from estates that had been set on fire by the peasants, out for vengeance on their landlords. The abstract love of the privileged for their poor fellows had taken a knock, but the remorse and guilt they felt still ran deep. The rich were like drug addicts though, and could only forget their existential pain in intoxication, continuing to party, living off the interest on the family fortunes that they'd inherited, travelling to sanatoria and rivieras, while in the evenings they were still served food and wine brought by their servants from the kitchens, which they'd often never set foot in themselves.

After the revolution, Nicolas Nabokov, the cousin of the writer, pondered in his memoirs, 'Were all of us, the entire upper class of Russian society, so completely insensitive, so terribly alienated, that we didn't realise that the delightful life we were leading was unjust in itself, and it was impossible for it to continue like that?'

After the outburst of fury in Petrograd in 1917, Lenin's world revolution almost succeeded. In Germany, Italy, the Balkans, and the collapsed Austro-Hungarian Empire, a furious throng traipsed through the streets with red banners and flags, clubs, bludgeons, knives, and firearms, to settle accounts for good with the old capitalist regimes. In the end, it was only after World War II that Stalin was able to install his communist satellite states in Eastern Europe, but the years 1918 and 1919 could have been the historic moment for the Occident to truly turn red — not with blood, but politics.

Many of the German soldiers who'd returned from the trenches and found the land of their birth in complete chaos, cowardly abandoned by Kaiser Wilhelm II, who'd fled to the Netherlands, pinned their hopes on the Spartacists led by the German communists Karl Liebknecht and Rosa Luxemburg. The red spectre was now belching, farting, and reeking from every pore, and crapping all over the old continent. Soon, Hungary had its own Soviet regime, under the leadership of 'The Budapest Lenin', gentleman-dictator Béla Kun. The communists were also stirring in the Carpathians, the Balkans, and in the new small republic of Austria, while in nearby Bavaria the beer-halls were jam-packed with furiously smoking Red Guards, communists, former deserters, defected soldiers, nihilists, students, and artists — the men sporting long hair, the girls often close-cropped — who called for Soviet republics, full of revolutionary zeal, sex, and fighting songs, while at headquarters fingers hovered over the triggers of the machine guns, ready for the global uprising.

But it would all end in the slaughter of the communists, followed by the establishment of the Weimar Republic in 1919

— the first parliamentary republic in German history — where an ex-paper-hanger and failed painter from Austria, with a black toothbrush-moustache, would soon succeed in filling those same Bavarian beer halls, drawing in people with his hypnotic and demonic talent for rhetoric — a born comic, with people literally doubled up laughing, sprawling over the wet wooden tables as he again conjured up some greedy little Jew — mostly rousing the same men to rapture who had previously huddled together in this place, deflated and disillusioned, to listen to the communist prophecies from other mouths, and who now stared hopefully up at the podium once again, while the Löwenbräu flowed from the beer taps like biblical liquid gold, spattering into the steins.

Hitler was soon christened the 'Bavarian Mussolini', the counterpart to the Italian who'd been sent by the gods, with his granite eyes, granite fist, and granite chin, who knew how to manipulate mass psychology — with short salvos from deep in his throat, the staccato of a machine gun — an art in which Lenin had been his forerunner. It was with Lenin, and nobody else, that this irascible barking began, and the dismissal of opponents, the propaganda, the spectacle that since then has never ceased. German democracy did its work. Hitler was elected chancellor. The revolution had succeeded after all, even if the outcome was somewhat different than some had hoped for and expected.

Now, was the world on the cusp of revolution again? Wasn't it a recipe for disaster that there were, once again, millions of stateless persons and refugees roaming the globe, with unemployment that had never disappeared, and a mass of people thundering towards Europe from Africa?

To many, the Russian aristocracy's flirtation with the underprivileged — those they'd ordered to fetch firewood every day, or to take their coats, or tuck hot foot-warmers in their beds — was only a fashion statement in those years before 1917, a perfume you put on; it cost them little. But when the revolution came, people learned: the rich started employing these 'red reins' *en masse*, not when it was too late, but preventatively.

After the revolts throughout western Europe in the sixties and seventies, western society slowly became the Realm of the Red Rein, where optimism reigned supreme, where people could finally think about themselves for once, and growth seemed uninhibited, a universe in which everything was possible, in which a generation ruled the roost that had never been through anything.

History had ended; everything was purely and exclusively focused on the shining future, shinier than the present.

Most people one came across were kind and friendly; workers stuck out their hands the way you'd blissfully stroke a stray dog's head on the street. People praised newcomers for the variety of their cultures — essential enrichment; by now, their own lives were as pristine and immaculate as newly starched sheets — if a blemish were to appear, an immediate panic would ensue. Never before had the liberties and delights of life smelt and tasted so good, certainly in the ever-swelling archipelago of restaurants — take two steps and the cuisine of the world was on your plate; only Philistines still cooked and ate at home. The aeroplane was the new bike; in the Realm of the Red Rein, people travelled to their holiday homes in France, Florida, and Tuscany, just as ordinary people would walk up the gravel path to their garden sheds. War and poverty were far distant phenomena; if the threat came closer, approaching the borders of their blessed districts, sometimes terrifyingly close to their streets and fine homes, then something had gone terribly wrong beyond the scope of their understanding. People would look around like a mother who'd lost her child at the beach, and a guilty party would soon be located.

From preschool, people were taught to love threatened plants, animals, and distant peoples, and were prepared step by step for a diffuse philanthropy, a warm empathy for humanity. By some wondrous ethical mechanism, people were even saved from guilt. Criticism of their actions stemmed from the malodorous crypts of bastardry, hate, envy, jealousy; they themselves did little or nothing wrong — a person who wished others well could never be a bad person.

In the Realm of the Red Rein, it wasn't particularly about political colour. The reins were taken up by all persuasions and creeds, from left to right; those who adhered to a leftish world view lived like the right, and those who were on the right lived like the right too — their actions barely differed, their lives were often completely identical. It was a phenomenal and magnificent spectacle, with a moving and sometimes almost poignant beauty. The members of the Brotherhood of the Red Rein took their red reins in hand and collectively drove an immense air-carriage, drawn by air-horses, with their hooves clattering in the pink clouds, as though they were swimming. There was enough room for everyone on the comfy, silky-soft cushions, for the family, their children, often for their friends too. They drifted over the countries of Europe like some unearthly phenomenon, in radiant, twinkling light. The masses looked up at them with their heads raised, at first filled with awe, open-mouthed, as though it were a reverse eclipse; but anyone who looked too long would get a sore neck, a stabbing headache, and after a while some were slightly blinded by the sight. Spots appeared before their eyes, not red ones but black and brown.

The most important principle in the Realm of the Red Rein was this: always, and without fail, you must act in accordance with the law. Within that boundary, anything was possible, even the abandonment of your own morality. In public, you could plead for diversity, write about it in books, pamphlets, and newspapers, you could even lead political parties that were almost exclusively driven by ethnic prophesising, but at the same time no one barred you from sending your child to the very best school, and always a white one. Often the entire network was desperately tapped — tips were feverishly exchanged on the silky-soft cushions of the air-carriage about universities all over the world, institutions that would give the children of the Brotherhood the best chances of success. These were the most precious things they possessed. The contacts that children made on holidays, beneath the smiling gaze of their parents, were maintained digitally for the rest of the year and on short vacations — a week skiing, a week snorkelling, a city trip. There seemed to be no limits for the children in the gilded air-carriage either; they glided over the world like eagles over ploughed fields, they knew each other, spoke each other's language.

In the Realm of the Red Rein, people mostly went to work like other mortals, but at the end of the month, many of the members of the Brotherhood came home with three, four, five, sometimes fifteen or twenty times more than those that still stared at them from the ground with their sore necks. It was the market, the law of supply and demand, that explained and determined and justified these great differences; there was nothing illegal about the fact that one person had to work an entire month for what another earned in a day. This had been true in the directors' offices at multinationals, banks and law firms since time immemorial. But now it had gained a foothold elsewhere too: the directors of semi-public enterprises, housing associations, utility companies, hospitals, care facilities, and even schools had begun to act like capitalists, with bonuses and chauffeur-driven cars, not with private capital, but the community's. Friends were taken on as consultants for daily sums that a butcher in an abattoir wouldn't earn in a month.

In the beneficence of the golden air-carriage, the *nouveau* soon spoke the same language as the older passengers; as well as tips about schooling, addresses were secretly exchanged for bankers and accountants — entirely honest, reliable, decent folk that could help them to pay the state as little of their thoroughly deserved earnings as possible. Many of these recommendations came with tips about buying property abroad, or making financial arrangements offshore; there was nothing illegal about this, it was all above board, people in every country were doing it. If the new European aristocracy with their barely taxed salaries and allowances wanted to stretch their legs and head to the nearby paupers' wards, it was as if they were taking a stroll back in time from the chic Nevsky Prospect to the outskirts of the Vasilyevsky Island of 1917, with the revolution already brewing.

Modern poverty was particoloured, both native and external; an ironic and sickening consequence of the actions of the members of the Brotherhood of the Red Rein was that these ordinary people were set against each other, fighting for jobs, for some air, for a respectable life. But it was different from Petrograd in 1917, where the bourgeoisie had gone around wrapped in furs, while bums were often left shivering and barefoot in rags. The difference between rich and poor on the streets in contemporary Europe was now almost invisible. Two boys in the same jeans, wearing the same trainers, staring at the same smartphone, were standing at a stop waiting for a tram. The tram came, they got in, and a little while later they got out at different stops. One boy came home to a house with a velvet cord in the drawing room; the other stumbled over a mountain of unpaid bills, staring at the toes of his far-too-expensive shoes. The clichés about poverty from Dickens to Dostoyevsky had slyly metamorphosed, but one thing had remained the same: those in the Realm of the Red Rein still professed a love on a mass scale that cost them nothing; they pleaded for a better life for others, some even screamed it from the rooftops; they even budgeted for the costs to bring this about, but once again they mostly had others pay for it — their own prosperity remained largely unmolested.

The discourse conducted by the Brotherhood of the Red Rein centred on gender, art, vegetarianism or otherwise, benevolence, and the necessity for meditation, all to distract attention from the real problem: the ever-growing differences between rich and poor; one's own pleasant life versus the awful lives of others. In the Realm of the Red Rein, they continually pointed to the politicians. Of course, they voted for the right party — a party that stood up for the weak; it was others that were holding back progress. At the same time, the lives of those they professed to love were further away than Saturn — those who cleaned their houses, served them in restaurants, washed the bottoms of their parents. When there was any criticism of their own decadent lifestyles — the absurd salaries, bonuses, and allowances, the nepotistic networks — the Brotherhood of the Red Rein took refuge in a sort of bizarre logic that was reminiscent of the red aristocracy under Stalin. Whenever anyone denounced their lives, they furiously dismissed this with the riposte that they didn't own the luxury goods, but only made use of them with the approval of the state. This dialectic came quite naturally to the Brotherhood of the Red Rein.

But something had gone terribly wrong in recent years. The passengers on their silk cushions in the golden air-carriage had suddenly glanced down and observed the state of things, such strange and unexpected things, so that all of them like a single being were driven to the corners of the carriage in panic; but the horses continued to canter and managed by a whisker to keep the whole thing upright. The passengers, clutching each other tightly so that no one would tumble out, looked in astonishment at how black smoke was rising from the earth, from explosions: not the detonation of fireworks, but real bombs. At first, everything seemed far away, pandemonium like in a silent film, but all too soon the thunder, the blasts, and the gunpowder smoke of the battlefield came closer by; and at the same time, another phenomenon unfolded below, but at first they couldn't work out what it was — a horde of ants, cockroaches, lemmings? — but when one of the passengers, an MEP from Brussels, took out his ivory opera glasses, which he always carried with him for his weekly visits to La Scala in Milan, and set the precious object to his eyes, twiddling the lenses open-mouthed, he suddenly exclaimed: 'People! There are *people* down there!' And for a little while, a terrible panic broke out in the golden air-carriage, a clamour, cries of fear, and telephone calls to family and children — with recommendations flying back and forth like fleas in a circus for how to secure their homes and possessions. A stream of people was advancing from the south to the north, and thank God passed the neighbourhoods and houses of the passengers in the golden air-carriage; this was a natural process, there was little they could do; water simply happened to flow downhill. The passengers had barely recovered when the most terrifying thing imaginable occurred; the opera glasses were passed from hand to hand, the ivory grew moist from their sweaty, trembling fingers. Among the continuous stream of people — poor creatures in search of a decent life, a plate of food, safety — a raging sea of balled fists suddenly rose, like weeds in a stubble field. This repugnant sight was accompanied by guttural screams and curses at those on the silk cushions in the golden air-carriage, where their fidgety buttocks sidled back and forth in cold fear. As well as their fists, people held up flags, while metallic echoes arose from songs sung in unison. The Bavarian beer halls of the old days hadn't only been brought back to life, now filled with the supporters of new political adventurers, who'd cribbed the arts of the black toothbrush moustache, but also seemed to be spreading out over the earth beneath the cantering hooves of the air-horses, like an aggressive eczema. But then — as though in a fairy-tale with a happy ending — the riff-raff thinned out from one day to the next. The offensive that the passengers in the golden air-carriage had initiated on a mass scale, using their smartphones like old-fashioned cannons, the networks that they'd made sweat and steam, the newspapers, TV, and other media that had sped to their aid, had transformed into a triumph of democracy, reason, control, and hope mostly. Even if there were autocrats in power and lunatics elsewhere in the world, and the drowning in the cold waves went on every day, the inhabitants of the Realm of the Red Rein began making plans again; they phoned their offspring, happily and optimistically, from their homes and holiday homes, with some studying abroad, or backpacking somewhere on the globe, and once again consulted their financial advisors, daring to take another look at the state of their securities portfolio after such a long time, and even bought some extra shares, immersed themselves in culinary delights as before, in a delicious Babel-like confusion of palates; while the theatres and concert halls were crowded too. The delight that people derived from the arts, which offered consolation for the sufferings in this world, had in fact never abated; the music of Bach, Mozart, Scarlatti, and others could still affect their tender souls, move them to rapture, like the Saint Petersburg aristocracy who had sat on the plush blue velvet in 1917, listening breathlessly to Chaliapin's bass voice in the Mariinsky Theatre — the opera *Boris Godunov* — while the Winter Palace was being stormed a short distance away, and the vermin were creeping from the gutters and readying themselves for the final struggle. And just as then, when they'd left the beautiful temples, when they'd exchanged the delirium of the arts for the delirium of ordinary life, lips curling in distaste, heads turned away and cursing the vulgus under their breath as they passed them on the street, not the Saint Petersburg pariahs this time, but those that had looked up at the passengers flying through the firmament in their golden carriage, feeling distaste, envy and hate, until everything before their eyes had turned black and brown, and they'd shown their true character, their pigs' faces, their uvulas weak from yelling slogans, after which they raised their collars and walked on swiftly, or hoisted a hand and vanished into the night by taxi.

It was quite a thing, human existence!

> *Whatever way you look at it, that's life.*
> *It's like the sea, an endless ebb and tide.*

———

I'd been drinking wine for the last couple of hours sitting here at my desk on Tchaikovsky Street 40. The thrumming renovation had finally ceased. The cats lay together in the linen closet in the bedroom; safe in there, content. I turned Hildegard Knef's voice down a bit. Not that I needed to: my Russian neighbours above and below had left, without my having been able to say goodbye to them; they'd disappeared like thieves in the night.

Many of my generation have never heard of Hildegard Knef. An international star, a diva, a writer, wife, mistress, mother, chanteuse, human. Every word of hers, every verse that she sings in her husky, smoky, Berlin voice, with the timbre of some old brothel madam, strikes my flesh and blood like bullets.

*Today, there may be happy hours,*
*But tomorrow will bring misery,*
*Because each new day is a clean slate,*
*So you'd better get ready.*

Julia had left at six to teach at the evening school. I walked to Yuri's on Furshtatskaya soon after. I thanked him again for arranging the Gippius thing. He started reminiscing about one of his Casanova conquests from the old days, and I came back with two bottles of Pinot Grigio. I drank it slowly, glancing at the pages of the manuscript of my book on the Russian Revolution of 1917. I'd managed to finish it after all, two weeks earlier than planned.

Of course, my friend was right, there in Cap d'Antibes among the parasol pine trees, staring out over the azure sea. Artists should talk about their own times. But what do I, the son of a capitalist, have to do with the masses in that earthly world? And anyway, the world these days seems more like 1905 than 1917: the feared tidal wave of vengeance, the envy of the common folk, the powers of darkness, all a trickle. The dance goes on — yes, the dance always goes on. Maybe this was another false rhyme of history, and we were on the cusp of a new biblical deluge of blood.

Tomorrow, I will send my manuscript to Amsterdam. The only care, the only love I'll have from now on, is for our three cats and my wife, who at this very moment was teaching German in a classroom where once children — between their maths and biology lessons — were trained to assemble and disassemble Kalashnikovs, revolvers, and hand grenades; a practice that has largely returned.

> *You have to figure out how you want to live.*
> *That's what it boils down to.*
> *And if you're in pain, don't complain,*
> *There's nothing you can do.*

What a fine language German is! And what a singer!

My second bottle of Pinot Grigio was now half empty. Luckily, there was a dash of red left from the previous day on the mantelpiece between the brass candlesticks. I chucked a couple of birch logs on the open hearth, with some wood chips to light it, along with the thick paper from my old manuscripts.

A literary fire!

It was mid-August, but behind my desk I still enjoyed the smell of burning and the flames. Have I already told you about our open fireplace? An artefact made of pure marble, with a chiselled nest and a pair of swallows feeding their three young from their beaks; the work of an unknown Italian master.

What life doesn't give us, art does!

*Whatever way you look at it, that's life.*
*So I say, live for today.*
*Whatever I've done, I tried to have fun,*
*And don't regret anything anyway.*

I once wrote a story about this building, and those who had passed through it. I can still see all of them before me.

You already know my downstairs neighbour, Gennady Nikolaevich, in his striped sailor's top, chopping up a gleaming antique cherry-wood dresser with an axe, while his wife looked on with her alcoholic clown's face, and also the rest of the occupants of the *kommunalka* who I'd said hello to on the stairs over the years. Good, honest people in general — with lives, pasts, feelings, desires, and expectations —who I always enjoyed a good chat with, who helped me out, who I sometimes helped too. Now they had all disappeared for good.

I would never again hear the civilised voice of my elderly upstairs neighbour, Eugene, a retired physics teacher, and a secret homosexual, who told me one day on the couch in his little three-metre by four-metre room about his father's suicide in 1950. He'd made it to Berlin as a 20-year-old soldier, but when he returned to Moscow after the war, he was seen as a traitor because he was not a body on the battlefield — had not fought hard enough or he would not still be alive — an offence that landed him in a penal colony twice. 'I was standing there with my little brother. My father was standing in front of the bathroom mirror. He cut his throat with a razor. Just like that, from ear to ear. The blood spurted out as though from a shower head. My little brother and I ran in terror.

We never saw him again.'

What stories, what misery.

The meagre few square metres that the residents of the *kommunalka* had been allocated one day by the Soviet authorities were privatised after the fall of the USSR, and have now been sold on with kickbacks, and everyone has disappeared to a pigeon-coop somewhere on the outskirts of the city.

The opera singer who lives in her four-hundred-square-metre apartment on the top floor with her son and mother was relieved by this turn of events. In a while, she told me in passing this week, our building will finally be back the way it was in 1900. It was only by some stroke of audacity that the bourgeoisie had ever been driven out and the common people had taken possession of everything.

The dark-haired soprano is called Galina Gorchakova. You can find her on YouTube, just like Hildegard Knef. I'm not making anything up, why would I? I'm beyond fiction. Her apartment is the former residence of Count Vasily Pavlovich Zubov, an intimate of the Romanovs, who kept the apartment before the revolution as a *pied-à-terre* to meet young women. The soprano bought out the Jewish residents who occupied the entire upper floor in the late nineties. With ready cash in their pockets, they emigrated to Israel. The diva got rid of everything that reminded her of Soviet times and restored her palace. One day, amid a cloud of Chanel, she took me to her music room; the walls were draped with light-blue satin and there were chairs with carved-out backs in the form of treble-clefs. As she smiled, she pointed out a white Bechstein grand piano from 1893 in the middle of the space.

The ostentation of the past was back.

Meanwhile, there were people living below her who'd had less luck, in their musty rooms with a communal kitchen, where the tiles dropped off the walls together with the plaster, the passages reeked of the food smells from six families, and cockroach poison, nicotine, and the unremitting stench of the parade of people defecating on the one toilet, like in the *kommunalka* on Vasilyevsky Island, where I'd spent my first nights of love with my present wife.

> *You're in this world to find some happiness,*
> *But you don't know where that is on earth.*
> *You may use your wits for money,*
> *Or you may feel that only love has any worth.*

For a long time, our building was a time machine: a grotesque mixture of rich and poor, where the shadows of the czarist age, communism, and these new times competed with each other beneath the rafters. All that was over now because of some prole in the city authorities.

But to return to our marble hearth. It has an historical allure.

One day, I began searching for our apartment in the books and archives, and came across a Frenchman, a certain Viscount Eugène-Melchior de Vogüé. After a diplomatic career in Constantinople, Syria, Palestine, and Egypt, he'd ended up at the French consulate in Saint Petersburg in 1878. A little later, he married a Russian beauty, went looking for an apartment, and where do you think that nobleman ended up? At Tchaikovsky Street 40, of all places, here on the third floor where I'd finished my wretched book yesterday. Our living room served as the viscount's political cabinet. He'd already been active on a literary front in his earlier postings. Now, he began to bombard France with books, writings, and articles about Russia from inside this very room. He familiarised his countrymen with the works of Dostoyevsky, Tolstoy, and other classic Russian authors. While the world was largely fixated on France in those days, it's not too much of a leap to say that the European advance of Russian literature — which would result in Dutch translations that I read as a teenager, that took possession of me and would ultimately bring me to Russia — actually began here between these high walls.

Everything in life is a coincidence; it is totally arbitrary.

The wine was finished, including the last dash of red. I'd eaten a couple of handfuls of cashews and a bag of paprika crisps and my stomach had fallen prey to a nasty fermentation. Bad stomachs make for bad minds. This is one of the few pieces of wisdom that life has taught me. The only remedy is something sweet; not actual sweets, but a sweetness of alcoholic origin. I found five mini-bottles of banana liqueur in the kitchen drawer below the one with the cutlery and the eighty old corks, buried among meat-skewers and aluminium foil. No idea where I got them. From an airport? Or a mini-bar? I poured the contents of one bottle down my throat, glugging it. A deliciously warm, full aroma of banana. And then another one immediately. A tongue-caress from Tenerife where I once lived, but that's another story.

I got a text from Julia: she isn't well, can I come and pick her up at school?

I had to go.

The flames in the open hearth would go out all by themselves.

That's perhaps the most beautiful and most comforting thing in creation: that sooner or later everything goes out all by itself. To be on the safe side, I closed the dividing door to the room where our dear cats slept. I walked out into the cool echo of the passage, but damn it … What was going on? I hadn't even locked the door behind me yet and all the lights had gone off. The stairwell was as dark as a coal mine. Keeping close to the banister, I descended carefully, step by step, my fingers gliding over the pre-revolutionary wood. But in the lobby, I still couldn't see my hand in front of my face. I pushed on in a cocoon of sweat, a shortness of breath, an irregular heartbeat. That's because of the drink; everything is because of the drink. And because of mankind. 'That's great, my boy,' I can still hear my father saying from his hospital chair, when the cancer had reached his throat and I'd told him about my plans in Moscow. 'But be careful. People in this world are sons-of-bitches.' All of us are growing older. That's for sure. Meanwhile, we're not only surrounded by lunatics and hypocrites, but by lies too. With the gait of a blind person, I walked straight towards the door to the street; it's a wooden monster, like at a factory. I wrestled it open, but then too … Darkness! The bluish-black dark enveloped me again, although it was not total … Darkness on earth is seldom total. People are like moles of hope, and hopelessness. The electricity in our part of the city was apparently out; that happened a month ago too. Some people say it's because they're busy renovating, others because we're still lumbered with the old Soviet junk. I moved between the wings of the tall houses, and stood up straight; I blinked my eyes. I saw something incredible, of such a moving beauty that my granite face streamed with tears, the ducts bursting like a pregnant woman's waters. There was a meteor shower falling from a point in the sky, carving long tails, a shower of sparks. The stardust of the Perseids. It comes at around the same time in August every year. And yet, I've still witnessed this natural wonder so infrequently. Blinded by the light on earth.

What do I hear? The sound of hooves?

The dark forms of parked vehicles were all around me; expensive cars, off-roaders. The rest of the traffic appeared to have been banished from Tchaikovsky Street. I breathed in the warm evening air with a deep gulp. An oscillating blue glow moved closer, a will-o'-the-wisp, with the swelling sound of hoofbeats. A truly regal sound! My nostrils swelled with the smell of stables. The city lights all around switched on just before the carriage reached me, with its brass lantern on a swishing arm; the windows of the houses growing yellow.

The carriage came to a halt in front of me. There was a Russian on the front seat with a bulbous head. He had an enormous black moustache, and was dressed in a cherry-red operetta coat, with imitation gold buttons and braiding. I'd seen him a few times — this Russian of around sixty, who looked as if he was an escaped extra from the Imperial Theatre. He's one of the coachmen on the pleasure carriages that pick up tourists on Palace Square in front of the Hermitage and take them on trips around the city.

'Hey, coachman!' I called. 'How much would it cost to get to the Sadovaya?'

'I'm going home.' The man on the front seat loosened the reins in his white-gloved hands for a second. 'I've been driving tourists around since this morning. Chinese — it's an epidemic!'

'It's a surprise for my wife …' I feverishly patted my body, found a five-thousand ruble note in my back pocket and held it up to this apparition from an operetta. 'Here, is this enough?'

Five thousand rubles, eighty euros. Death on instalment, life on credit.

'Just there, or back as well?'

'There and back. I want to pick up my wife.'

'Well, chief, get in ...'


And we were driving, we were driving!

I stared at the broad-shouldered back of the coachman, who occasionally drew his whip from the sheath and gave his two horses what's for, while making a shrill whistle between his teeth. We glided at a trot through Tchaikovsky Street towards Tauride Garden. By Zinaida Gippius's corner house, we turned right, but what a speed! Before I had a chance to take it in, we'd already passed it. I glanced back; there were figures moving behind the high windows.

The earthly palace has vanished, but it is still occupied.

I breathed in another gulp of the August evening air, taking delight in its scent, the withering sap of an approaching autumn. The sky was uniformly grey, lit from below by the pale sheen of streetlamps. The meteor showers above must have been ongoing, I'm sure, but what a person doesn't see doesn't exist, or at least they don't need to know about it — all the rest is philosophy!

A couple of years before his death, the godfather once showed me his telescope in the villa that his wife and children had left. The editor-in-chief of the biggest newspaper in the country was always surrounded by chaos and din, but he most liked to stare at the eternal stillness of the universe alone.

Nobody and nothing in life are quite what they seem. The fraudsters are always around us, the boasters, the preachers of false love, the travelling salesmen of humanity. A masquerade! A charade! What is it the Russians say? Write the way you breathe and breathe the way you write.

The acid in my stomach rose; I let the third bottle of banana liqueur glide down my throat as we set off, trotting towards Nevsky Prospect through streets like monstrous alleys, where the clattering of hooves echoed off the walls. Once again, the warm, sweet anaesthesia. But then I was struck by a sledgehammer blow from inside, as though a black curtain had dropped inside my cranium, its cords snapped, the dust flying. There was Gippius, alone in her apartment in Paris, an old woman after more than twenty years of exile. It's 1942, the Krauts are striding through the streets; she's been talking to her husband about Russia, he's been telling her how much he misses his country, and dies shortly after. 'I was entirely calm, I didn't shed a tear, not at the time and not later. Maybe my heart's made of ice and will never melt again.'

That's the devilish thing about life too, that people with a heart say they have a heart of ice. And the reverse!

I found Knef again, scrolling through my phone. I wormed the earphones into my ears, the husky voice resuming exactly where it left off:

> *We all have the right to be happy.*
> *You have to take whatever road you must.*
> *And only God can say if things will turn out okay.*
> *But it's up to you, however tough.*

———

'Coachman!' I took the earphones out; I couldn't shake that damned image of a lonely Gippius. I wanted to hear my own voice, to be certain that I was not drunk and dreaming.

The man half turned to me.

I asked, 'How much longer?'

The Russian said with gusto, 'Ten minutes, squire!' and cracked his whip over the horses, which gleamed black with sweat, stallions by the look of it.

The streets like alleys were now behind us; as we drove onto Uprising Square, the Nevsky was chock-a-block with traffic to the left and right of us. I was blinded by the commotion, the jumble of lights from the shops, the illuminations over the road and the headlights of cars, as if I were seeing this profusion for the first time.

As we went round the roundabout in front of the station — where the trains leave for Moscow, and where the criminals and politically oppressed gathered with chains riveted to their ankles, for transportation to Siberia before the revolution — the clock read ten to ten.

Right on time, everything well in hand.

This guy was going to pick up his wife in an open carriage drawn by two black stallions! Rarely has anyone integrated as quickly and as well as her. After a year, she read and spoke Dutch fluently. She was a walking encyclopaedia of my fatherland. A sponge for history, arts, even cabaret and variety. But because her master's degree was seen as inferior because she came from a country where people couldn't think independently, she spent the first few years selling shoes. She was a forerunner, a pioneer, a trailblazer for the legions that would later follow: the hordes from the Eastern Bloc who'd work as waiters, chambermaids, plumbers, cleaners, and nannies to satisfy the needs of Western civilisation; but apart from their labour, they were meant to leave everything else behind at home, certainly when many of them turned out to have come from entirely different worlds and started to develop pretensions. Where did they come from? Where was their *gratitude*?

*So you'd better make up your mind how you want your life to be,*
*That's what it boils down to.*
*And if you're in pain, don't complain*
*Because there's nothing you can do.*

What traffic, but watch out, boys! If you're not careful, you'll hit our fine horses!

I recognised almost every building, every shop. Images of the past and present flitted through me as if on the shuttles of a loom. The kaleidoscope of someone who's perhaps lived here too long, whose time has come, who one day may have to bugger off out of this country, but where to?

The delicatessen paradise of the Elisseeff brothers! There isn't a finer store anywhere, at least not in Saint Petersburg. You can go there for pastries, chocolate pralines, fine meats, smoked salmon as fine as tissue paper, the very last black caviar, and other comestibles. It was around ten, but the chandeliers were still lit in the gold-leafed emporium that has survived all revolutions. If I had a child, a grandchild by now, I'd have popped by occasionally with the little girl or boy to enjoy the moving fairy-tale figures made of brightly coloured wood in the shop window, before going in for a lolly, a bag of toffees, or an ice-cream.

I enjoyed the sights flashing by. We slowed down behind a line of cars, and once more I was overcome by terrible confusion, not because of what I was thinking this time, but what I saw.

It couldn't be the drink — just two bottles of white wine, half a bottle of red, and a few drops of banana liqueur for the sweetness; I'd never used drugs, but it felt as if I were hallucinating.

Impossible!

On the broad granite pavement to the right of me, a young man wearing a fur hat on his fleshy, red head is shoving this ancient woman along in a prehistoric-looking wheelchair. The young man is me and the lady in the wheelchair decked in fur from head to toe in spite of the August heat is none other than Madam Pokrovskaya.

'Hey, coachman!' I yelled before he could giddy up with the whip in his hand. 'Stop! I have to get out for a moment!'

The White Nights were over, the devil no longer tugging at the sheets, I know that this is a city of phantoms, but I was *not* drunk, though still it was me walking there. A 27-year-old version of myself, wheeling that terribly elderly Russian woman from the home where I'd fruitlessly handed out bibles, on a mission for Siderius. She'd begged me to take her outside for a trip through the city.

When I'd brought her back to the director and asked if there wasn't anything she could do for her, maybe get in touch with the poor woman's daughter, she burst out in a satyr's laugh. The woman was completely nuts! When she'd still been able to walk, she gave all the feral cats in the neighbourhood food in the courtyard, costly victuals meant for her. The daughter was only in her head, it was all a delusion, she'd never had a child in her whole life!

———

I stepped out of the carriage, the man on the front seat yelled at me that he couldn't stay here long, that it was prohibited. But I urged him to wait, and trailed after my phantom apparition.

They hurried away in front of me with the rickety chair.

I was sober as a judge. But my calves were as heavy as stone from the alcohol. Once again, that nasty, sweaty shortness of breath, the irregular heartbeat. I waded forward through the throng; the pedestrians coming towards me in the liquid, blue light of the lamps, parting to the left and right of me, and although I kept shouting angrily at him to stand still, my 27-year-old self didn't have any notion, but I started to sprint and then I laid a hand on his shoulder.

The guy in the fur hat turned around to face me. He looked at me aggressively, with a mouth full of brown, stubbed teeth and that ugly, fleshy head. The pensioner in the wheelchair turned towards me too, looking up at me like a weasel. She had no teeth at all, her head a shrivelled blue plum. They were tramps who live by begging off tourists, immured to the world, wrapped in fur summer and winter.

'What is it?!' the guy said, incensed.

His words were borne on his stinking breath.

I apologised profusely; it was a misunderstanding!

As I was about to hurry off, the man laid one of his mitts on me. He moved threateningly towards me and grabbed me with his other hand too, and asked what in the devil's name I was after. He bellowed like a bear that I'd provoked. I laid my hands on him, he wanted compensation, three hundred rubles! The woman in the chair started bellowing too, as if I were trying to rape her.

I plunged my hand into my back pocket and gave the guy a thousand-ruble note, which he studied as though he was seeing money for the first time.

After I was back inside the carriage, the coachman pulled off right away. I could tell from his body language that he was irked. I yelled up to him that I'd pay him a little extra. I popped the earphones back in, pressed play, and closed my eyes amid the waves of light from the city.

I was startled awake again by honking that pierced the German diva's voice. We carried out a deft turn halfway down the Nevsky, surrounded by tooting cars, and drove into Sadovaya, a renowned street where, in the month of February 1917, the first insurgents died in their droves in the snow, cut down by machine-gun fire. What an assault to the senses. That I'd seen myself pushing a wheelchair on the Nevsky! Was it that damned banana liqueur? What did you say, coachman? I'm having awful trouble hearing you.

'Which number?!'

But I didn't know which number; I did know where the building was though. My wife's evening school was thirty metres ahead.

'Pull up here, coachman, stop!'

I got out and walked into the lobby of the institute, which stank of cigarettes. A school as they should be, with sea-green tiled walls. People still learnt here, from books, and by heart. A group of boys of around twenty years of age stormed down the wide stone stairs. They already had moustaches, some had hipster beards; they had the voices of adults, but their pumped-up joy was reminiscent of infants. If another war came, these would be the soldiers, or else their children or grandchildren. Only idiots believe that the rhyming of history will one day cease, and be replaced by fairy-tale prose.

Julia came down the stairs amid a floating haze. She held her books pressed to her chest, like a student in an American film. She was talking to one of her students and hadn't noticed me. I was concealed behind a pillar, spying from my position, and again felt as nervous as almost thirty years ago when I waited for her for the first time in the lobby of another school. She's past fifty now, but I can still see in my wife's current form who she was back then. And if I look closely, I can even see the girl of five, just like in the black-and-white photo on my desk, where she's pictured with her grandma, who'd cry with joy each time she arrived in old East Prussia from Leningrad, 'And who do we have here then? What treasure has come to visit us?'

Thirty years — everything has changed, but everything has remained the same.

Suddenly, my throat felt parched. As soon as the student left, I stepped forward and popped up in front of my wife, like a jack-in-the-box.

'What's the matter with you?' She pointed at my moist face.

'These damned contact lenses! The tears keep running because of my dry eyes. I'll have to go to the optician again soon.'

'How much have you had to drink?'

'The usual.'

'Well, how much is that?'

'*Whatever way you look at it, that's life,*' I begin to sing out loud in my fine singing voice. '*Today, there are only happy hours …*'

Then my wife burst out laughing.

'Knef?'

'Our immortal Hildegard!

I planted a smacking kiss on her mouth and led Julia outside, onto Sadovaya, where my coachman was waiting for us on the front seat of his open carriage, with a fine vermilion-black silhouette.

'What's this?'

The man dismounted and charmingly opened the door for us, we got in, and in the blink of an eye we were riding.

'Hey, what's this about?' My wife still had her books pressed to her tummy. 'Have you won the lottery or something?'

I took the two remaining mini-bottles of banana liqueur from my trouser pocket, unscrewed the tops and gave one to my wife. As I glugged the contents down in one gulp because of my parched throat, Julia took a sip.

'Sweet!' she said. 'Delicious and sweet! Where are we going?'

'Home ...' After another circus-like turn, we were already flying down the seething Nevsky, but in a different direction now.

My wife stopped asking questions. I saw how she was enjoying the unexpected trip through her own city, the clattering of hooves, the whistling of the coachman, the panting of the stallions, the wind rushing by.

'We're going pretty fast!' she cried, with her hair fluttering.

I thought of the five grand in my father's money-box in the bottom of the dresser in our bedroom. Death on instalment, life on credit. If we died, we'd regret two things the most: not showing each other enough love, and not travelling enough together. I asked my wife where she'd like to go.

'What do you mean?'

I told her I'd finally finished my book, that I really had to get away for a while, away from these streets, these former battlefields.

She was terribly surprised.

The world's big, but Europe's enough for us.

A carousel of potential future pleasures spun through her mind. She thought out loud. Thuringia, the lavender fields of Provence, the coasts of Bulgaria, Croatia or Romania, the hills of Kent, the arid vistas around Toledo, Tuscany. Italy. We decided to look for a house for a month, somewhere in Liguria.

'Moesha and the boys can come too, can't they?' My wife looked at me imploringly with her almond eyes.

It used to be the girls; now it was the boys.

'Of course,' I said. 'Moesha and the boys can come.'

At that moment, the two stallions squeezed out two ginormous deep-yellow turds while at a full trot and in stereo. They were as round as bullets, gleaming gold in the evening light, they fell between the kicking legs. We traced a circle again on Uprising Square and eventually turned right in the direction of Tchaikovsky Street.

Not named after the composer, but after the revolutionary.

# ACKNOWLEDGEMENTS

In the writing of this book, I've made extensive use of previously published literature on pre-revolutionary, revolutionary and post-communist Russia, as well as exhaustively mining my own biography. Sometimes things have coincided, sometimes they haven't. I particularly owe my thanks, and in some cases sadly beyond the grave, to the authors of the following works from which I have borrowed words, ideas, and insights, listed here in non-alphabetical order: Orlando Figes, *A People's Tragedy, The Russian Revolution 1891–1924*, Jonathan Cape, London 1996; Edward Radzinsky, *The Rasputin File*, Doubleday, New York 2000; Curzio Malaparte, *The Kremlin Ball*, De Arbeiderspers, Amsterdam 2017; Sima Sneevliet, *My Years in Stalinist Russia*, BZZTôH, Den Haag 1994; Henk van Renssen, *The Revolution Collector*, Uitgeverij Podium, Amsterdam 2006; Ben Knapen, *The Long Road to Moscow*, Elsevier, Amsterdam 1985; Helen Rappaport, *In the Midst of the Revolution*, Uitgeverij Unieboek/Het Spectrum, Houten 2016; Douglas Smith, *Former People: The Final Days of the Russian Aristocracy*, Uitgeverij Balans, Amsterdam 2016, and of course Zinaida Gippius, *The Splendour of Words*, Privé-domein 94, De Arbeiderspers, Amsterdam 1984.

*P.W. Saint Petersburg, 28 August 2017*